Daoism, Dandyism,
and Political Correctness

SUNY Series, Translating China
―――――――――
Roger T. Ames and Paul J. D'Ambrosio, editors

Daoism, Dandyism, and Political Correctness

THORSTEN BOTZ-BORNSTEIN

**SUNY
PRESS**

Published by State University of New York Press, Albany

© 2023 State University of New York

All rights reserved

Printed in the United States of America

No part of this book may be used or reproduced in any manner whatsoever without written permission. No part of this book may be stored in a retrieval system or transmitted in any form or by any means including electronic, electrostatic, magnetic tape, mechanical, photocopying, recording, or otherwise without the prior permission in writing of the publisher.

For information, contact State University of New York Press, Albany, NY
www.sunypress.edu

Library of Congress Cataloging-in-Publication Data

Name: Botz-Bornstein, Thorsten, author.
Title: Daoism, dandyism, and political correctness / Thorsten Botz-Bornstein.
Description: Albany, NY : State University of New York Press, [2023] | Series: SUNY Series, Translating China | Includes bibliographical references and index.
Identifiers: LCCN 2022059361 | ISBN 9781438494524 (hardcover : alk. paper) | ISBN 9781438494531 (ebook) | ISBN 9781438494517 (pbk. : alk. paper)
Subjects: LCSH: Philosophy, Comparative. | Taoism. | Dandyism. | Political correctness.
Classification: LCC B799 .B68 2023 | DDC 100—dc23/eng/20230509
LC record available at https://lccn.loc.gov/2022059361

10 9 8 7 6 5 4 3 2 1

Contents

Introduction		1
1	What Would Zhuangzi Have Said about Political Correctness?	15
2	Daoism and Dandyism	37
3	The "Equalization of Genders"	59
4	Sincerity and Authenticity	85
5	The Authentic and the Sincere in Daoism	101
6	The Authenticity of the Dandy	119
7	The Dandy and the Snob	131
8	The "Ethics" of Coolness	159
Conclusion		187
Notes		191
Bibliography		207
Index		221

Introduction

Political correctness (PC) is a measure that attempts to prevent all expressions or actions that could offend or marginalize certain people or groups of people and aims to spread justice and fairness by making the public sensitive to those most vulnerable in society. Starting in the 1970s as an ironic self-criticism of leftists, PC would soon be appropriated by various political groups. It would also generate much criticism. Many PC policies are used to define and correct language, especially linguistic markers of race, gender, and sexual orientation. The belief that altering language usage will change the public's perception of reality and, finally, reality itself, has led to an important reform of gender terms, personal pronouns, and gender pronouns. Certain terms and pronouns were amended and new ones defined. Since the late 1980s, the idea of "inclusive language" has been an important part of Western culture. In 2016, the State of New York issued a list with thirty-one "protected genders" among which there was also the "gender fluid" and the "gender gifted."

How would Zhuangzi (also Zhuang Zhou or Chuang Tzu),[1] a Chinese philosopher who lived in the fourth century BC, have reacted to these linguistic reforms? Zhuangzi is a pivotal figure of Daoism, which is, alongside Confucianism, one of the great philosophical systems of China. Zhuangzi was a language skeptic, which means that he did not believe that language could convey the true meanings of the world. This view set Daoism in opposition to Confucianism, which is famous for its vast "language correction project." Confucianism required clear standards for the use of names because Confucians thought that "if names be not correct, language is not in accordance with the truth of things."[2] For the *Zhuangzi*, the name is not the real thing and "names are arbitrary." The *Zhuangzi* provocatively holds that "a dog could be a sheep."[3]

For Confucius, the rectification of language is equivalent to moral cultivation. Does the *Zhuangzi*'s position toward Confucianism join some of the criticism with which the PC discourse is confronted in our times? Critics of PC, such as John Lea, believe that PC's purpose is "to induce correct opinion rather than to search for wisdom and liberate the mind" (Lea 2008, 29). More radically, Doris Lessing writes that PC, just like Communism, "debase[s] language and, with language, thought" (Lessing 1994). Does this criticism reflect the *Zhuangzi*'s position about language? Would Zhuangzi have argued that PC creates a (linguistic) dream world made of rules, policies, and words that is no more real than "Zhuangzi dreaming that he is a butterfly"? The Butterfly Parable, which is the arguably most famous text in the *Zhuangzi*, says: "Once upon a time, I dreamt I was a butterfly, fluttering hither and thither, to all intents and purposes a butterfly. I was conscious only of my happiness as a butterfly, unaware that I was myself. Soon I awaked, and there I was, veritably myself again" (trans. Giles 2019, 47).[4]

The Butterfly Parable is the last text to appear in the *Zhuangzi*'s chapter called "Adjustment of Controversies" (also translated as "The Equalization of Things" or as "The Smoothing out of Differences"), which deals with the topic of "transformation" (*hua* 化). In the parable, Zhuangzi does not know whether he is a butterfly dreaming that he is Zhuangzi or whether Zhuangzi is dreaming that he is a butterfly. This means that Daoism undermines identity, reality, and language, and thus also gender identity and gender reality, as they are expressed through language.

Daoism and Dandyism

The provocative sentence that "a dog could be a sheep" fascinated the Anglo-Irish writer Oscar Wilde, who was one of the first readers of the *Zhuangzi* when it appeared in its English translation by Herbert Giles in 1890. The young Wilde wrote one of the first reviews of the book and arguably designed his theory of "dandyism" in accordance with some of its principles. Dandyism was a challenging fashion movement, and it was very influential throughout the nineteenth century in the upper strata of English and French societies. One of dandyism's most prominent characteristics is that it questions the rules and codes of correctness in language and behavior. The present book will show that dandyism also has a very peculiar approach toward today's PC.

The link between dandyism and Daoism has been noted by several scholars, and all of them concentrate on Oscar Wilde.[5] Some point out that Wilde did not only write the review of the *Zhuangzi*, but that there are many parallels between Wilde's dandyism and Daoism in his work. Jerusha McCormack picks up the "correctness" topic and depicts both Zhuangzi and Wilde as "contrarians," that is, as people who "think against prevailing conventions in a way that appears to be systematically perverse, hence 'contrary' to the dominant discourse" (McCormack 2017, 77). She concludes that, historically, Wilde's anti-Victorianism mirrors Daoist anti-Confucianism because "the kind of society advocated by Confucius and that of high Victorian England had many similarities" (78).

Is there a connection between Daoism and the unwritten philosophy of the nineteenth-century dandies? In some way, the connection is counterintuitive. Daoism, as it rejected the Chinese clan system, "sought a return to a more ancient and animal-like world that rejected all artifice, culture, and order, and took a very passive attitude toward human affairs" (Li Zehou 2019, 67). Can this back-to-nature movement really be compared with the world of the masters or urban life, the dandies? I believe that it can, and the connection can best be established by looking at what both say about political correctness.

Daoism was against Confucianism, and Wilde fought the puritan Victorian moral earnestness of his society, ultimately being imprisoned for homosexuality. This means that both Zhuangzi and Wilde combated similar "sanitizing" social tendencies and undermined a certain form of "correctness" by using peculiar counter-methods reaching from the aesthetic to the anarchic. McCormack's parallelism is driven by the fact that Wilde read Giles's translation of the *Zhuangzi* and wrote a review of it. For McCormack, "Zhuangzi's thinking was certainly crucial in shaping Wilde's concept of the dandy" (93). Indeed, it seems that the *Zhuangzi* made a lasting impact on Wilde. In a correspondence, Wilde addressed his mock-rival James Abbott McNeill Whistler as "Dear Butterfly" (Wilde 1962, 170) and wrote to his friend Ada Leverson that *The Importance of Being Earnest* is a play "written by a butterfly for butterflies" (382). However, McCormack also wonders how Wilde's earlier thinking could have developed along similar lines even before having read the book: "Wilde's thinking at this point could hardly be said to be influenced by Zhuangzi. Yet the tenor of the argument as well as its mischievous style are uncannily close to that of Zhuangzi's exposition of the ambiguities of 'the real'" (78). For some scholars, the fact that such elements are present in Wilde's early work even before having read the *Zhuangzi* is reason enough to question the existence of any Daoist influence in Wilde's writings: "The critiques that deny Chuang Tzu's influence largely develop along the rationale that Wilde had already formed most of his own views on art, life and society before he came to read Chuang Tzu" (Murray 1971, 4).

McCormack establishes numerous parallels between Wilde and Daoism but rarely refers to a broader concept of dandyism that, in Wilde's time, had already been in place for three generations. The other scholars follow the same approach. In this study, I want to widen the spectrum and look not only at Wilde but at dandyism more generally because earlier dandies are not less "Daoist," even though no direct Daoist influence on them can be detected. The parallels are indeed amazing. Not only can dandies be contrasted with Confucian moralists or with pedantic logicians like Huizi, but Confucian moralists and the Logicians from the School of Names have clear equivalents in what earlier generations of dandies had designated as their enemies: the snob and the careerist.

In the present book, I put a special focus on the founder of dandyism, George "Beau" Brummell. Brummell fought hypocrite aristocratic culture not, like Wilde, during the Victorian era but roughly seventy years earlier, during the English Regency period.

Baudelaire explains that dandyism appears "in periods of transition, when democracy is not yet all-powerful, and aristocracy is only just beginning to totter and fall" (Baudelaire 1986, 28).[6] The English Regency period, the time during which dandyism most consistently developed, was an unstable time swept up by great social, political, and economic change, which creates a parallel with China. Daoism thrived during the Warring States period (475–221 BC), which was a time of political division in which feudal systems were decaying. Politically, the situation resembled that of the Holy Roman Empire in its decadence, but, paradoxically, it was also an era of great cultural and intellectual expansion. The thoughts and ideas of this period remain important to this day in many Asian countries.[7]

The *Zhuangzi* presents a variety of "counterheroes," such as the drunkard who masters the "art" of falling from a cart without getting hurt, or the swimmer who dives into the most dangerous waterfalls without drowning. These protagonists excel at "useless arts," and the dandy could very well be another example of such unlikely characters from Daoist "knack stories." Brummell spent five hours in front of the mirror binding his tie, and, equally meticulously, waxed his shoes down to the soles. He excelled at these activities like nobody else, but his art remains useless. What is this philosophy that attempts to make statements by engaging in useless activities? The concept of dandyism can be better understood by viewing it in light of Daoism. Both the Daoist and the dandy do nothing, but they do "nothing" in a particular way. "Of petty uselessness great usefulness is achieved," says the *Zhuangzi*.[8]

Both dandyism and Daoism adhere to an idle but fluid moving around, for which, in the nineteenth century, the word *flâner* was coined. The dandy is a flâneur, and in the *Zhuangzi*, *you* (遊) stands for a similarly aimless roaming, rambling, or sauntering. *You* has been translated as "going rambling without a destination" or "free and easy wandering." While Confucians focus on moral and personal duty, the *Zhuangzi* promotes carefree wandering (*xiaoyaoyou* 逍遥游). The flâneur never stops but sees men and women pass by while he is walking. Similar to the Daoist engaging in *you*, the flâneur's view "is constituted in multiple respects by our relation to the landscape" (Moeller and D'Ambrosio 2018, 11).

As the flâneur moves around in life "with unspectacular excellence and spontaneity" (Moeller and D'Ambrosio 2017, 164), he has no time to confer names or pronouns upon the men and women that pass by. The dandy is not a language reformer but looks at society, men, women, transgender people, and many others in a detached way. In terms of gender, the dandy is a peculiar case because he is neither gay nor transgender or cross-dresser. But the flâneur is not simply gender-neutral either; he might have been "useless" for women but still exercised considerable attraction on women. "Of petty uselessness great usefulness is achieved."

As the Daoist-dandy strolls through society, he sees social reality not in terms of rules, speech codes, and other essences but rather as a unified totality of cultural existences that remains full of ambiguities. And both dandies and *you*-ing Daoists play with these ambiguities, which is why they are, by nature, opposed to all sorts of official correctness.

Wilde sees "uselessness" as a protest against the new businesslike lifestyle that keeps people running—not roaming: running after money but also running after the right ethics, through preaching, philanthropy, and mutual surveillance. In his review of the *Zhuangzi*, Wilde criticizes much of what we would today call "neoliberal culture." A rigorous and puritanical economy-based culture, not very ethical with regard to its economic principles (the Victorian age was also the great age of British colonialism) but issuing politically correct ethical appeals wherever it could: "The doctrine of the uselessness of all useful things would not merely endanger our commercial supremacy as a nation but might bring discredit upon many prosperous and serious-minded members of the shop-keeping classes. What would become of our popular preachers, our Exeter Hall orators, our drawing-room evangelists?" (Wilde 1919, 186) There is, in Wilde's writings, a certain spirit of "live and let live" that contrasts with political correctness, which can be found in Daoist authors as well as in another Warring States philosopher who formulated an alternative to Confucian and Mohist thought. Yangzi, the founder of the Yangist school,[9] said that "if nobody would sacrifice a hair, if nobody would try to benefit the world, then the world would become orderly" (in Mair 1994, xxiii). This "order" will be established organically, that is, not by insisting on formal rules but by means of a tolerant cultural play.

Brummell and PC

What would Brummell, the foremost dandy, have said about political correctness? The *Trésor de la langue française* defines the dandy as somebody who has a total "disregard for social conventions and the ethics of the bourgeoisie." An anonymous author writing for *Blackwood's Edinburg Magazine* defined Brummell as "magnanimously mean, ridiculously wise, and contemptibly clever" (Anonymous 1844, 769). The secret of dandyism is not ethical engagement but rather the playful enactment of selfishness. The dandy is famous for his transgressive play not only with social rules but also with names as well as with genders. In one anecdote, Brummell goes to a certain Mrs. Thompson's ball without being invited but hopes to be able to get in with his friend the Prince Regent George. Unfortunately, George is late. Brummell makes "his best bow" and, "leisurely feeling in all his pockets to prolong the chances of the Prince's arrival," presents Mrs. Thompson with the invitation card to a certain Mrs. Johnson, who is Mrs. Thompson's rival in the East. "'That card, sir, is a Mrs. Johnson's; my name is Thompson." Brummell remains "perfectly cool" and replies: "Dear me, how very unfortunate! Really, Mrs. Johns—Thompson, I mean, I am very sorry for this mistake; but you know, Johnson and Thompson—and Thompson and Johnson, are really so much the same kind of thing" (from Jesse 1884, 1:101). This is Brummell's version of "The Equalization of Things." The dandy is very much aware of the importance given to names and titles, but he intentionally disrespects them. The dandy is incorrect, but this does not mean that he simply neglects all conventions and acts carelessly. On the contrary, the dandy masters the conventions and ethics of the upper class better than anybody else. He challenges the rules of correctness, but he does so in such a polished way that it shames the most fervent defenders of correctness. His behavior can therefore be termed "polite incorrectness."

Political correctness is about being a perfect gentleman, and, in particular, about how to use the perfect language in all circumstances. The dandy does not combat this concept of correctness by simply being "incorrect" but rather creates his own parallel idea of the "incorrect gentleman" that he practices to perfection. Dandyism does not engage in a Confucian "correction" of names but is rather tempted by what Daoism calls the playful "chaotification" of names.

The Power of Language

Much of Western thought is obsessed with the power of language. Wrong essences (essentializations) need to be corrected by modifying language, and PC consistently follows this tendency of Western thought. From a Daoist point of view, PC invents new terms not in order to overcome essentialist thinking but to create new essences. For the *Zhuangzi*, human reason sets formal limitations to everything, and the mind puts essences in order so that something solid will be established around us. The mind constructs a reality; however, from a Daoist point of view, this is not "real" reality. Political correctness is therefore part of a project of reason that essentializes reality through words. Daoism attempts to transcend such linguistic distinctions. Like the "way" of dandyism, the Dao cannot be the "correct way." Daoist "heroes" like Robber Zhi are blunt and irreverent, constantly speaking up against hypocrisy and Confucian stiffness; they are thus the opposite inverse of the politically correct. In the *Zhuangzi*, Robber Zhi says to Confucius that "there's no robber worse than you. Why doesn't the world call you Robber Confucius instead of calling me Robber Zhi?" (trans. Graham 2001, 237). Knowing the Way does not require etiquette; it does not consist of learning the formal rules of good manners or correct behavior. "Knowing the Way" is a matter of "useless but efficient play," and both Daoism and dandyism develop this philosophical concept.

Political Correctness and Irony

Political correctness is an attitude serving the purpose of social well-being: it aims to control and modify behaviors and expressions that might offend or hurt certain categories of people, most of whom presumably belong to minority groups. Since the late 1980s, the term has been used to describe a preference for inclusive language, which is why an examination of PC in philosophico-linguistic terms is interesting. PC concentrates on various issues in which it seeks to obtain equality and social justice, often revolving around questions of religion, class, or disability. In everyday life, matters of race, gender, and sexual orientation have become dominant. In this book, I refer to the topic of gender most often because a reading of PC through Daoism turns out to be most pertinent when concentrating on the implications of gender in language. The term "politically correct" was originally picked up from communist sources and was "adapted from the concept of 'correct thinking' as in the English translation of Mao's Little Red Book" (Suhr and Johnson, 9; see also Perry 1992). There is thus a connection with "'correct lineism' as used within the Communist Party" (Suhr and Johnson). According to Paul Berman, PC was "an approving phrase on the Leninist left to denote someone who steadfastly toed the party line" (Berman 1992, 5). This means that PC came into use as a self-critical statement among leftists in the 1960s. Later, in the media and in public usage, PC began to describe programs associated with ideas of diversity and multiculturalism or the respect of minorities. The transformation is rather surprising. However, before adopting its present function, the term had been subjected to irony and parody. Gloria Steinem (quoted in Hess 2019, 127) states that, initially, the term "'politically correct' was invented by people in social-justice movements to make fun of ourselves," which means that PC was not meant to be sincere at all and had begun as a measure of self-ridicule and irony. In the 1970s and '80s, leftists used PC as a self-critical satire. Far from being a sincere political movement, PC was a leftist joke aimed at holier-than-thou liberals—by those same liberals. Also, it was not directed at the present but rather at the recent past by "acting out an ironic replay of the Bad Old Days (Before the Sixties) when every revolutionary groupuscule had a party line about everything" (Hall 1994, 164). Typically, PC people would address "some glaring examples of sexist or racist behavior by their fellow students in imitation of the tone of voice of the Red Guards or Cultural Revolution

Commissar" (164). As a critique, PC was thus directed at those who "over-politicize" issues that were originally nonpolitical: family life, marriage, sexual relations, religion. And the critique's targets were leftists: leftists ironically criticized leftists.[10]

Within the political context of the 1980s, PC morphed into something else. At the time of Reagan and Thatcher, PC became a "backlash against the 60s" (Hall 1994, 165), which means, first, that PC became ethicized, and second, that once the political right had taken up the theme, it became thoroughly politicized.

Political Correctness and Leftism

A further peculiarity is that this process went hand in hand with a crisis of the left. In the early 1980s in Western countries, leftist thought took a procapitalist turn, as it ceased defining itself as incompatible with capitalism. The old foundations of leftism were perturbed. In the wake of this, another event would determine the course of the left in an almost equally dramatic fashion. When Margaret Thatcher and Ronald Reagan came to power, something unprecedented happened to the "individual." In the new laissez-faire style liberalism, individualism was given the status of a supreme value, and, surprisingly, this individualism appealed to everyone, regardless of their position on the political spectrum. The hedonism of the preceding hippie culture had laid the foundations for an individualist lifestyle, and by the end of the 1970s, individualism and identity search were no longer the exclusive values of the bourgeois right. It had become the lifestyle of conservative neoliberals as well as of leftists as the left could no longer counter this individualism with ideologies inspired by collectivism. Individualism had become the lifestyle par excellence. The ideological confusion that emerged from this change of direction, together with the procapitalist turn taken by leftist thought in general, has been a hallmark of leftist politics ever since. Having become both procapitalist and individualist, the left had to abandon most traditional socialist ideas. Its parties no longer spoke to, or for, the popular masses, which had already begun turning from the left anyway. The 1980s saw the "decline in active participation in mass political movements and a weakening influence and power of the 'old' social movements of the working class and industrial labor," writes Stuart Hall (1994, 167). Party discipline was no longer what it used to be. Now it was not leftist parties but rather "individual" and independent social movements that began launching political initiatives. This development continues today.

The new economic and cultural constellations, which deprived the left of its traditional values, created a vacuum, and this vacuum would need to be filled. From here on, all that was left (for the left), was to speak up: not for the poor masses but for *other individuals*. Its principal occupation would become the fight against racism, intolerance, and the exclusion of individuals who were different, weak, or disadvantaged. Political correctness, semantically manipulated by the right, could serve as a welcome tool. The individuals that needed to be saved were not necessarily *literally* individuals, but they could also be represented by small coherent social groups motivated by ethnicity or gender. What the psychologist Jordan Peterson (Peterson et al. 2018, 37) has called the "new tribalism" emerges from these constellations.

Identity politics replaced socioeconomic theories like Marxism. However, the new cultural sensitivity could be just as suffocating as Marxism. Literature would now often be examined through the lenses of race and gender, as well as the new paradigm of multiculturalism. Though initially the new cultural sensitivity was supposed to broaden academic inquiry, often it "only narrowed our intellectual horizons," as writes Nathan Harden in his book *Sex and God at Yale*. Harden describes in his book on the new Ivy League academic culture a curious mixture of open-mindedness and closed, rigid formalism, which seems to resemble the culture that Alan Bloom had already announced in 1987 in *The Closing of the American Mind*.

Conservatives used PC in a different way: they imitated leftists by depicting themselves as oppressed and as victims, not of capitalism, but of the PC left. As a result, reasonable discussions about PC became gridlocked. The New Right thinking of the same era would reproach leftists for politicizing education (and pretty much everything else). They were not wrong, although their point falls a little flat: those who label leftists as PC are just as engaged in politicization.

This book tries to wrench the discussion from this gridlock, and to do so, it approaches PC from an unusual angle, represented by dandyism and Daoism. From a Daoist point of view, both the left and the right ethicized and politicized culture and were unwilling to accept culture for what it is: chaotic. Left and right launched dead-serious battles over PC, and each camp defended its position with the help of ethics. Today it is difficult to even imagine that PC or anti-PC could be about aesthetics and not about ethics. Dandyism in particular, seems to adopt the behavior of the earlier pre-PC left, as dandies make fun of their own class, exalting and exaggerating a certain snobbish behavior, spicing it up with some biting irony. There is also a parallel with the *Zhuangzi*. According to Moeller, many texts in the *Zhuangzi*, especially the famous story of butcher Ding, were initially parodies. Later, some readers ceased seeing the irony and the humor, and the texts lost much of their subversive power (see Moeller 2020b).

The Aesthetics of Transgression

So is it true to say the dandy is not politically correct but is therefore "politically incorrect"? As mentioned, the *Trésor de la langue française* defines the dandy as somebody with a total "disregard of social conventions as well as the ethics of the bourgeoisie." Chateaubriand held that "Brummell reveals the proud independence of his character by keeping his hat on, rolling on the sofas [and] stretching his boots in front of the ladies who are sitting in front of him, all of them in admiration" (Chateaubriand 1836, 273). The dandy is also famous for his transgressive play with names and titles. The Johnson-Thompson anecdote of Brummell going to a ball without being invited has been related previously. The narrator (Jesse 1844, 1:101) depicts the adversary as losing control over the situation while Brummell stays cool, makes his "best bow, leisurely feeling in all his pockets" as he searches for an invitation card. The "incensed lady" Mrs. Thompson takes the card and "haughtily throwing it from her in a climax of vexation and anxiety to get rid of him," says that it is not her card, whereupon Brummell tells her, always "affecting the most innocent surprise," that some names are simply (almost) equal. There is an equalization of names, and Brummell stays perfectly cool when spelling it out in front of the lady. A similar confusion of names or titles emerges from the anecdote of Brummell attending a ball that was organized by a certain Lady Jersey. Brummell called up her carriage, mentioning the name "Mrs. Fitzherbert" instead of "mistress" and "laid a strong emphasis on the insulting epithet" (Jesse 1844, 256). Forgetting about names is part of the dandy's phlegm, and it can be considered his version of "no-mind." McCormack notes that the "difficulty of 'naming' is also central to many of Wilde's plays. Is a woman 'good' or 'bad'? Who is Jack, after all?" (McCormack, 95n3). In *Dorian Gray*, Basil calls Henry "Harry" for no particular reason. The dandy is aware of the importance of names and titles, but he disrespects them on purpose.

The dandy is incorrect, but this does not mean that he simply neglects all conventions and acts carelessly; on the contrary, though the dandy has a total "disregard of social conventions and the ethics for the bourgeoisie" (Trésor), he masters the conventions and ethics of the bourgeoisie better than anybody else. The dandy is determined by a paradox. He is revolted and likes to provoke powerful people; however, contrary to the simply "incorrect" person, he not only occupies a firm place in the highest social strata where such conventions are applied but is even admired by its members because, in general, he *does* follow the rules very well. He is integrated and accepted, but the reason is not that he is politically correct. The gap between him and the rest of the "simply correct" community remains constantly obvious. The dandy *seems* to follow the rules, that is, he pretends; however, he does it so well that his pretense becomes genuine. He goes along with conventions but at the same time makes it clear that he does not take them seriously. Following the rules is for him an aesthetic play, which means that he does not accept the rules' ethical justification.

In a century of conformity, the dandy exercises a cult of difference but does so not by reforming but rather by parodying the rules of conformity. Reformers were plentiful, and most of them were moralizers and modernizers. The dandy breaks the rules of correctness; but, contrary to the opponents of PC that are increasingly prevalent in our times, he challenges correctness in such a polished way that it shames the most fervent defenders of this correctness. When Brummell finds the champagne of bad quality, he raises his glass and says, "John, give me some more of that cider" (Jesse 1844, 1:105); or he feeds the caviar to the cat and the truffle stuffed capon to the host's dog when the quality is inferior (Jesse 1910, 1:99, 2:25). The dandy's incorrectness is aimed at those who believe themselves to be very correct. He is thus reminiscent of Diogenes of Sinope, who rebuffed the powerful with his cynicism. To a lady who politely remarks that he must be embarrassed if somebody were to see him talking to such an unfashionable person as herself, he replies: "Don't mention it; there is no one near us" (Jesse 1844, 1:112). There is also some ironically applied megalomania. Brummell is reported to have said to Colonel McMahon, the prince's private secretary, about the prince regent: "I made him what he is, and I can unmake him" (1844, 1:257).

The dandy shocks—but with style. Through exaggerations, the dandy takes the concept of the perfect gentleman to an extreme, which means that he empties the concept of the gentleman of its ethical content. He keeps the form but fills it with absurdities.

The dandy is provocative and against correctness, but he is not the rugged chap who bluntly claims to be politically incorrect and behaves accordingly. His provocations are not of the dramatic or kitschy kind (kitsch will be dealt with in various contexts in this book), and Marie-Christine Natta is even convinced that "provocation plays no role" in Brummell's life (Natta 1989, 26–27).

The anti-PC rugged chap might seek to instigate a revolution. Meanwhile, the dandy has no intention of instigating a revolution of the politically incorrect because revolutions are always ethically motivated. The dandy has only an aesthetics. He sublimates the revolution into something that looks revolted without reaching the state of revolution and calmly continues playing the game of high society; by doing this, he changes the rules slightly. The dandy has no political program and no theory, not about aesthetics nor gender. He just does what he finds appropriate, and he does it with such consistency that observers sometimes imagine mysterious and unwritten rules behind his random behavior.

Chapter 1

What Would Zhuangzi Have Said about Political Correctness?

Daoism on Language

The *Zhuangzi* is opposed to the orthodoxy represented by Confucius's *Analects* and the Mohists, Xunzi, as well as some other Chinese philosophers who required clear standards for the use of names. Against this, the *Zhuangzi* suggests that the name is not the thing and that to some extent, all names are arbitrary. Logically, any rectification of language becomes useless. So, how would Zhuangzi have approached PC?

Early Confucian texts like the *Analects* and the *Mencius* highlight the necessity of making social roles (that is, titles or names) correspond with their enactment, and Confucius insists that "if names be not correct, language is not in accordance with the truth of things. If language be not in accordance with the truth of things, affairs cannot be carried on to success."[1] In state affairs, the first thing to do is to "correct terms" because otherwise "speech will not follow" (*yan bu shun* 言不順) and "affairs will not be accomplished" (*shi bu cheng* 事不成) (Analects 13.3).

The proposal to rectify names[2] (*zheng ming* 正名) is certainly the most striking feature of Confucian social theory: "By carefully modeling language distinctions, social-political authorities try to make us follow the traditional codes correctly" (Hansen 2000, 65). Against this, the *Zhuangzi* depicts Confucian philosophy as obsessed with the rectification of names or with the correspondence of names and actuality (*ming shi* 名實).[3] Among Confucius's most notable examples of *zheng ming* is that "a prince should act as a prince, a minister should act as a minister, a father should act as a father and a son should act as a son" (*Analects* 12.11).

Against this, the *Zhuangzi* suggests that fixed language standards are, first, unattainable, and second, unnecessary or even bad for communication. With regard to names, as with anything else, the *Zhuangzi* values a philosophy of spontaneity (*zìrán* 自然). Names are dynamic, as the existence of nicknames demonstrates best. The *Zhuangzi* criticizes, as Graham notes in an apt comment, what it perceives as excessive scholasticism and recommends "to educate the spontaneous energies rather than use the heart [the mind] to think, name, categorize and conceive ends and principles of action" (2001, 7). The main purpose of these premises is to disable nominalism and, even more radically, as says Coyle, to disable "any correspondence theory of truth" (2016, 200). The Vienna Circle philosopher Rudolf Carnap reproached Heidegger to create semantically empty sentences and pseudostatements.[4] Zhuangzi would not contest that Heidegger's expressions such as "the Nothing nothings" fail to correspond to really existing things. However, the precise language of logicians does not correspond to really existing things either. Logical language is semantically empty, but logicians refuse to acknowledge this. Logicians are talking about objects that have no fixed contents.

Nominalism in PC and Chinese Philosophy

PC describes behaviors and policies that are intended to prevent the discrimination or offense of members of certain groups in society. PC puts a strong emphasis on language. Certain words need to be avoided, and new words need to be created in order to improve human behavior. The ultimate objective of this language reform is to make language match an ideal reality. What does it mean to make language match an ideal reality? Within this project, two approaches need to be distinguished. First, PC acknowledges an existing reality, such as, for example in the realm of gender, the reality of the "non-binary person," and subsequently "reconfirms" this reality through a correction of language by providing an appropriate name or an appropriate pronoun for this person. Second, PC is also an activist movement that tries to *reform* reality through the correction of language. Stuart Hall has called this approach "extreme nominalism" because PC seems to believe that "if things are called by a different name they will cease to exist" (1994, 168). Here the idea is not simply to make language match an existing reality but rather to *change names in order to change reality*. The dynamic of PC constantly operates through both poles. The first intention is to correct language to make it more compatible with the reality "out there," a reality that is believed to prefigure the linguistic reality. The second intention, the "extreme nominalist" one, is to correct words in order to *create* a reality that conforms with abstract ideas of justice and equality. Both intentions are distinct, but they often manifest in a single gesture, which is why it can sometimes be difficult to disentangle them. In this chapter, I will submit both poles to a Daoist reading.

I will start with the first one: the attempt to make language more compatible with reality. PC has many language policies through which it attempts to minimize offense to individuals or groups. PC's lists of prohibited words can be long, but I want to concentrate here on how PC handles gender because, as mentioned, I believe that a critical reading of PC gender language through Daoist philosophy is most enlightening. The favorite focus of language correction projects are identity-based topics such as gender, race, and religion—gender probably being the most popular. Some transgender or gender-nonbinary people use pronouns different from the ones they were assigned at birth, and sometimes they use "they" in the singular or "zhe" and "zher." The task of correcting pronouns could not have been solved by simply using a "genderless pronoun" such as "it," which already exists. The problem with "it" is that it does not properly reflect the complexity of gender reality and has, apart from that, objectifying connotations. Consequently, entirely new gender terms had to be created to match gender language with gender reality. In 2016, New York's Human Rights Commission issued a list with thirty-one "protected genders," some of which do also have their own pronouns. Among the new gender terms are not only "bi-gendered" and "cross-dresser" but also "pan-gender" and "androgyne." Some of those, like "transgender," had been extant before this list although not as official gender terms. Others, like "two-spirit," "gender fluid," "gender gifted," "demisexual," or "graysexual" are entirely new inventions. It is now illegal to discriminate against anyone on the basis of gender identity and gender expression.

How would Zhuangzi have judged this project? Zhuangzi was a language skeptic, which means that he did not believe that language could ever convey the true meanings of the world. Beyond that, in general, Daoism has no strong attachments to any kind of unitary self, and it can thus be assumed that it would have no strong attachment to a unitary form of gender either. By nature, Daoism would be against identity politics. The *Zhuangzi* insinuates that any identification with social conventions can be avoided and that notions of authenticity and the self can be circumvented. Instead of constructing or discovering an "authentic self" that might ultimately reify authority, the *Zhuangzi* puts a special emphasis on "forgetting (*wang* 忘), losing (*sang* 喪), and negating (*wu* 無) one's social self" (Moeller and D'Ambrosio 2018, 2).[5]

It has been said above that PC operates through two poles: (1) correcting language in order to make it more compatible with the reality, and (2) correcting language in order to *create* a reality that conforms with ideas about what is good. Confucianism has a similarly twofold interest in language correction. *Ming shi* is the correspondence of names and actuality whereas *zheng ming* is the correction of reality through language. Ge Rongjin recently claimed that Confucius's *zheng ming* theory "attempts to correct actual situations that have undergone changes by means of old names" (in Sigurdsson 2020, 16). Mencius, a Confucian, makes this logic of "extreme nominalism" even clearer when explaining that words contained in certain teachings will first enter the mind and later become actions: "What arises in the mind will interfere with policy, and what shows itself in policy will interfere with practice" (Mencius 2003, 143).[6] Using the right words can change the world.

When it comes to the correspondence of names with reality, Confucians are not the only thinkers in ancient China to develop such "nominalist" approaches. They are not even the most radical ones, but the "School of Names," another of the One Hundred Philosophical Schools of the Warring States period (5th century–221 BCE) took nominalist thinking to an extreme. The School of Names (also referred to as the school of "the Logicians") is a traditional label for a group of thinkers who concentrated on the relation between object and name.[7] Logicians speculate with words. The School of Names is notorious for logic chopping and the invention of paradoxes,[8] as well as for discussions concerning how one can distinguish the "same" from the "different." The philosophy of language and epistemology of this school sees philosophical disputation as "a process of debating whether the thing in question is 'this' (*shi*) or 'not-this' (*fei*), the same as or different from some model, paradigm, or analogy" (Fraser 2017). Huizi (Hui Shi), a "logician" and the most prominent representative of the School of Names (though also, oddly enough, a good friend of Zhuangzi), saw logic as an investigation of the underlying structure of reality.

Huizi's thought came close to that of the Mohists, who were a paramilitary group selling consultancy services to leaders in times of crisis. Mohists defended very authoritarian positions and were specially trained in the arts of defensive warfare. They were also famous for matching their actions to their beliefs. Mohists are part of what Chad Hansen calls the "analytic period" of ancient Chinese philosophy (2000, 4): criticizing Daoist antilanguage positions, later Mohists in particular, concentrated on realist analysis. The Mohists were utilitarian and insisted on logic, rational thought, and science. Caring for all was an important moral premise, too. Huizi adopted Mohist positions and probably pushed Mohism even more toward a technical analysis of the nature of language, logic, and validity in argumentation. Though Mohism was more opposed to Confucianism than any other school, Mohists took the reform of language the furthest. An essential task became the description and classification of word uses in order to regularize the way that terms are used in actual speech. In the later Mohist writings, great effort was made to assign precise and unambiguous definitions to words. When ambiguity could not be eradicated from ordinary terms, new words were coined, and technical vocabulary was devised to clarify grammatical and logical features of language. Gongsung Long from the School of Names, who was unrelated to the Mohists but influenced by Huizi,[9] believed that "any fully perfected language must conform to the doctrine of the 'rectification of names,'" which means that every word must be used to refer to a particular predefined referent (see also note 5). A word can only possess a single referent, and each thing can only have a single name (Eno 2016).[10]

The above Chinese thinkers adhere to unique knowledge systems dependent on their culture, but in most general terms, they do have counterparts in the West. Examples would be the Alexandrine Grammarians of the second and third century BC or contemporary analytic philosophy, which emphasizes the study of language and the logical analysis of concepts. These knowledge systems accept language as the perfect means to map reality. Opposed to these are, in the West, philosophies that profess language as an insufficient means to capture reality and that thus come closer to Daoism. Prominent among these is the Continental philosophy of language initiated by Hamann, Herder, and Humboldt as well as its developments undertaken by Heidegger and modern hermeneutics.

Confucius, the Mohists, the School of Names, as well as all the other Chinese schools mentioned in the preceding paragraphs, require clear standards for the use of names to avoid chaos. Against this, Zhuangzi holds the position of a linguistic liberalist. It has even been said that Zhuangzi "stands out among thinkers, Chinese and Western, for his positive appreciation of chaos" (Jochim 2016, 65). However, this does not mean that Zhuangzi thinks that chaos is best. Daoism's relationship with chaos is peculiar. The *Zhuangzi* does indeed suggest a "chaotification" of reality; however, what will be chaotified is only the *linguistic* reality, which will lead to the appreciation of a reality that exists beyond language. Daoism does not believe that total chaos will arise simply because we refrain from matching the name with the thing. Linguistic liberalism does not generate disorder. On the contrary, it is the regulations that create chaos. The *Daodejing*[11] argues that "the more laws and regulations are promulgated, the more thieves and robbers there will be" (chap. 57). This also concerns the regulations of names. Fixing names is not only futile but can also be dangerous. The more names are regulated, the more likely it is that some people will take undue advantage of it and appropriate names they do not deserve. In the *Zhuangzi*, even Confucius is depicted as if he were very much aware of this. Doing things with the only purpose of "getting a name" for it, undermines virtue, be it simply because it is hypocritical. In the opening story of the *Zhuangzi*'s chapter 4 called "In the Human World," an overzealous Yan Hui seeks advice from Confucius in political affairs; his hidden ambitions to "get a name" are subsequently revealed. To keep names in an initial state of "chaos" is always the better option.

Gender and Culture

If objects have no definite content, then genders must also be objects without fixed content. From a Daoist point of view, language is not a reality: "real" reality lies behind language or, perhaps more precisely, beyond language. Supporters of PC will not *necessarily* say that the new language they create is a reality. If they do, they will adhere to the second option, the "extreme nominalist" one, which will be discussed below. But most of the time, language is, for them, supposed to correctly *reflect* a reality that lies behind language. For the *Zhuangzi*, language cannot reflect this reality for the simple reason that any reality behind and beyond language is fluid and not objectifiable. It is not chaos in the sense of meaningless nonsense. As mentioned, the real chaos is the petty knowledge acquired by the reasonable faculty of mind, which counts, quantifies, and invents rules and names. But behind that language, there is a kaleidoscope of an ever-shifting multiplicity of things, and the Daoist sage attempts to observe *this* reality and not merely a reality shaped by linguistic conventions. Knowledge must be knowledge of the dynamic multiplicity of things and not of linguistic entities and pronouns, which is why the *Daodejing* says: "Those who know do not speak; those who speak do not know" (chap. 56). In other words, Daoism wants to shift the level of reason from the consideration of linguistic essences to the consideration of cultural existence. It believes that all essences, including names, are merely products of the mind. Consequently, genders have no essence either, but they are only what we believe them to be; any language reform making gender terms or pronouns match with "real" genders becomes redundant. There is language with its conventions, but it is only language. PC insists on these conventions though it also believes that some of these conventions need to be corrected.

For the Daoist, behind the reality of linguistic conventions is the reality of culture; and culture is somehow "chaotic," if only because it does not always follow conventions or abstract rules. Culture is not created according to rules but is dynamic and constantly emerging. In principle, we can never say that "this is true" or "this is false" in a culture because culture is constantly changing. Applied to genders, this means that we can never say what gender somebody actually has: gender only *emerges* from a culture—but there is no reason to mold this culture into language. Jordan Peterson expressed this thought in the famous Munk Debate called "Political Correctness Gone Mad?"[12] when saying: "Sex, ethnicity, race. What about how they interact? Gender is infinitely differential. Endless number of ethnic variants. You're going to control for the interaction between all of those?" (Peterson et al. 2018, 37). Culture is the reality of human life, containing emotions, choices, values, desires, perceptions, attitudes, interests, expectations, possibilities, and sensibilities. New components constantly emerge, some fuse, and others are rejected. There are no fixed elements such as identities or genders, but identities and genders are produced by our ways of behaving and our ways of seeing while we are living in cultures. For the Zhuangzists, identity is, as says Hans-Georg Moeller, "like child play that grows into a much more serious and complex life form" (2020).

There is a superficial similarity between the Daoist approach and PC, which can be misleading when trying to understand the relationship between Daoism, language, and PC. As a matter of fact, both Daoism and PC have the same starting point, as for both, language does not match reality. However, the Daoist finds that any matching of the former with the latter is impossible because reality is unstable. Matching reality with language will cause us to lose reality. Against this, PC believes that once we have matched reality with language, we can grasp reality and perhaps even shape it.

Daoism holds that cultural realities are concrete and therefore necessarily different from the abstract and static codes of political correctness. *In culture*, phenomena, behaviors, standards, and gender roles constantly emerge as they are lived and experienced. In a Daoist understanding, only this culture corresponds to the real world, and language cannot fully grasp this culture. It is interesting to observe that sometimes linguists attend to this realm, too, and call the cultural situation of the real world the "normal discourse." In normal discourse, things are not yet clearly opposed to each other; they are not yet essentialized at their ontological core. Normal discourse is the "fluid" language that is spoken in cultures. Sometimes conflicts between normal discourse and official language occur. Linguists know that in normal discourse, some coinages (for example, strange bureaucratic terms) cannot be sustained because reality is more fluid than the official language suggests. Daoism suggests looking at the "ordinary views." These views are not determined by our (linguistic) preconceptions, rules, and standards, but they reflect reality as it emerges and is "flowing" in front of our eyes. To grasp this reality, we must "give up our devotion to our own views and occupy ourselves with the ordinary views" (*Qiwulun*). Rules about "things" (for example, about genders and pronouns) can be no guidelines, but what matters is the ordinary use of things (or of gender terms and pronouns) within cultures. This is why Izutsu concludes that the sage or the Perfect Man experiences the world in the form of an "ontological chaotification" (1983, 377).

The Pursuit of Freedom

The situation becomes slightly more complex when we consider the second approach. PC does not merely try to match language with a preexisting reality, but it also actively strives to change reality by changing language. What Stuart Hall has called "extreme nominalism" is also an appropriate description of Confucianism and the School of Names. A part of PC is clearly characterized by this activist approach, as it attempts to create a new, ideal reality by inventing a new language. It abandons oppressive words and replaces them with new words connoting justice and equality. This can happen in any realm and in many ways, but for matters of consistency, I want to stick here to gender language because such a focus delivers clearer results when comparing PC with Daoism.

When it comes to gender, the "extreme nominalist" part of PC insists that our identities should not be restricted by the names "male" or "female" and that a new reality with new gender identities should be created by inventing new names. The main driving force of such thinking is the pursuit of freedom. Everybody is free to choose the gender and the gender names he/she desires. In this case, the question is, of course, whether it would not be better to turn attention away from names altogether, in order to have maximum freedom. This is precisely what Daoism suggests. For PC, this is not a viable option because, for PC, identity and authenticity are supreme goods that must be established through names. We will see in chapter 4 that in the Enlightenment tradition from which PC emerges, authenticity and freedom have always been linked.

In its pursuit of freedom, the PC approach can initially seem like a "reverse Confucianism" and thus as being closer to Daoism. The person will not have to, in a Confucian manner, live up to the name he/she was given, which by definition is considered to be fundamentally what they are; for example, a father, a son, a biological man or woman. Instead, a new name is invented to designate whatever the person intends to live up to. Gender roles appear first, only to be defined and given names later. This is a "culturalist" position, which is, once again, confusingly, similar to that of Daoism. *In culture* gender turns out to be incompatible with a static "either male or female" scenario. *In culture*, gender is not fixed but rather a spectrum. However, instead of consistently remaining on the level of Daoist chaotification, which insists on the vagueness of any cultural gender spectrum, PC's final step turns out to be very Confucian: PC attributes an identity to this "cultural reality" by issuing a name. PC believes that only when we have attributed the right name to each shade of the cultural gender spectrum can we speak of peoples' "gender identities." For this very reason, in the end, PC is *not* attached to culture but proceeds to a linguistic rectification. Both Daoism and PC thus have the same starting point as both agree that gender is very much socially constructed. However, PC attempts to attribute the right name to the thing, which runs contrary to all Daoist intentions.

Seen from this angle, PC is not similar to but rather the contrary of newspeak whose purpose is to enhance the power of the state over the individual. George Orwell's newspeak, described in his 1949 antiutopian novel *1984*, is a simplified language meant to deprive people of their cognitive faculties by eliminating indirect allusions or multiple meanings from words. Though newspeak also invents new political terms, the main purpose of all these terms is to eliminate nuances and thus to ethicize the world in terms of good and bad ("goodthink vs. crimethink"). PC replaces words, too, but this tends to have at least one reverse effect: most often it makes language more complex. Sometimes PC might be about simplification, but most often it is about complexification. It introduces new words that *add* instead of eliminate shades of meanings. PC language and newspeak thus share the fact of being the outcomes of an "extreme nominalist" thinking because "normal discourse" (oldspeak) is altered in order to change the existing world. However, PC also alters language in order to reflect the world more properly through language, and this intention is absent in newspeak. Seen from another angle, PC simply *is* newspeak because, in the end, reality is always more complex than language, no matter how precise the language is meant to be. This is what appears from the Daoist point of view. Thus, both newspeak and PC eliminate ambiguities, but both do so in different ways. Newspeak describes the world in terms of dichotomies whereas PC often adds new terms in order to clarify the ambiguity. Daoism simply leaves ambiguities intact and pushes aside all linguistic questions.

Sex and Gender

Finding the "real" in culture is a complex task, especially when it comes to gender. It can appear that PC wants to overcome a biological or a scientific reality that is valid only in science and that wants to create a new "cultural gender reality" (later fixed through language). Most of the time, this is indeed the case, but sometimes the approach is fuzzy, as is best shown by the distinctions that have been made between sex and gender. This should be briefly addressed here in order to characterize an—admittedly rare—subapproach of PC that has a peculiar relationship with science.

"Sex" refers to the biological ("scientific") differences between males and females whereas gender refers (though not exclusively) to the "cultural" roles that males and females play in society. In many languages, there is no word for "gender" as distinct from "sex," but in English-speaking countries, "gender" would give its name to a large theoretical body of work named "gender theory." One of the tasks of gender theory is to explain that sex and gender do not necessarily overlap, which means, most of the time, that the cultural reality does not match the biological one and that names and pronouns need to be adjusted. Biology limits sex to a binary scheme, but in culture, the genders are nonbinary. The reverse approach is also possible. Sex can be established as nonbinary on the biological level, and the task of PC is to adjust the cultural genders to this biological reality. Here biology turns out to be more complicated than what conventional gender language assumes. If we only adjust gender language to a new scientific interpretation of sex, we will have a correct language and, necessarily, also a better cultural reality. This is another version of PC. The website healthline.com, which provides resources for people with transgender issues, explains that "the human gene expression actually has much more diversity than the starkly binary physical ideals we've been using to categorize people and their experiences. It reveals that a "perfect" man or woman is a socially created narrative that ignores the full scope of what it means to be human" (Clary 2018). We move away from the Confucian "Perfect Man" who lives up to his name and find, instead, the "Perfect Man" inscribed in our genes. The "Perfect Man" is here no longer necessarily a man or a woman but can be something more complex. But he/she/they is still defined as *something*, and this "something" is believed to predate culture. For PC, the "correction of names" can thus also mean that the name must be matched with the genes, in which case, the world of genders is adjusted not to ethical-cultural models but to scientific models. Instead of seeing a blurred gender spectrum as a cultural fact, the blurred gender spectrum becomes a scientific fact.

Gender Existence

What matters for Daoism is culture, and in this book, I will be drawing parallels between culture as a concept and what Daoism calls the Dao. Confucianism has created an elaborate system of moral values based on the assumption that essences are marked off from other essences. Against this, Daoism suggests that people who believe in the existence of such systems of moral values are deceived by external and phenomenal aspects. Without saying that Daoism is existentialism, I find it useful here to contrast essence with existence. Of course, my idea of existence does not have the same kind of "authenticity value" that it has in existentialism. Far from it. Daoist existence is rather, as I have already stated, a cultural totality that remains full of ambiguities. In a Daoist view, existence is a process through which life manifests itself as it unfolds, and rules, systems, names, and pronouns cannot grasp this reality.

This does not mean that in the "real world" everything is relative because nothing is fixed and because nothing can be spelled out. Daoism does not suggest relativism, but it is merely skeptical of systems, rules, and essences because these items can never truly reflect reality (nor can gender terms or gender pronouns). Daoism criticizes those who believe they have identified *the* principal rule of ethics, justice, reality, and correctness. For Daoism, there is no such "correct" principle, but our right behavior always emerges while we are playing social roles in culture. Daoism does not abandon all standards, but the Daoist sage simply finds that the real world is not a system of rules with permanently correct linguistic distinctions. The real cultural world is rather a limitless space where things constantly melt into one another. Daoism criticizes those who believe, as the "logicians" do, that the correct matching of names and things leads to knowledge and that the relations of "same" and "different" determine what is real and right.

It has been previously shown that it is rather tricky to put this topic in relationship with PC because, superficially, the Daoist and the PC approaches are similar. When it comes to genders, PC, too, wants to look past a male-female binary that it considers "not real," arguing that external and phenomenal aspects should not deceive us. "Externally" s/he might look like a man, but "in reality" s/he is not. PC wants to modify the gender terms that are commonly used, which is to say, are *culturally* used, in our language. Superficially, this approach does indeed resemble the Daoist one because PC, too, is skeptical of what is generally taken for granted. The (linguistic gender) reality that we perceive is not necessarily the real gender reality, but there is another reality behind it. However, the *Zhuangzi*'s skepticism goes further than that of PC. Instead of inventing new gender terms and pronouns that reflect what still only *appears* to be (more) real, Daoism recommends the "chaotification" of reality altogether. In this chaos called reality, linguistic reform is neither possible nor necessary. What matters is rather the cultural experience of genders through which a "gender reality" emerges.[13]

"Daoist Feminism"

The Daoist thought model can also be illustrated by contrasting it with a gender-related phenomenon from which PC partly derives: feminism. Many feminisms issue a deontology of abstract rules that are supposed to be valid on a universal scale. As a result, gender and gender relations become essentialized, and feminism ends up with a world of black and white. The French philosopher Bérénice Levet criticizes this approach and insists that "any ambition to create an abstract form of equality authorizes the multiplication of norms, quotas, and the intrusion of laws into our lives, as well as all the destructions of language and spiritual works" (2018, 126). Levet argues that equality cannot be spelled out in a formal fashion but that it must always be enacted within certain cultural places, that is, within a certain cultural "reality." These real places are more "chaotic" than what the rules of feminism suggest. Levet is not against the equality of men and women; just as Daoism is not against the equality of things, as emerges from the "Discourse on the Equalization of Things." "Daoist feminism," should it ever exist, would rather strive to attain a reality of gender equality without *essential* distinctions between men and women, and this would be achieved by letting all linguistic distinctions lose their solid contours. The existing distinctions would not need to be modified, supplemented, or rendered more complex. Instead, their nonessential character would have to be recognized as the only reality, which would then lead to a "chaotification" of distinctions. An equalization of things does not mean that all things must be identical. It is rather the feminists who support this by creating an abstract form of equality. They are like those who misunderstand the Daoist principle of equality and whom Yong Huang describes as such: "They fail to realize that, to equalize things, what one needs to do is not to make them identical but to recognize their equal value, however different they are. [The equalization of things] does argue for the unity or interconnectedness of things, which, however, is different from their identity" (2010, 75). In summary, the Zhuangzian view of equality of things is the result of a great awakening to the reality of things, and this would also have to be applied to the reality of gender.

Confucian Gender Theory

There are reasons to suppose that Confucianism takes a more rigid view of genders than Daoism. Sin Yee Chan (2003) finds expressions of gender essentialism in the *yin-yang* distinction when aligned with gender because it attributes "invariable or core characteristics that define that particular gender identity" (319). Though the *yin-yang* distinction does not appear in the *Analects* or the *Mencius* (it is only mentioned in *Xunzi*), it became an integral part of Neo-Confucianism. Early Confucianism did not link *yin-yang* to genders, but, according to Chan, the Confucian Tang philosopher Dong Zhongshu (772–841) "tried to seek cosmic justification for the social-political hierarchy that genders became codified as the exemplification of *yin-yang* forces" (332–33). It was believed that *yin* and *yang* can accurately represent the essential characteristics of genders. The distinction was thus guided by essentialism, which is all the more disconcerting as it often implied hierarchies. Following the gender norm was the way to achieve cosmic harmony (330), and "any divergence from the presumed pattern would be seen as a deviation and, therefore, wrong or bad, or at least undesirable" (321). With the "genderization" came the ethicization: "For example, Zhu Xi (AD 1130–1200) wrote, 'Good and evil can be applied to describe *yin* and *yang*. It can also be applied to describe the male and the female'" (315).[14] With the advent of Neo-Confucianism, the denigration of the *yin* force, and hence the female gender, would be further accentuated. Chan does not accept the "fluid distinction" argument, which only seemingly cancels the essentialism. According to this view, *yin* and *yang* are relational, which means that there are no fixed rules as to the weight assigned to each of them.

Henry Rosemont insists on this dynamism, pointing out that "nothing is either *yin* or *yang* in and of itself, but only as it stands relative to something else. An elderly man is *yang* with respect to an elderly woman, but *yin* with respect to a young man. (. . .) This relationality clearly militates against the view that the early Chinese thinkers are essentialistic in their accounts of women and men" (Rosemont 1997 quoted in Chan 2003, 319). Chan rejects this argument and believes that the essentialism continues even within the dynamism:

> That males can sometimes be in the *yin* position does not mean that it cannot be true that all males are *yang* when

compared with females. Put another way, remember that *yin* and *yang* imply different characteristics or attributes. (. . .) Consequently, in Rosemont's example, since an elderly man is stronger than an elderly woman, he is *yang*. But he becomes *yin* when compared to a young man. This, however, does not mean that all males are not strong in the absolute sense. (319 and 320)

Chan's point is to say that if *yin* and *yang* would really be strictly relational, then the distinction itself would be vacuous. As an alternative, Chen points to androgyny, which is a more Daoist ideal. Obviously, when androgyny is the ideal, gender becomes irrelevant, and only then do all people "have equal opportunity in developing all desirable character traits, regardless of gender" (333). "Isn't it better that the Confucian role-system combine instead with the ideal of androgyny?" (336) asks Chan.

That this is a Daoist position has best been explained by Roger Ames. In his article "Taoism and the Androgynous Ideal" (1981), Ames first criticizes the concept that Daoism is "feminine" as opposed to the more "masculine" Confucianism. Feminine is here supposed to mean "tolerant, yielding, permissive, withdrawing, mystical and receptive" (Ames 1981, 21). Ames sees the androgynous as a more plausible Daoist option, be it only because political rulers, to whom the Lao Tzu was addressed in the first place, could not be merely feminine. Instead, the ruler should be "androgynous in his orientation. (. . .) [Likewise], for the consummate person, the ideal for the individual in this society must also be androgynous" (33). Since the sage-ruler is the "model of the world," in both the Lao Tzu and Chuang Tzu, a "reconciliation of opposites concomitant with the embodiment of the constant *tao*" (36) is more advisable than simply reflecting the "feminine." Only then, the people are "free to pursue their own realization" (34). Ames supports this point of view with the following passage from the *Laozi* (chap. 28):

> One who knows masculinity and yet preserves femininity
> Becomes the river gorge of the world. . . .
> One who knows whiteness and preserves blackness
> Becomes the model of the world. . . .
> One who knows glory and yet preserves tarnishedness
> Becomes the valley of the world (37)

The sage-ruler remains non-active with regard to femininity and masculinity and thus represents a "reconciliation of the feminine/masculine dichotomy" (37); only then can the people be transformed on their own. For gender, this means that the gender spectrum is no longer fixated on two genders (not even the "dynamic" ones of *yin-yang*), but that all essentialism has been taken out of the gender equation. Gender will be a pure matter of "self-so-ness," naturalness, spontaneity, and *ziran* (自然).[15] Its identification will not be obstructed by knowledge about rules and about "correct" identifications. All that remains is natural genuineness and self-transformation (*tu hua* 獨化).[16] The Daoist option is compatible with the desires of liberal feminists as well as with those "people who choose to deviate from gender norms, whom Chan addresses at the end of her reflections on Confucianism and gender. For the "androgynous ideal," "femininity and masculinity, like other desirable personal traits such as curiosity and prudence, are optional. Their normative force is conditioned on their noninterference with individual freedom and choices. Confucians, on the other hand, may be more strict about the normativity of gender traits" (2003, 229).

Listening to the Cultural "Background Noise"

In a Daoist sense, culture is a sort of prelinguistic "background noise" that will never entirely overlap with distinct language. I take the word "background noise" from Frank Stevenson's article on the *Zhuangzi* in which he compares the Daoist "chaos" with Michel Serres's elaboration of chaos theory in physics. Daoism sees the Dao as chaos: "Dao is already not silence but also not yet a full-fledged 'rational discourse'; it is the noise (. . .) out of which 'language' or 'meaningful sounds' emerge" (2006, 308). I understand culture precisely as such a background noise. Culture is like an uncarved surface, or a "field of undifferentiated language" and therefore a sort of "pure language" that will only later become "discriminated into self-opposed meanings (this/that, true/false, right/wrong)" (308). This also applies to male/female distinctions and their corresponding pronouns. Gender terms do not *reflect* a preexisting factual reality; nor *are* they a reality: they only express, in Eliade's terms (see note 13 above), experiences through "religious" symbols.

Moeller explains that there was in ancient China a "semiotics of presence" that knew no ontological gap between representation and presence but conceived "of *both* the signifier and the signified as equally present. The realm of the present includes everything that 'is' (*you*)" (2004, 145). There is, in this semiotics, no "ontological split" separating "a mere 'symbolical' realm of representation (such as, for instance, language) from a truly present realm of things or ideas" (141). As a result, names and the nameless coexist, just like presence and nonpresence do coexist.[17] Daoist thought employs this semiotics of presence, and it is clear what consequences this has for the present discussion of genders. Genders exist in culture, and the Western semiotics of representation (as opposed to the "Daoist semiotics of presence") attempts to represent these genders through names and pronouns. In a "Daoist semiotics of presence," such representation is not necessary. Not everything that exists needs to be presented: most of New York's thirty-one gender terms could also be left nonpresent, which would not mean that their existence would be denied.

In the "Discourse on Equalizing Things," which is a meditation on the relativity and the "equilibrium" of all things and meanings, the *Zhuangzi* advocates the collapsing of the distinction between so and not-so as well as of what is admissible and inadmissible.[18] As mentioned, the result of this collapsing of distinctions is not mere relativism. Relativism is thinkable only when there are essences that relate to each other or when there are essentially different genders that relate to each other like stable essences. The *Zhuangzi*'s project is different. It wants to shift the level of reason from the consideration of essences to the consideration of existence, which means that it wants to *transcend* relativism to reach a stage of equalization of all things. This is the necessary outcome of a view that holds all essences to be merely the products of our minds. In that case, genders have no essence but are only what we believe them to be. And if this is true, why would one need a language reform to establish the right use of names and pronouns?

It would thus be completely wrong to say that Daoism creates relativism and that PC establishes absolute meanings through rules and names. Allan Bloom, an early and fierce critic of PC as well as one of the harshest critics of "postmodern" relativism, has shown that PC and relativism are linked. Bloom unconsciously formulates a Daoist argument. PC suggests that everybody is right (in his/her own way), and it creates special rules meant to defend the "being right" of every individual, and in Bloom's view, *this* creates relativism. PC establishes essences and substances and subsequently equalizes them, which is precisely the relativism that Daoism wants to transcend. For PC, not only do genders have an essence, but these essences will become even more fixed through gender language. In this way, PC just creates a new, abstract reality, which becomes most obvious when some people feel that this linguistic reality does not entirely correspond to what they would spontaneously identify as real. As pointed out previously, some linguistic coinages cannot be sustained in "normal discourse." In Canada, the Ontario Human Rights Commission ruled that "refusing to refer to a trans person by their chosen name and a personal pronoun that matches their gender identity" can be considered discrimination. Gender identity and gender expression are protected by the Human Rights Act and the Criminal Code. Jordan Peterson famously resented the idea that the government might force him to use these neologisms and called this PC policy "authoritarian." In Daoist terms, Peterson did not want to accept the reality created by the mind and believed in the existence of a "cultural reality," "lived reality," or a "normal discourse" that is more real than the linguistic one.[19] By saying this, he did not want to make any essentialist statement about transgender men/women or about any other gender. Peterson did not mean that a given individual who may subjectively be perceived to be male but requires a specific pronoun other than he/him, would, for Peterson himself, still essentially be a man and should therefore be referred to as such. On the contrary, Peterson referred to a gender existence that is more "chaotic" and more fluid than the abstract reality prescribed by language. Peterson did not claim that his own standard was right and that he would simply stick to it. He only resented the fact that PC wants its own standard of right and wrong to become the universal norm to which all others must conform. One can also say that Peterson pointed to the fact that normal discourse cannot always absorb new linguistic realities, to which PC would answer that normal discourse needs to be changed; and to which a Daoist would respond that cultural discourse is chaotic anyway and in constant change. So why *should* it be changed? The aim must rather be to find a reasonable and polite way to play our social roles within this cultural discourse.

In the *Zhuangzi*'s view, "authoritarian" approaches like that of the Canadian government reflect an opinionated mind that tends to lead projects to disasters (on this as well as the respecting of differences see Huang 2010, 79). Culture is fluid, and a social rambler, roamer, or flâneur like Peterson refuses to stick to a single view. His vision is fluid as it "is constituted in multiple respects by our relation to the [cultural] landscape" (Moeller and D'Ambrosio 2018, 11).

The Zen Buddhist View of Language

Though this book's declared aim is to consider Daoism, it is useful to sketch, at the end of this chapter, the principal lines of the Zen Buddhist view of language. I will also occasionally refer to Zen ideas in order to strengthen the arguments that will emerge in further discussions. Similar to the Daoist approach, reality as seen by Zen defies linguistic description, and together with this, apparently solid laws of identity. Huineng, the founder of the Chan (Zen) school, was illiterate, and one of his "main teachings was that a person should not be reliant on words. One could not become a wise follower through thought and reasoning since language and the written word were man-made shackles. They were limited, dealt in generalities, and were one-sided, preventing people from grasping the true nature of reality" (Li 2019, 204). The mind essentializes reality, and Zen Buddhism is against *svabhava*, which is self-essence or self-nature. For example, there is no substance in the external world manifesting qualities that could be called "the qualities of woman." What exists is only what phenomenally appears as a woman, and to see woman "really" as woman does not mean to delimit the fluid phenomenon "woman" to fixed and unchangeable womanness. On the contrary, woman should rather be seen in its indetermination. Woman has no permanent ontological solidity but only a phenomenal existence. Woman (or any other phenomenon) can manifest itself in its "fullest density of existence" (Izutsu 1982, 14) and thus in its freshness; but this will never be attained through language.

When the mind cannot attain this existence due to the essentialist tendency of the ego, it will abide with objects in their delimitation. However, there is a nonarticulated field in which phenomena (cultural movements, men, women, etc.) articulate themselves freely and independently of the dichotomizing activity of our intellect. While our mind tends to go for either the male or the female, "real" gender reality is not bound by such limitations.

This thinking is based on the Buddhist idea that there is no self and that the belief in a self leads to suffering: "By oneself the evil is done, by oneself one suffers; by oneself evil is left undone, by oneself one is purified. Purity and impurity belong to oneself, no one can purify another" says the Dhammapada" (chap. 12, Müller 1880, 46).[20] Zen Buddhism thus tries to perceive a point where all things are just what they are: mountains are mountains and rivers are rivers, which is an absolute antinominalism. Mountains and rivers do not correspond to their names but are truly what they are, independent of language. Zen Buddhism calls this state the self-determination absolute nothingness.

With regard to pronouns, it is not "he" or "she" but rather the pronoun "I" that raises most suspicions not only in Zen Buddhism but in Buddhism in general. Other pronouns can be submitted to the same critical treatment, but the "I" is clearly seen as an expression of the self that needs to be avoided. Long before the rise of Zen, Buddhism in India had subjected the usage of the first-person pronoun to a thorough scrutiny. "We constantly conjure up such ideas as 'I' and 'mine' and many most undesirable states result," writes Conze (1959, 18). Buddhism finds that the "I," which is our ego, does not correspond to any reality. Later, this anti-first-person pronoun reasoning became the most serious question for Zen. A typical Zen Buddhist question is thus: "Does the grammatical subject of all these sentences represent the real personal subject in its absolute suchness?" (Izutsu 1982, 67).

Concerning the irrelevance of the "I," Buddhism and Zen agree. However, there are discrepancies with regard to other "names." As a matter of fact, Zen's opposition to nominalism emerges from a fierce combat against some conventional Buddhist linguistic theories. In the history of Buddhism there is a fight between nominalists and antinominalists that echoes the above-described fight between Confucianism and Daoism. The semantic theory of the Buddhist Nyaya and Vaisesika schools held that a word is a symbol for something existent. Whatever is knowable is namable: as soon as we have a word for ox, the ox exists. Nyaya-Vaisesika's theories can be added to the previously mentioned philosophies that believe that language is the perfect means to map reality. In the Indian cultural sphere, these schools were opposed by Upanishadic philosophy, Advaita Vedanta, Sunyavada (see Theodor and Yao 2013, 27), as well as by the Mahayana philosophy of language that is contained in the Madhyamaka (Middle Way) School and Ideation-Only School. Nagarjuna, the founder of the Middle Way School, deconstructed the nominalist usage of terms with the help of the concept of *sunyata* (emptiness). The Middle Way school portrays a position between two metaphysical positions claiming that things ultimately either exist or do not exist. The Ideation-Only school taught that the myriad *dharmas* (the rules vaguely corresponding to *li* in Chinese philosophy) are ideation only. This means that language has no ontological significance and that words are merely signs established for the convenience of life: they have nothing to do with the structure of reality, but what exists is a continuous stream of consciousness whose meanings constantly change. Ordinary people live with linguistic conventions and take for granted the linguistic reality imposed upon us. Sometimes, they want to change it and invent new words and pronouns. However, as long as they do not recognize reality in its limitlessness, they will always stay imprisoned within their closed linguistic reality.

Chapter 2

Daoism and Dandyism

You (遊) and Flâner

Western philosophers like Wittgenstein developed themes that were apparently Daoist,[1] and some Western writers' personalities or lifestyles have been said to be similar to Zhuangzi's. Victor Mair (1983a, 86) sees François Rabelais and James Joyce as Zhuangzi's confreres, and affinities between Daoism and Cynicism have also often been stated (see Raphals 1994; Kjellberg 1994; Yang 2007).[2] I want to demonstrate in this book that Zhuangzi, the "free-wheeling scamp" (Levinovitz 2012, 480), is also reembodied by protagonists of the Western cultural phenomenon of dandyism. One way to establish parallels between dandyism and Daoism is to look at the concept of *flânerie* to which dandyism is linked and to compare it with the Chinese concept of *you* (遊). Daoism recommends *you* as a sort of literal and metaphorical rambling. Both *you* and *flâner* are playful forms of wandering and bring about fluid—as opposed to fixed—experiences of the surrounding environments. I will later show that this fluidity even concerns gender. *You* appears in the title of the first chapter of the *Zhuangzi*, the "Xiaoyao You" (逍遙遊), and has been translated as "going rambling without a destination" (Graham) or as "free and easy wandering" (Watson). The fact that Daoism puts forward the "Way" as a model of Enlightenment turns walking into an important metaphor. However, *you* is not just any kind of walking. Goal-oriented walking is different from *you* as much as *flâner* is different from hiking. Normal walking (*xing* 行) proceeds along a particular path, whereas *you* is meandering.

You is the most suitable approach for anybody who wants to appreciate the fluid character of society and who intends to live a meaningful life within this fluid culture.³ While Confucians focus on moral duty, the *Zhuangzi* promotes carefree wandering. Instead of committing himself to moral training, the correctness of social relationships, sincerity, and political administration, the Daoist engages in aimless roaming. In the end, his wandering leads to a unification with "the Way" (*Dao* 道).

The *Zhuangzi* develops the theme of nonlinear walking also independently of *you*. In chapter 4, titled "In the Human World," there is an enigmatic madman who mocks Confucius and announces: "Drawing a straight line upon this earth and then trying to walk along it—danger, peril! The brambles and thorns, which so bewilder the sunlight, they don't impede my steps. My zigzag stride amid them keeps my feet unharmed" (trans. Ziporyn 2009b, 32). The madman has the recommended crooked or zigzagging style of walking, whereas Confucius is "drawing a straight line." For Paul D'Ambrosio, this straight line "refers to a preconceived plan that does not allow for as much flexibility when maneuvering through the world. And just like this story of the madman in the Zhuangzi, the straight lines that are drawn by an aspiring Confucian are completely imaginary" (D'Ambrosio 2017, 33).⁴ The zigzagging manner of walking also signifies the Daoist empty heart-mind: instead of being bound by an artificial straight line, one follows the natural tendency of things.

The Flâneur

The Western flâneur is mainly a literary type from nineteenth-century France, and though he is French and linked to Paris, the originally English dandy plays an important role in all flâneur culture. Around 1840, the year Brummell died in France, the French dandy was supplemented (though not replaced) with the flâneur, a type of dandy who maintains a closer contact with modern consumer culture. With the flâneur, the dandy—who normally hates the masses as much as commerce—goes public and exchanges exclusive clubs and sumptuous aristocratic residences for the shopping arcades of the modern metropolis. The flâneur thus becomes the first psychogeographer of literature.

The transformation of the dandy into the more "democratic" flâneur happened during the French Restoration, when the brothers of the executed Louis XVI came to power and reigned in highly conservative fashion. During this time, France underwent a wave of Anglomania, and *flânerie* became what would today be called a subculture or counterculture. It also became the basis of "literary dandyism." The concept of the strolling dandy was probably established by the French writer Jules Barbey d'Aurevilly who devoted an entire book to the iconic figure George Brummell. The flâneur is a "popular" character, but still he remains a real dandy. He is a useless man of leisure and an idler who wanders through urban environments with no real purpose other than observing the emerging modern capitalist society. Despite this uselessness, Sainte-Beuve could write in his entry to the *Grand dictionnaire universel* (1866) that flâner "is the very opposite of doing nothing." It appears that the "doing nothing" of the dandy has paradoxical connotations similar to those inherent in the Daoist (and also Confucianist) "effortless action" or inaction called *wuwei* (無為).

Wuwei is a paradoxical "slogan" mainly appearing in Lao Tzu's *Dao-De-Jing* and literally means nonaction. It is a fluid "doing by non-doing" that is closely linked to *you*.[5] Bo Mou calls *wuwei* an "act without pretentious 'acting'" (2020) because to have *wuwei* means to act in a nonexcessive but conscious natural way, and this effortless or spontaneous way can be obtained through cultivation. Wilde's *The Critic as Artist* (2005) bears the subtitle "With Some Remarks upon the Importance of Doing Nothing."[6] The piece is obviously inspired by *wuwei* or inaction and a Daoist view of virtue as something passive and not active. In the realm of aesthetics, doing nothing in art is more than simply being inactive, but beauty tends to "show itself in this calculated and sudden glare, as the coincidence of activity with passivity" (Scaraffia 1981, 78).

Though the French dandy emerges from within a wave of Anglomania, it is no coincidence that France became, after England, the most fertile ground for dandyism. Already immediately after the French Revolution there were *muscadins*, *jeunes gens*, and *incroyables* who attempted to create a new fashionable aristocratic subculture. These young eccentrics organized hundreds of balls during which they launched exaggerated and manneristic fashion trends and greeted the new regime with an outbreak of luxury and decadence. This happened during the postrevolution *terreur*, but "where[as] the terrorist paranoically revealed the reality underlying a fiction, the *incroyable* pointed to the fictionality of reality itself. In his wit and detachment, we begin to recognize the modern dandy, but his stance was neither apolitical not apathetic" (Amann 2015, 13).

The *incroyables* were not politicians, and both the modern dandy and the flâneur are at least as apolitical as them. Phlegm and indifference would soon become a trademark of dandyism, and with the flâneur this phlegm developed into a dynamic activity that could now be acted out in more popular social environments and on a large scale. While moving through the cities, the flâneur develops a phlegmatic way of walking that will become characteristic of an entire dandy culture. In agreement with the older dandy style, there is neither judgment nor engagement; however, the flâneur expresses this indifference through continuous and flowing body movements.

The fluid style of walking manifests thus strong affinities with the Daoist *you*. The Daoist, when engaging in *you*, moves around in life "with unspectacular excellence and spontaneity" (Moeller and D'Ambrosio 2018, 164), and his view "is constituted in multiple respects by our relation to the landscape" (11). He is detached and never attracted by particular objects. While walking, he contemplates mountains, rivers, lakes, and seas, but he remains at a distance and never gets involved. Similarly, the dandy sees fashionable people, street fights, beggars, modern cars, and political demonstrations, all of which pass by and leave him indifferent.

The flâneur never stops. While he is walking, he sees people and objects pass by but always remains detached. He moves around in the midst of the modern city's population, which is marked by uniformity, speed, and anonymity. His movements remain fluid because he is just watching and not gawking. The act of flâner integrates something that has been explained in the preceding chapter about the Daoist skepticism of language. The flâneur's vision of the world is never backed up by a narrative but remains composed of fragmented pieces of experience. The experience of *flâner* cannot be crystallized in language. The reality of the flâneur is not a linguistic reality but is something experienced in a manner more akin to a not-yet-spelled-out dream. According to Elisabeth Wilson, the dandy observes "bits of the stories men and women carry with them, but never learns their conclusions; life ceases to form itself into epic or narrative, becoming instead a short story, dreamlike, insubstantial or ambiguous" (Wilson 1995, 73). Walter Benjamin goes even further and holds that for the flâneur, objects get divorced from their history and their production and that their fortuitous juxtaposition therefore suggests not logical but rather mystic and mysterious connections. Benjamin calls this approach the "phantasmagoria of the flâneur" in which time becomes "a dream-web where the most ancient occurrences are attached to those of today" (Benjamin 1972, 546). The dandy creates his own time, which is a consecution of flashes of the present as says Guiseppe Scaraffia: "Time is for the dandy a continuous rush of presents of 'here and now' thus threatening the modern cult based on progress and on ideological, moral and religious anxiety" (1981, 43). In the next chapter I will show that the Daoist conception of the dream as an egoless nonnarrative in which events simply "flow" without being connected by a rational (linguistic) superstructure, bears strong similarities with this "phantasmagoria of the flâneur."

Finally, because there is no narrative, there is no *moral* narrative either. Any moralization of *flâner* is impossible, which is, for Wilson, a typically modern and urban way of experiencing one's cultural environment. The flâneur roams beyond language. He sees men and women passing by but has no time to confer names or pronouns upon any of them simply because the totality of the gender reality that he perceives is too fluid. He apprehends a juxtaposition of images but does not attempt to mold this flow of images into language. As a result, he has no suggestions about "good" or "bad" language either. The dandy is no language reformer. As a matter of fact, he does not want to reform anything but prefers to look at the whole of society from a more detached perspective. He merely provokes and twists the ordinary view of things which, in his opinion, is too determined by rules and a belief in moral essences. Slingerland highlights a statement from the *Zhuangzi*, which suggests that the sparrow is the "wisest of birds because it is wary of people and yet it lives among them, protected within the altars of grain and soil." Slingerland concludes that "the Zhuangzian sage is a bit like this sparrow, living among people, but not getting drawn into attachments that may, in the end, turn into traps" (Slingerland 2014, 157). This description would also fit the flâneur. Language with its names and pronouns is such an attachment that can quickly turn into a trap.

The Useless Dandy

Modern dandyism was initiated by England's foremost dandy, George "Beau" Brummell. The word "dandy" already appears at the end of the eighteenth century and is vaguely related to revolutionary and counter-revolutionary activities of the 1790s in London and Paris.[7] However, with Brummell, dandyism becomes a more complex and quasi-philosophical activity. It has already been mentioned that Brummell spent five hours in front of the mirror binding his tie and that he meticulously waxed his shoes down to the bottom side of the soles. This can be complemented by a series of other curiosities. The shine of his shoes was said to have been maintained with champagne froth, and his search for perfection led him to devise a stirrup fixed under the shoe to stop his pantaloons from wrinkling. Virginia Woolf tells the story of Brummell drawing "his head far back and [sinking] his chin slowly down so that the cloth wrinkled in perfect symmetry, or if one wrinkle were too deep or too shallow, the cloth was thrown into a basket and the attempt renewed" (1935, 86). His friend, the Prince of Wales and future king, watched this spectacle for extended periods. Furthermore, Brummell employed three different glove makers for each pair of gloves, one each for the palms, fingers, and thumbs. He also employed three hairdressers, one to cut the front of his hair, one to cut the sides, and one to cut the back.

All these initiatives are useless, and it would be ridiculous for anybody to take pride in them. However, looking for a use is either a utilitarian or an idealist approach, both of which would miss the point of dandyism. Being a dandy is never useful. Nor is it an ideal or a virtue because ideals and virtues are always attained through doing, that is, through a doing that strives to come as close as possible to an ideal. Since the dandy is not *doing* anything, since he simply *is* a dandy engaging in useless actions, his actions cannot be established in terms of ideals. Baudelaire made this very clear when writing in his diary (*Mon Cœur mis a nu*) that "to be a utile man has always seemed to me something quite hideous [which is why] a dandy does nothing" (1986b, 97). Elegance and beauty should not be seen as the dandy's ideals either because such ideals could also be obtained in much easier ways.

Because the dandy is useless and has no ideals, he cannot take pride in anything, which makes him not morally superior but morally neutral. However, he perceives this neutrality as a superiority. As soon as something is *done*, and especially when it is done by following certain rules meant to bring actions closer to ideals, some people will take pride in being better at it than others. Soon there will be dandy competitions and dandy rankings. Next there will be jealousy and cheating. All these competitive projects are either idealist or utilitarian (probably more the former than the latter) and have no place on the rambling dandy's agenda. Oscar Wilde, arguably the last dandy, issued explicit rants against this competitive aspect of modern culture that had become so common in his Victorian England.[8] Therefore he praised the *Zhuangzi* for its renunciation of *all* competition. Competitiveness is not only problematic because of the jealousy, cheating, and petty-mindedness it creates. The issue with competitivity, as Wilde saw it, is not that the apparent winner will be rewarded but rather that moralistic views sneak in where one might not initially expect them: the loser must be rewarded, too. The main problem with competitions is their appropriation for the purpose of ethics. *For ethical reasons*, the winner must share his gain. Consequently, Wilde found that the *Zhuangzi* formulates refreshing counter-positions that mock the morals of "philanthropist busybodies" because Zhuangzi

> has nothing of the modern sympathy with failures, nor does he propose that the prizes should always be given on moral grounds to those who come in last in the race. It is the race that he objects to; and as for active sympathy, which has become the profession of so many worthy people in our own day, he thinks that trying to make others good is as silly an occupation as "beating a drum in a forest in order to find a fugitive." (Wilde 1919, 179)

For Wilde, the perfect gentleman is entirely liberated from morality, just as Zhuangzi is liberated from the bondage of Confucian moral dictates. Wilde himself represents the "alternative Victorian gentleman," able to live freely and liberated from the prison house of morality. Dandyism's refusal of competition alienates it, not only from the ranking obsessions proper to Victorian culture but also from the ethical PC culture of our day. Correcting names and distributing titles are very kindred activities, and getting the "best name" or the "best title" has been the result of many a language correction project. For the *Zhuangzi*, the robber has more insights into philosophy than Confucius, and many common laborers and workmen teach the "gentleman" (particularly in the *Zhuangzi*'s chapter 19, "The Full Understanding of Life") about the true meaning of the Way. There are no hierarchical prejudices, which clearly represents an "anti-ranking philosophy." To this critique of competition, Wilde also attaches a critique of scientism. In his time (much as today), moralist prescriptions tended to be fused with scientist tendencies. According to Simon Reader, Wilde's provocations therefore aim "to resist the empiricist investments of his late nineteenth-century moment" (2017, 17); indirectly, Wilde speaks up against the same empirico-moralism that we find today in our own ranking culture.

Historical Parallels

As mentioned, Baudelaire explains that dandyism appears "in periods of transition, when democracy is not yet all-powerful, and aristocracy is only just beginning to totter and fall." For Baudelaire, dandyism becomes the "last spark of heroism amid decadence" (Baudelaire 1986a, 28). Dandyism developed during the Regency era when Prince Regent George (the future King George IV) ruled because his father George III was deemed unfit. The term "Regency" can refer to various stretches of time. The formal Regency lasted from only 1811 to 1820, but very often, the period from 1795 to 1837 is seen as the Regency era as well.[9] This means that the Regency's beginnings can be seen as falling into the time almost immediately following the French Revolution. The entire span of this broader Regency era is characterized by distinctive cultural and political trends.

When Brummell experimented with his new concept of dandyism, the social mood in England had become more pessimistic than it had been during the English Restoration period. The French Revolution had undermined the British ruling classes' self-confidence, the American colonies had been lost, and it was feared that the Irish would declare independence. All this put many members of the upper class into a state of ruminating self-examination. Furthermore, society and the economy were in bad shape. Between 1789 and 1839, the English population had doubled, and 50 percent of the populace lived in cities in often appalling conditions. Inflation had widened the gap between rich and poor. The Regency era was also an unstable period because the war against Napoleon as well as other wars had severely affected commerce and politics. Society's shift from the traditional aristocratic society to a modern bourgeois society sparked another crisis: the middle class wanted to get involved in all stages of the nation's decision-making process, which created conflicts. Still another crisis lay in the fact that not only political leadership but also spiritual leadership, so far provided by the church, were both bankrupt. Despite all this, the period is remembered as a sort of mini-Renaissance of culture because amidst all these constraints, the Prince Regent fostered the arts. Beyond this, in such an environment of economic and religious decline, art and the aesthetic could become a new political creed or even a new quasi-religion.

This was not the first time that a dandylike aestheticism emerged as an answer to a societal crisis. In 1660, Oliver Cromwell's puritan regime was succeeded by that of King Charles II, whose flamboyant merriness resembled that of the later Prince Regent George. This was during the restoration of the Stuart monarchy when King Charles II returned from his European exile. Like France with its postrevolutionary *muscadins*, *jeunes gens*, and *incroyables*, England had created a premature dandy culture in which dandies were called fops, *macaronis*, or (more formally) "restoration gallants." However, overall, these were negative terms: *macaronis* were believed to achieve no more than the "unembarrassed copying of foreign fashions [which] was an insult in the face of a growing sense of nationalism" (Ashelford 1996, 147). These predandy tendencies are only superficially related to the philosophically more complex concept of dandyism that emerged later with Brummell. After the Regency era came the Victorian era, which saw a more consistent rise of the middle class, whose main ideal was no longer the aristocratic gentleman but rather the trustworthy and puritan businessman. It became Oscar Wilde's task to recast the concept of the dandy in this new context, which mainly meant that the dandy became more countercultural and closer to the flâneur. For Baudelaire, dandies were the "rejected members of a great extinct civilization" (1986a, 29).

Some historical similarities with Daoism are striking. Daoism thrived during the Warring States era (475–221 BC), which was an era of political division that ended when the Qin state conquered its competitors. The rule of the King of Zhou was shattered by feudal princes, and the feudal systems themselves were equally verging on decay. Despite the immense political decline that took place during this period, the era was also one of great cultural and intellectual expansion. The Hundred Schools of Thought (*zhuzi baijia*, from the 6th century to 221 BC), though already emerging before the Warring States era, flourished during this time when China was fraught with political chaos. The period remains a golden age of Chinese philosophy because the "chaotic" situation permitted relatively broad intellectual freedoms. Daoism developed a philosophy suggesting that its practitioners not get involved in worldly affairs—or, in other words, be "useless." The era ended with the rise of the Qin dynasty (221 BC–206 AD), which was the first dynasty of imperial China. The Qin dynasty was hostile to any form of theorizing and also purged all dissent.[10]

Aesthetics and Transformation

In England, the dandy responded to the social changes in a strange fashion. Especially Brummell developed increasingly absurd approaches to social questions. Dandyism is humorous and uses paradoxes and epigrams to poke fun at society's hypocrisy. It is very much about wit and "practical jokes," and it uses a kind of deadpan humor often reminiscent of the *Zhuangzi* and Zen Buddhism. Just as Zhuangzi's sages reject almost all judgments and convictions that characterize common sense, there is in dandyism a desire to foil all ways of conventional reasoning. Brummell took great pleasure in confounding his audience by saying something unexpected and making them laugh at his absurdities. For example, one day seen limping on Bond Street, Brummell was asked what the matter was and replied that he had hurt his leg and that the worst of it was that "it was his favorite leg" (Jesse 1844, 1:111–12).

For both dandyism and Daoism (and also Zen Buddhism), the protest and the liberation were "aesthetic" because they took a fresh look at conventional shapes and conventions. They took an aesthetic attitude toward life. For Chinese art influenced by Daoism this is very obvious because the appropriation of unconventional forms was meant to function as a liberation from constraints, as explains Li Zehou: "Clumsy strokes in painting and calligraphy, odd looking rocks in landscapes, [and] plot twists in drama" broke with the "sweetness of harmonious relations or the tranquil norms of moderation" that was now found hypocrite (Li 2009, 93). Similarly, Brummell and Wilde use "aesthetic" arguments to counter their moralistic environments. McCormack describes Wilde's anti-Victorianism as an approximate mirror image of Daoist anti-Confucianism as Wilde counters the overwhelmingly social and moral preoccupations of his age with aestheticism: "In fact, the kind of society advocated by Confucius and that of high Victorian England had many similarities. Both preached the supreme value of Duty within a rigid male hierarchy whose ideal was exemplified by the image of the 'gentleman.' Both believed in subordinating the individual to the group, and dedicated art, together with all other disciplines, to the service of morality" (McCormack 2017, 78).[11]

Peculiarly, McCormack does not see such aesthetic qualities prominent in Daoism: "Unlike Zhuangzi, what Wilde concludes is that man's life must be lived within the realm of the aesthetic: not only through art, but as an art in itself" (87). However, the insistence on the "aesthetic" *is* also obvious in Daoism where useless activities can be scheduled as aesthetic, be it only because they circumvent moral statements. First, aesthetic experience is a pervasive guiding force in everyday life. Second, the *Zhuangzi* and the *Liezi*[12] contain many stories about Daoist artists and artisans and their abilities, which shows that the focus is on aesthetics. "Zhuangzi allowed a truly aesthetic attitude toward life, nature, and art to emerge within the context of the Confucian aesthetic tradition," writes Li Zehou (2009, 90). For Li, the *Zhuangzi*'s philosophy is clearly "aesthetic in character" (105); even more, "the 'realm of heaven and earth' is actually an aesthetic realm of life" (88), and the Zhuangzi was even "appropriated by Confucianism to serve an aesthetic function" (105).

The aesthetic element is necessary for the implementation of Daoist principles. In a nonaestheticized life, the Daoist indifference towards death, the nondifferenciation between dream and reality, or between gain and loss, are difficult to maintain. It takes a dandyist-Daoist aesthetization of life to put such principles into practice. This is why these principles "had the potential to be exceptionally apt and fruitful" (90) in art and literature.

Daoist aesthetics will be more closely examined in chapter 5, but one clearly Daoist aesthetic strategy, which also manifests a parallel with dandyism, can already be presented here. Both Daoism and dandyism develop a "transformative relationship" between those elements that they encounter in everyday life and the realm of the fantastical. This is a matter of aesthetics because the level of the fantastical is attained through an act of aesthetic transformation. In principle, the dandy develops a relationship between the real and the fantastical by upsetting the rational order of his environment, which means that his absurd statements and actions make the "normal" environment strange and transform it. In the *Zhuangzi*, transformation (*hua* 化) is the topic of many stories and most directly graspable in the Butterfly Parable and in the story of Master Yu who, diseased and deformed, does not resent his transformation through death.[13]

Tzvetan Todorov depicts the fantastical as an intermediary state between the logic of the real world and the nonlogic of the supra-natural suggesting that the fantastical always takes place within a "temporal space of undecidedness," that is, between the logical language of the real world and its counterpart, the irrational. Within this undecidedness emerges the new logic of the fantastical (1973, 33). Todorov's description fits the productions of the dandy as well as the transformations described in the *Zhuangzi*. Both dandy and Daoist transform the conventional world, but neither through magic or science, nor by overturning the existing order of things and by instigating a revolution. They rather transform the world through personalization. In other words, they are not magically creating something out of nothing but are transforming the world by transforming themselves. Sarah Mattice explains that butcher Ding does *not* "find a magical chopper that does not need to be sharpened, and that the wheelwright and calligrapher are "not engaged in creativity as novelty. [The wheelwright] trains by imitating the great works of old, until the point at which she is able to develop her own style, in and through tradition" (2017, 257). At the core of these transformative processes is aesthetics in the sense of doing things in a certain way or in the sense of having a certain lifestyle. These activities transcend reality through aesthetics. Mattice analyzes that in the Daoist knack stories, heroes are trying "to live in such a way as to integrate the everyday with the fantastical, and then leap beyond these distinctions into the dao" (257), and the dandy's approach is similar. The dandy does not create an imaginary world but rather makes the existing world more aesthetically pleasing, more humorous, and more playful through his actions. Another parallel is that the results of these aesthetic activities are always simple, natural, and never overdone.

First of all, in both Daoism and dandyism, one transforms the world by transforming one's self: transforming the world does not mean to convert others but rather to improve one's own person. The *Zhuangzi* proposes that "correcting others yet concealing one's own virtue results in virtue remaining unexposed" (chap. 16, "Mending Nature," trans. Mair). Accordingly, Wilde suggests (in his *Zhuangzi* review) to transform one's proper self by seeing the world in a different way. Wilde speaks here out against those moralist busybodies who try to change the world through preaching, philanthropy, and moral conversions. Still the dandy and the Daoist remain settled within social contexts also after their transformation. The reason is that for Daoism and dandyism the self and the world are interconnected. Through an act of self-transformation (*tu hua* 獨化), the world will be changed; but for this, one needs to be *in* the world.

For Daoism, seeing the world (the cosmos) differently means to stop thinking of the self in a conventional way: it means, for example, to "forget about success and reputation, [and] personal interests" (Lundberg 2016, 213). Both Zhuangzi and Wilde remain integrated into the environment they are living in. Changing one's way of living does not require emigration or retreat from society. Both are indifferent toward the world, but they do not flee it; they transform the world by implementing their own lifestyle. Li writes: "What we often see (. . .) is either, on the one hand, 'dying for the sake of humaneness, retiring for the sake of righteousness' (the sacrifice of the individual in the service of society); or, on the other hand, reclusion, flight from political struggle to the pleasures of nature" (2009, 88). Neither revolution nor the life of a hermit are valid options, and transformation through aesthetization transcends both options. One *can* seek solace in real life. This is what Li means when writing that "in the world of thought and the emotions, art, literature, and aesthetics" there are only very few hermits (101).

The same is true for words. Here we come back to the topic of language. Our selves are integrated into language, and we cannot flee it. There might be some names that we dislike, and we should not adopt them. However, Daoism recommends neither a linguistic revolution nor linguistic emigration: "The Zhuangzi does not suggest that one should stay away from these designations entirely. Rather one should be careful and sparing with picking them up or residing within them" (D'Ambrosio 2018, 35). Language will not be reformed but rather transformed. Most useful is the aesthetization of words, which can also include subversion. Words can be seen in another way and put into other contexts.

Another important precondition for this aesthetization is indifference. In French, "the world" (le monde) can also mean "the people." The dandy abandons all idealist and utilitarian notions and sees reality as constantly floating, not fixed, and always "passing by," which is aesthetic. It is not exaggerated to say that the dandy's relationship with "the people/the world" leads to a stoic perception that is reminiscent of a Hegelian *Weltgeist*. There are no essences, which means that there is no higher instance in this world than the world spirit. Therefore, in his *L'Amour impossible*, Barbey even literally introduces the notion of the "esprit du monde" when making his dandy hero Maulévrier say: "The idea of God leaves us cold; nature leaves us cold; we only have the *esprit du monde* that has no true interest to offer to us and to whom we have nothing to prefer."[14]

The esprit du monde is an aestheticized version of the world, and for the flâneur, this world is the street with its people: "The collective is an eternally restless, eternally moving essence that, among the facades of buildings endures experiments, learns and feels," writes Benjamin in his *Passagenswerk* (1972, 994). For the Daoist, the world that is only a *Weltgeist* is the cosmos. Both dandy and Daoist attempt to sense this aesthetic spirit of the world.

There is still another component that makes Daoism aesthetic. If we identify "aesthetic" with a generally contemplative attitude refraining from ethics-inspired action, that is, an attitude that is always calm and aims to capture the broader picture of situations before acting, then we can call Daoism "aesthetic." Daoism engages in aesthetic contemplation. However, contemplation is equally important for dandyism—and not only for the flâneur. Wilde insists that "from the high tower of Thought we can look out at the world. Calm, and self-centered, and complete, the aesthetic critic [thus the dandy] contemplates life and no arrow drawn at a venture can pierce between the joints of his harness. He at least is safe. He has discovered how to live" ("The Critic as Artist," 2007a, 179).

With Oscar Wilde and some of his British contemporaries, "Aestheticism" becomes an official cultural movement, and it is necessary to address this evolution briefly. Already, the mini-renaissance of culture that took place during the Regency period had turned aestheticism into a new quasi-religion. Now, roughly eighty years later, British Aestheticism or the "Aesthetic Movement" achieve the same feat once more when declaring that for literature, art, and music, aesthetic values are more important than sociopolitical themes. This period is also known as the "Yellow Nineties" due to the leading British quarterly literary periodical *The Yellow Book*.

Wilde was at the forefront of this "art for art's sake" philosophy that challenged the Victorian idea of art as a transmitter of ethical values. Aestheticism abandoned any notion of transcendent truth, although it also combated realism. As a result, Aestheticism would soon be classified as "decadent." British Aestheticism can thus be seen as a last flaring up of the flaneur culture because, like the flaneur, this movement was linked to the emergence of modern consumer society or to what Marxist philosopher Guy Debord would later call the "society of the spectacle," that is, a society in which everything is mere representation and in which nothing is authentic.

Interestingly, British Aestheticism came with a marked interest in Asian—especially Chinese—culture because travel writing had by now shaped the British imagination for decades. In particular, the British aesthetes appreciated the antirealist visual representation shown on the patterned blue and white china that became very fashionable at the time. A widespread *Chinamania* inspired, for English artists, the abandonment of linear perspective, fragmentation, and the disruption of compositional elements. It is not an exaggeration to say that the nonrealistic depictions on blue china anticipated visual modernism in the early twentieth century. Through these Chinese images, aestheticists found an antirealist art free from moral concerns, which was exactly what they aspired to. Young Oscar Wilde kept a collection of many pieces of blue and white china in his Oxford dorm and famously made the remark that "I have to live up to my blue china" (Ellmann 1988, 44). The sentence became a widely circulated aphorism, and English periodicals pictured Wilde as the "Chinese in Victorian popular culture" (Ding 2012, 99).

Culture and Anarchy

It has been previously said that culture is chaos and that the Daoist sage attempts to grasp this chaos as such. To see culture as chaos appears counterintuitive if we think of Matthew Arnold's classical opposition of culture and anarchy. However, Arnold's *Culture and Anarchy* (1869) accords with a puritan, Victorian cultural agenda, as it defines culture—in an almost Confucian way—as the pursuit of humanity's total perfection through moral strictness: "For more than two hundred years the main stream of man's advance has moved towards knowing himself and the world, seeing things as they are, spontaneity of consciousness; the main impulse of a great part, and that is the strongest part, of our nation, has been towards strictness of conscience" (Arnold: 106). Arnold explains that "the ruling force is now, and long has been, a Puritan force, the care for fire and strength, strictness of conscience. (. . .) Hebraism, rather than the care for sweetness and light, spontaneity of consciousness, Hellenism" (112).[15] This represents precisely the view that the Hellenist Oscar Wilde combated. Arnold's views would also be in line with today's PC policies. The entire movement of British Aestheticism was opposed to Arnold. More specifically, it opposed Arnold's conception of art as something moral or useful as well as against the realist conception of art for truth's sake. Proponents of Aestheticism thought that art should provide sensuous pleasure rather than convey moral or sentimental messages. Arnold as well as John Ruskin and the Scottish poet and Christian minister George MacDonald became the enemies of Aestheticism, and the contrast between the two schools is most manifest in their opposing views of two items: culture and anarchy. The Aestheticist view of "culture as chaos" is fundamentally different from Arnold's idea of anarchy and corresponds more with Wittgenstein's idea that "if you want to philosophize you have to step into the original chaos and feel at home there" (1980, Aphor. 542). For Wittgenstein, instead of philosophizing about language that is already essentialized, it is better to philosophize about cultural chaos.[16] Daoism provides precisely *such* a concept of chaos and anarchy. For example, the *Zhuangzi* says: "Forget distinctions. Leap into the boundless and make it your home" (chap. 2). Henry Skaja even holds that the *Zhuangzi* might be the "first documented instance of a true anarchist in China" (2016, 106), and Roger Ames suggests that *wuwei* (無爲) could also be translated as "anarchy" (though he eventually refrains from this translation) (2016, 7). However, once again, the overthrowing of authority that anarchism normally requires is not radical. There is, for Daoism, no authentic "anarchic" way of living, and the relationship with authority must be submitted to aestheticization, too. This means that authority will be challenged only indirectly, as Moeller and D'Ambrosio explain: "Rather than directly challenging authority or trying to either abolish it altogether or to find the 'right' and 'authentic' kind of authority, the *Zhuangzi* looks at it as a problem that must be dealt with. A Daoist strategy of dealing with authority is aimed at enacting and living with it as sanely as possible by not blindly worshipping, idolizing, or craving it" (2018, 10).

Wilde more explicitly adhered to anarchism after reading the Russian revolutionary Peter Kropotkin. In his prison writing *De Profundis*, Wilde describes Kropotkin's life as one "of the most perfect lives I have come across in my own experience" and sees Kropotkin as "a man with a soul of that beautiful white Christ that seems coming out of Russia" (2000, 124). In "The Soul of Man under Socialism," Wilde expounds not so much a socialist worldview but rather a libertarian one and argues for the abolition of all authority since "all authority is quite degrading. It degrades those who exercise it and degrades those over whom it is exercised" (2007c, 244). In a questionnaire that the Symbolist review *L'Hermitage* had submitted to various writers in 1893, Wilde remarked that "once he had been politically a supporter of tyrants, but that now he [is] an anarchist" (Woodcock, 2004, 304). George Woodcock, in his *Anarchism: A History of Libertarian Ideas and Movements*, devotes four pages to Wilde and shows that the Irish author is interested in a certain aspect of anarchism: "If Proudhon and Tolstoy represent the anarchist as moralist, Wilde represents the anarchist as aesthete" (408). In the light of Wilde's later writings, his youthful statements about the

Zhuangzi appear more pronounced and seem to indicate an early inclination toward anarchism. In the review Wilde writes: "It is clear that Chuang Tzu is a very dangerous writer, and the publication of his book in English, two thousand years after his death, is obviously premature, and may cause a great deal of pain to many thoroughly respectable and industrious persons" (1919, 187).

With his proto-anarchism, Wilde is in good company. In France, Neo-Impressionists (George Seurat and Paul Signac) fused aestheticism and anarchism and pushed their progressive aesthetics toward avant-gardism (a project that the British Aestheticists had never attempted). And like Wilde, Neo-Impressionists justified their aesthetic thoughts on the basis of Kropotkin's "anarcho-communism," which was a crossbreeding of communism and anarchism (see Roslak 1991, 383). Later, Cubism and Futurism would become even more explicitly anarchic (see Antliff's article "Cubism, Futurism, Anarchism").

Daoism confronted Confucianism, which emphasized the right enactment of social roles in order to create harmony. Dandyism confronted a Victorian cultural agenda that defined culture as the pursuit of humanity's total perfection. In the comedy *The Ideal Husband*, Oscar Wilde (2003) lets Mrs. Cheveley speak of a "modern mania for morality. Everyone has to pose as a paragon of purity, incorruptibility, and all the other seven deadly virtues." Matthew Arnold's classical study, both influenced by and influencing the puritan Victorian era, pits culture in opposition to anarchy and suggests that cultural harmony (that is, the opposite of anarchy) can only be achieved by following the right rules. Arnold defines culture in a "Platonic" way, as a state of civilization containing truth and beauty. Truth is to be obtained through a civilizing process, which perfectly reflects the values of the Victorian middle class that "recommended norms by which people are supposed to shape their emotional expressions" as well as opinions about how to obtain "calmness and composure of spirit" (Stearns 1994, 2, 25). Such emotional shaping was not seen as oppressive, but self-restraint was rather perceived as a source of individualism. It is calmness, but it is not the contemplative calmness of the dandy or the Daoist. Rather, the new Victorian ethics was brought about through the amalgamation of the merchant classes' capitalist values with religious Puritanism. As it was based on self-restraint, it fundamentally differed from dandyist phlegm. In Puritan self-restraint, spontaneity is totally disabled, whereas dandyist and Zhuangzist spontaneity are not only compatible with but even *based on* phlegm and "no-mind" from which emerges spontaneity. This kind of spontaneity was the type of social behavior that Victorian puritanism feared the most because it clearly went against the Republican ideal of "rational, ascetic, and self-governing individuals" (Takaki 1971, ix).

Self-restraint and the complete lack of spontaneity became decisive for the formation of an English (but also American) culture that increasingly required one to "repress one's emotions, to think more clearly and to effect a more 'objective' intellectual analysis" (Dinerstein 1999, 253). Daoism inverts Arnold's formula in the most obvious fashion. Anarchy *is* culture whereas everything else is just petty knowledge. Culture is the chaotic reality that hides behind all "civilized" rules and linguistic conventions. This view is not like Arnold's Platonic view but rather Nietzschean. While Arnold's idea of culture as "the best that has been thought and said" (1869, 5) dismisses the anarchic reality of culture, Daoism sees culture as the concrete reality of human life with all its emotions, expectations, and contingencies. Arnold's formula also frames culture in terms of rankings because Arnold speaks of "the best that has been thought and said." In comparison, the Daoist concept of culture is not elitist.

Puritan ideas of progress and civilization subsist in today's discussions of PC, as had become very clear in the previously mentioned Munk Debate with Peterson, in which the actor and writer Stephen Fry, who had portrayed Oscar Wilde in the movie *Wilde*, also participated. In the debate, Michele Goldberg points out that PC is progress, and that Peterson describes "almost any efforts to rectify or acknowledge discrimination against women or sexual or gender minorities as a politically correct assault on the natural order" (Peterson et al. 2018, 14). Against this, Peterson criticizes the fact that PC depicts Western civilization as an "oppressive, male-dominated patriarchy" (50). Fry seems to present, in this debate on PC, Oscar Wilde and, in particular, Wilde's Zhuangzian penchant when defending a more "anarchic" concept of culture. Fry attacks progressive ideas of civilization and suggests that "progress is not achieved by preachers and guardians of morality but (. . .) by madmen, hermits, heretics, dreamers, rebels, and skeptics" (57). Furthermore, "If you have a point of view, fight it in the proper manner, using democracy as it should be, not channels of education, not language" (71). Finally, culture means to "play gracefully with ideas. I think that's disappearing from our culture" (89).

Polite Incorrectness

Daoism criticizes the "Logicians" who have petty knowledge about what is real and right or about the correct matching of names and things. Against this, the dandy abides with nonknowledge. The dandy is "intelligent but does not want to be considered as such," writes Schiffer (2010, 21). Nonknowledge is linked to nonaction (*wuwei*), and in Daoism, nonaction depends on emptiness (*wu* 無) as opposed to fullness (*you* 有). *Wuwei* means to have no knowledge of one's action; it is action without any prior conscious knowledge of what one is trying to do. In other words, in *wuwei* one acts without a mental picture of a goal because the action has no definite purpose. To some extent, *wuwei* action is always impulsive. In this section I want to take a closer look at how dandyism implements the aesthetic aspect of this action guided by nonknowledge.

Whatever the dandy says, he does not show his convictions. Such behavior is also known as understatement and is typical of polite people. Just like politeness, nonknowledge as understatement is an aesthetic gesture. However, in dandyism, politeness receives a twist precisely through this nonknowledge. Sometimes, through nonknowledge, insolence can emerge in parallel with understatement, which is paradoxical. For example, Baudelaire asks in his published diary (1986b, 712): "What do I think of voting rights? Human rights? (. . .) A dandy does nothing. Can you imagine a dandy talking to people for a purpose other than scoffing at them?" Baudelaire combines understatement and restraint with provocation and thus welds together the polite and the impolite to create a dense compound of "polite incorrectness." This paradoxical concept has also been put into another formula: the dandy has the "art of pleasing while displeasing" ("l'art de plaire en déplaisant").[17] The dandy's secret is to create a peculiar mixture of exquisite politeness and indecency. Some examples of polite incorrectness have already been provided in the introduction. Brummell shouting "John, give me some more of that cider!" or feeding the caviar to the cat and the truffle stuffed capon to the host's dog. At first sight, polite incorrectness is a dangerous project, but the dandy gets away with it because he also very much insists on the moral emptiness of his actions. The dandy avoids making any "real" statements because "real" statements will always contain some moral components. His statements and behavior are always playful and "empty," thus he can be impolite without ever being insulting.

Again, the dandy does not want to make a revolution that turns the correct into the incorrect. He is not a reformer who wants to change the world by converting, preaching, or insulting. The dandy simply wants to impose, and be it only for a moment, his "greatness without convictions," and he attains this grandeur not through morally correct actions but rather through absurd actions. Marie-Christine Natta has called her book on dandyism *Grandeur sans convictions* (2011). Once the dandy follows these principles, he can afford to be blunt and irreverent and yet never cease to be polite. The dandy's politeness can even look strangely genuine and is never merely hypocritical. Brummell perturbs the social order through his inappropriate behavior, but simultaneously, he finds an aesthetic way of dealing with the rules of high society. He dislikes "the people" (le monde) but develops a playful and aesthetic "rule following attitude," capable of combing the contradictory forces of submission and transgression. Again, this is "polite incorrectness," which also overlaps with what Camus has highlighted as an important trait of dandyism: aesthetic anarchy. It is not simply disorder but is rather "the perfect fusion (. . .) of order with disorder" (Scarafia, 1981, 78). Camus characterized dandyism as a sublimated form of anarchy: it is not real anarchy, but the anarchy is always played. Camus also said that dandyism is a repressed revolution, which will be discussed in chapter 8.

The system is more coherent than it appears at first sight. The dandy's move toward politeness is not arbitrary but necessary because once ethical ideals have been abandoned, once political (moral) correctness has been purged of its politico-ethical input, politeness emerges almost automatically. This marks the biggest contrast with PC. The latter can never be polite because it has not been emptied of its politico-ethical connections. On the contrary, the ethico-political connections have been reinforced. The dandy is an aesthetic anarchist. While the *regular* anarchist is politically incorrect because he sees anarchism as a political and moral program that fights certain rules, *aesthetic* anarchists like Brummell *can only* be polite. Not only is the apolitical and the amoral always polite, but politeness is always apolitical and amoral; it attempts to exclude ethical interpretations from its aesthetic outlook. The dandy *must* choose politeness. Instead of creating the *morally* perfect gentleman (as PC strives to), politeness tends to pass over potentially disturbing ethical questions. Correspondingly, Eugenia Paulicelli holds that "that politeness is a matter of grace incorporated into the dandyist phlegm" (2019, 95). Dandies like Brummell, Wilde (but also Bulwer-Lytton's Pelham from the important dandyist novel *Pelham or the Adventures of a Gentleman*, 1840) have this one thing in common: they are not only indifferent and witty but also amoral and *therefore* always polite. We arrive at the paradoxical formulation of politeness as a necessarily anarchic activity. Polite people disparage morality, philanthropy, education, government, and an entire sociopolitical discourse based on the idea of usefulness. Polite people tend to be not involved in social practices and applaud contemplation. It is clear that PC has the completely opposite agenda.

Paulicelli writes that "that politeness is a matter of grace" (95). Grace has here two meanings: it means "refinement" and also "kindness" when used in the sense of "by the grace of God." In Latin languages such as French, "être gracié" means "to be pardoned," and Marc Le Bot uses "grace" in precisely this sense in his article on dandyism. The dandy benefits from a sort of grace because he is fundamentally disinterested in ethical activities: his provocations are pardoned because he is fundamentally polite (see Le Bot, 1990 6). Alain de Botton, in his popular *The Book of Life*, suggests a similar concept when depicting the difference between politeness and PC as a matter of grace. Politeness will accord grace whereas PC doesn't: "Politeness recognizes [that] we will naturally and inevitably sometimes have mean or dark thoughts about other social groups. The philosophy of politeness doesn't panic, because it accepts that our brains are in many ways primitive. It doesn't believe that such thoughts can ever be entirely removed" (2008). Politeness benefits from grace (Le Bot) and also accords grace (de Botton). This is only possible because politeness does not look for moral perfection. Among the features of politeness that De Botton names, I want to highlight three because they concord with the dandyist-Daoist philosophy of aesthetic anarchism:

1. Politeness is not about rules, but it can best be attained in a playful fashion.

2. Usually, politeness is gently taught and not imposed upon through language correction initiatives.

3. Politeness is universal, not selective.

Point number (2) shows that while dandyism invests in polite incorrectness, PC functions rather through impolite correctness. Point number (3) suggests that unlike PC, politeness is not only directed at minorities and the underprivileged but at everybody or at "the world." It accords with the dandyist-Daoist spirit of universality. Consequently, De Botton writes: "The ambition of politeness, (. . .) is more expansive: it commands that one should be deeply courteous to everyone, whatever creed, color and background they might be. No one is left out and therefore no one can feel embittered.

Chapter 3

The "Equalization of Genders"

Finding the Right Gender Terms

The Daoist "equalization of genders," should it one day exist, would not imply that genders are *literally* the same. One topic addressed in the *Qiwulun* is that we tend to falsely believe that things in the real world are incompatible because *in our language* the corresponding words do not match. In reality, culture, society, and the cohabitation of humans with each other are always more chaotic than is suggested by the language describing them. Dichotomies, especially, rarely grasp real life. Being Zhuangzi or being a butterfly, having this identity or another, preferring life or death. In concrete situations, such choices are often not black and white, even if language often presents reality to us in the form of essentially distinct entities. Language can thus easily mislead us, which is why we must equalize things, that is, negate the differences that language has established. Only then can we recognize the more fluid character of reality and manage to live in it.

It has already been said in chapter 2 that, at the outset, PC's intentions are—perhaps ironically—similar. For example, when it comes to gender terms and pronouns, PC wants to grasp a reality that the static linguistic male-female or he-she model cannot grasp. As a matter of fact, PC tries very hard to overcome linguistic statism, although there is an important difference with the Daoist approach: PC tries to overcome language through language. Among the thirty-one gender terms that New York City recognizes, there is even "gender fluid," that is, a gender that fluctuates—controlled or uncontrolled—between any of the other genders. Or there is "gender gifted," which refers to a person who does not actually fluctuate but has the mental and physical capacity to do so. The problem is that PC still attempts to grasp this dynamic reality by means of language. True, initially, Daoism and PC follow the same impulse. In parallel with Daoism, PC wants to smash the preconceptions that limit our ideas about what reality is. However, to solve this problem, PC merely creates a new linguistic reality. Reason or the mind gives in to the natural disposition of representing reality in terms of oppositions such as male/female or right/wrong; but this is not what reality is. The PC mind discriminates among things and passes judgments that go beyond the traditional distinctions, but it cannot imagine that reality *could* also be different from anything the linguistic mind can grasp. Therefore, from a Daoist point of view, PC invents new terms, not in order to overcome essentialist thinking but to create new essences. The firm basis of all linguistic PC procedures thus remains, in fact, essentialist thinking, which is why PC remains unable to account for gender reality in terms of cultural existence.

Concentrating on language is not only Confucian but also a very Western approach. It has been mentioned in chapter 1 that Western thought from Antiquity to analytic philosophy has often emphasized the study of language and the logical analysis of concepts in order to approach reality. It is not exaggerated to say that, in general, Western thought is obsessed with the power of language. Technocratic newspeak or bureaucratic forms of rationality, as well as the ambition to create a "right" or "correct" language, are only the most visible outcomes of this "tradition." Daoism is clearly opposed to this. From a Daoist point of view, nonknowledge (which also means nonknowledge of the right language) is always the better option. In the introduction it has been said that in the early 1980s, leftist thought took a procapitalist turn, shifting away from the battle against capitalism and choosing instead to concentrate on the elimination of racism and intolerance. I suggested that the origins of PC culture can be found in this change. The new economic and cultural constellations of the 1980s had created a value vacuum for the left. However, it was not only some traditional leftist values and objectives that were lost but also the left's traditional enemies. Many leftists and liberals decided—perhaps unconsciously—to begin focusing on the enemy within: and principal among these would be the "incorrect person" or the person who uses "incorrect language."

This turn had dramatic effects in terms of culture. Slowly but steadily the new leftist ideologists replaced a dynamic culture of politeness, trust, compassion, and empathy, as well as a culture of play, wit, and irony, that had until then still existed, with a civilization in which people and peoples' language need to be constantly checked, formatted, and evaluated to make sure that they were still "correct." Essences believed to be wrong, as well as words representing those essences, became unacceptable, and the enemy within—the incorrect person who uses such words—became essentialized through these mechanics.

For some women, the enemy within became the man, which is merely an extension of the cultural turn described in the preceding paragraphs. The behavior of the man, and especially his language, needed to be checked more than anything else. The problem is that this development suppresses something that exists (though less and less) in the real world and in culture: trust between genders; the play with gender and politeness; or the smooth and fluid (though sometimes "chaotic") cohabitation of genders. Before, all these items had been present in the form of rather free-floating cultural activities; now, with PC, genders as well as correct intergender behavior, have become fixed. Though new gender terms were invented to adapt to a complex reality, genders actually became essences that were even more regulated than before. The introduction of new gender terms and pronouns represents only the surface of this development.

Daoism's gender agenda, if it had one, would be completely opposed to PC. The Daoist "Equalization of Things," were it applied to gender, would bring about an equalization of genders *on an existential or cultural level*. An actual equalization of *all genders*, as may initially have been sought by PC, follows automatically because Daoism would never make statements about the essence of genders or about the linguistic rules linked to these essences. Daoism would rather talk about how genders *exist* in culture; it would not attempt to equalize essences, which is what PC has come to seek. It would also recognize that the existential state in which all things are equal is in constant flow.

In ancient China, not even formalist Confucianism took the language correction project to the extremes that we can observe in PC. It is true that rule-bound and impersonal public institutions were supposed to prevent corruption, and this certainly also concerned language. But even in Confucianism, spontaneous and trust-based social behavior, casual remarks, or the practice of *wuwei*, would never be excluded. Even more, at some stage in the Confucian-Daoist debate, both Confucian and Daoist thinkers "rejected the earlier ideal of guiding behavior by social conventional discourse. They appealed to a natural, intuitive, or innate guide to behavior. This development led to the doctrines of Mencius and the Laozi form of Daoism" (Hansen 2000, 4). There is no simple choice between, on the one hand, the Confucian's obsessive overcommitment to roles or inflexible overidentification with roles, and, on the other, the Daoist's ironic and playful attitude toward roles. As a matter of fact, *wuwei* emerged from Confucianism and became an important concept in Taoism only later. Virtue can only be attained by not consciously trying to attain it, which means that one has to let go, not forcing it but needing to act naturally (see Slingerland 2007, 6). Sincerity (*cheng* 诚) does not just mean to blindly identify with social and linguistic conventions: "Confucians do not expect people to simply become aligned with whatever society prescribes. In fact, the Confucian tradition is largely born out of criticism of the notion that simple obedience in action can constitute morality," writes D'Ambrosio (2015, 372).

PC wants to equalize essences, which is an infinite pursuit because, in order to be as precise as possible, all essences need to be split up into subessences, and these subessences must be "equalized" in turn. New genders, new norms, and new quotas constantly need to be created and updated. The inevitable result of this process is the production of gender stereotypes, be it only because the pool of representative persons for one gender becomes smaller and smaller. How many species of the "gender gifted" do we actually have in each of our societies? There are a tiny number of asexuals, and according to some accounts, only about 0.018 percent of people are born intersex (Sax 2002). Real transsexualism occurs very infrequently . . .

Feminist Equality

Taking essences for granted and combating them by creating sub-essences creates stereotypes. Bérénice Levet sees this same process of stereotyping currently at work in feminism. Though it clearly runs contrary to feminism's initial intentions, campaigns like that of #metoo end up depicting women as "idiotic, completely innocent virgins who are frightened at the slightest saucy remark of those mean gentlemen. They require being treated as children" (2018, 36). Levet's analysis shows that the self-essentialization of women is a necessary consequence of essentializing feminism. And the man who does not stick to the rules of PC behavior—that is, who does not apply the newly established linguistic essences—is essentialized in return.

For Daoism, the existential state in which all things are equal (*qi* 齊) is not biased, it is not shot through with prejudices.[1] This is probably the point that is most difficult to understand. PC proponents believe that the existing gender reality has flaws because there is too much inequality. This amounts to saying that in existence, genders and other things have been essentialized in the wrong way. Feminists and PC conveyors are convinced that "out there," in cultural reality, essences need to be corrected and to a large extent through a reform of language. The new reality created will be value-neutral because wrong essentializations will have been amended. However, the contrary is the case. First, by creating a new linguistic reality, PC produces a no-less-essentialist view of cultural existence, for example, by inventing new genders and pronouns. If somebody who follows correct linguistic rules calls a person who looks like what is traditionally perceived to be a man "she," he[2] believes he has circumvented his personal, subjective preconceptions about what a woman normally looks like or should look like. He believes he has attained a state of "objective" judgmental neutrality since he no longer sticks to the old "male looks = male essence" paradigm. The problem is that "objectively," the man can still "somehow" be considered to look like a man and not like a woman. This man/woman's existence in real life is still different from the essence produced by the pronouns. Inventing a new pronoun only for him does not solve the problem either, because his existence is cultural and always enacted in a multidimensional cultural context and thus more complex than any essence that a pronoun can convey. His gender is in fact fluid: not because he specifically identifies with the term "gender fluid" (which in this example, he does not) but because the reality presented by him and everything around him is fluid; and no pronoun can accurately retrieve this reality. In Daoist terms, we can agree on certain gender terms and pronouns because they make sense within the cultural situation in which they are enacted. But we will agree on them not because we believe that they correspond to some essence. Strictly speaking, gender terms will not be *created* but will *emerge* though cultural play. Therefore, to recognize the existential state in which all things are equal is not biased, it is not a confirmation of prejudices, but rather a coming to terms with reality.

Daoism suggests that this "coming to terms" is not a matter of affirmation but of forgetting (忘), which introduces a strategy that needs to be examined more concretely. What would an "equalization of genders" in a Daoist sense mean in real life? It would mean that the fixed gender identity simply "does not matter." The only thing that matters is the cultural interaction that we have with, for example, the aforementioned nonbinary person. The interaction should be civilized, polite, respectful but never "correct" because correctness presupposes essences. Moeller puts this in the brief formula that "heaven and earth do not 'care'—and neither does the Daoist sage in the Laozi." Not to care is "the condition for a smooth and thus frictionless integration of the human world into the larger cosmos" (2006, 139), and "forgetting" is the key. In this concrete situation, it concerns the forgetting of gender terms and of pronouns so that only spontaneous cultural play remains. Another way of expressing this is to say that the gender term needs to be emptied (*xu* 虛) of all ethical connotations.³ Then gender relations will function "all alone" without constant appeals to ethics. They will be smooth like *you* and function through cultural play and not through ethical regulations that attach correct essences to words. In still other words, to see a gender in its indetermination, one must see it through no-mind (*wuxin* 無心),⁴ that is, without constantly thinking about the correct rules. One can also apply *zuowang*, which is "sitting and forgetting": "What we forget is the thing we hold most dearly: self, with all its opinions, beliefs, and ideals (. . .) personal ambitions and desires," says Shi Jing (in Kohn 2015, 162).

Of course, all this has also much to do with tolerance. The mind turns into an empty mirror without preconceptions and reflects and envisions all the plural ways in which things can fit together. The necessary result is tolerance. Daoism is open-minded and nontotalitarian. PC and certain feminisms take the contrary approach because they essentialize gender relations and pronouns and attach ethical meanings to them. Of course, the declared aim is precisely to avoid prejudices and preconceptions. However, when it comes to avoiding prejudices, the Daoist (or Zen Buddhist) policy of no-mind is much more efficient: because what can be more efficient than saying that gender terms and pronouns do not matter? For a similar purpose, dandyism uses the "phlegm," which is the dandyist version of no-mind. By contrast, PC ethicizes gender terms, which makes them static and thus more prone to becoming the sources of prejudices and preconceptions. From a Daoist point of view, instead of inventing thirty-one new gender terms, one should simply be silent about gender. Culture or civilization will do the rest. "Whereof one cannot speak, thereof one must be silent," says Wittgenstein (2012, 27). Pronouns and gender terms do not matter because essences produced by language are simply nothing. They might be temporarily useful in purely practical terms, but as essences, they should be encountered with indifference.

Dandyism functions along parallel lines. The dandyist no-mind is the phlegm or the '*dédain*' (disdain), which constitutes the *je ne sais quoi* of the dandy. The *dédain*, which is a sort of cynical reserve, deconstructs not only the environment with its rules and conventions but also the dandy's self. And because everything is deconstructed, style and politeness move to the foreground. Style and politeness are the only "solid" things that remain, as is well illustrated by the case of Bulwer-Lytton's Pelham, who "cared not a straw that he was a man of fortune, of family, of consequence; he must be a man of *ton*, or he was an atom, a nonentity, a very worm and no man" (1840, 14). The dandy does not care; he has his *dédain*, but eventually, this *dédain* is responsible for his *ton* or style. This is another paradox about politeness, which can be associated with the previously mentioned one that politeness is a matter of anarchism. The dandy is polite because he does not care and because his phlegm creates politeness. Oscar Wilde's "philanthropist busybodies" chose the opposite approach: they care too much and, as a result, are intrusive, try to convert everybody, and issue rules about correctness, which can be found rather impolite. For Wilde, there should always be a gap between action and emotion, as Wilde explains in *The Critic as Artist* (2005, 185). The artist, to produce good art, is always wearing a mask, which means that he does not really care (Wilde's argument will be further examined in chapter 5). There is an obvious parallel with the Zhuangzi's *zhen* (真) person who forgets and is therefore empty of any particular content, that means, who does not care. In a passage in the *Zhuangzi*, Yan Hui, Confucius's favorite student, asks Confucius about Mengsun Cai, who is a famed mourner in Confucius' own home state of Lu (chap. 6:7, "The Great and Most Honoured Master"). Hui is intrigued because Mengsun mourns so well without actually feeling sad. Confucius (who is here a mouthpiece of Zhuangzi) replies that Mengsun simply cries because others cry: "Meng-sun presented in his body the appearance of being agitated, but in his mind he was conscious of no loss. The death was to him like the issuing from one's dwelling at dawn, and no (more terrible) reality." Paradoxically, he can only mourn so well because he is not really sad. The key is that he does not care and is wearing a mask.[5]

For Zen or Chan Buddhism, the "dédain" or phlegm in the sense of "not caring" are fundamental, too. Zen Master Shou Shan (926–993) once showed his disciples a bamboo staff and said: 'If you call it a bamboo staff, you fix it [linguistically]. If you don't call it a bamboo staff, you go against the fact. . . . What will you call it?' The right answer to this koan has not been transmitted, most probably because there is no answer. All we can do is "not care," or have a *dédain*, about the right name for the object. There is another, similar, koan, which is followed by an answer, but the answer is as absurd as anything a dandy could say or do. A monk asked the Chinese Zen Master Feng Hsueh (Fuketsu, 896–973): " 'Speech spoils the transcendence (of Reality), while silence spoils the manifestation. How could one combine speech and silence without spoiling Reality?' The Master replied: 'I always remember the spring scenery I once saw in Konan. Partridges were chirping there among the fragrant flowers in full bloom' " (in Izutsu 1982, 107–108). While Confucianism builds up a system of moral values, Zen Buddhism and Daoism deny the existence of such systems because they are based on external, phenomenal, and linguistic presuppositions. We must forget about moral systems, that is, we must have a dandyist phlegm or *dédain*: only then can we become not immoral but amoral.

After all, the Daoist "forgetting" about ethics is not as strange as it sounds. We all employ the previously described amoral phlegms in everyday life, and Moeller talks about them in his *The Moral Fool*, which will be analyzed further on in this chapter. Moeller brings up the example of traffic (2009, 12–13), which supports the present argument. When somebody violates traffic regulations, we normally do not tend to see the violation in terms of ethics; the person is neither good nor evil, but s/he just violated a rule and should be punished for this infraction. S/he should not be punished for unethical behavior. It would of course be possible to interpret traffic infractions in terms of ethics, but in this situation, most of us would prefer to have a no-mind or a *dédain* for ethics. In a way, we become "moral fools" because we recognize that any ethical considerations would bring traffic into a moral realm where we don't want it to be. Importing the notion of moral correctness into traffic by establishing the idea of "politically correct traffic behavior" would not add to the smoothness of the unfolding traffic game but rather impede it.

We are not moral fools in the sense of the PC person who is another kind of moral fool and for precisely the opposite reason. The PC person is fooled by morals whereas the Daoist moral fool does not care about morals. Ethicizing traffic would also be counterproductive. This is true because first it would incite some people to be more correct than others and launch a combative rhetoric that would most probably interrupt the traffic flow; second, the correctness would have to be defined in increasingly specific terms to avoid any incorrectness, which would make driving difficult. It would spark a never-ending production of new policies, guidelines, signs, and symbols. In the end, the requirements of correctness would paralyze traffic.

"Traffic" here can metaphorically stand for culture. In culture, rules need to be followed, but there is no reason to ethicize these rules. The cultural rules guarantee the smooth functioning of society, and punishment for infractions is enough to maintain their efficiency. Through correctness, the adherence to rules (for example, the use of pronouns) becomes an ethical matter, which is necessary neither for smooth traffic flow nor for smooth gender relations. I believe that what Jordan Peterson resented when rejecting the idea that the government could force him to use gender neologisms was the unnecessary ethicization of gender relations.

In Daoist as much as in dandyist terms, ethicization is always counterproductive. Dandyism follows the rules of society merely with the purpose of being "somehow" accepted by society. The dandy always avoids seeing these rules in ethical terms. The rules are for him purely aesthetic, which is why he can play with them. One cannot play as easily with ethics. Wilde clearly distinguishes ethics from aesthetics when writing that "there is not a single real poet or prose-writer of this century (. . .) on whom the British public have not solemnly conferred diplomas of immorality" (Wilde 2007a, 251).

Wilde does not trust ethics and finds hope not among the virtuous but rather among those who are "ungrateful, discontented, disobedient, and rebellious" (234). This Daoist-dandyist aestheticism creates a phlegm or an amoral attitude toward all rules and actions. This attitude represents an essential component of dandyism from Brummell until D'Annunzio, who repeatedly emphasized that being amoral is very different from being immoral (see Paulicelli 2019, 43). At the same time, "amorality" does not prevent Daoists and dandies from following the rules of ethics. As the dandy switches his agenda from ethics to aesthetics, he simply "does not care," which means, paradoxically, that he *can* follow the rules. That said, while he does not care morally, he still does care aesthetically. This is why he will not simply engage in careless behavior. On the contrary, the fact of not caring about ethics leads him from correctness to politeness. The moral fool is always an aesthetic nonfool; and aesthetic nonfools tend to be very polite.

The *Daodejing* argues that "the more laws and regulations are promulgated, the more thieves and robbers there will be" (chap. 57). Wilde makes a similar remark in *The Soul of Man* when writing that "the more punishment is inflicted the more crime is produced, and [that] most modern legislation has clearly recognized this, and has made it its task to diminish punishment as far as it thinks it can" (Wilde 2007c: 245). Ethicizing the punishments is counterproductive, just as the ethicization of traffic rules would be counterproductive. The Daoist criticism of ethics is therefore an "aesthetic objection" (Moeller 2009 64). It might be a slightly exaggerated statement, but the Daoist or the dandy would probably look at traffic from an aesthetic point of view. Traffic is neither good nor evil; it just functions or does not function. And apart from the utilitarian perspective, it provides a perception of aesthetic flow. Being detached from ethics is the particularity of aesthetic phenomena. Just like nature, beauty is neither good nor evil. Beauty should not be ethicized. When beauty is ethicized, it often becomes kitsch, which happens most obviously in propaganda art. Kitsch will be dealt with in the next chapter in the context of a discussion of authenticity and sincerity in aesthetics.

Gender and Ethics

What does this mean for gender? Instead of searching for the correct fixation of the genders' essences, Daoism takes the cultural existence of genders at face value. This, too, represents a shift from ethics to aesthetics. Effectuating such a shift is more difficult than it sounds, and it can only happen through a consistent process of "chaotification." PC does precisely the contrary: by changing names, it creates a new "reality" through the establishment of new ethical essences. The problem is not really the rules themselves but rather the ethical character of the rules. The dandy aestheticizes the rules, and as a result, following or not following the rules is no longer a matter of ethics but of aesthetics. This can also be applied to gender: the Daoist would reject an ethical gender identity but still maintain an aesthetic gender identity. From a Daoist perspective, not being attached to a "gender self" does not mean that one has no gender. Being detached from a "gender self" does not suggest that "anything goes" and that everybody can change genders at any moment. This is rather the idea of PC's "gender-fluid" person, whom the Daoist sage would find odd. Daoism would simply hold that an individual cannot be defined through gender and that therefore gender identity cannot be reduced to names or pronouns. This gender skepticism is not limited to biological gender: for Daoism, gender identity cannot be defined through thoughts, actions, habits, or feelings, either. Instead, a person's gender identity *emerges* within certain cultural contexts, and its perception depends on cultural play as well as on the points of view from which it is observed. Gender identity is thus not ethical but aesthetic.

Daoism "chaotifies" the existing (linguistic) reality of genders and "equalizes" genders in the sense of *cultural gender equality*. Its aim is to grasp the original state of a chaotic unity that contains no definite limits. This "chaotic unity" might also be a reality in which person X uses a male pronoun when addressing person Y, who is a biologically male individual who wants to be recognized as a woman. However, when person X uses "he," he is still aware of the fact that Y's "maleness" is not an essence. X leaves the presumed maleness or femaleness of this "man" thus in a chaotic state; he does not attempt to rectify its name. He simply refuses to create a new essence for that "man." For the Daoist, person Y wanting to be addressed as a woman, as well as the question of giving in to the request or not, are not matters of ethics but of aesthetics. And in aesthetics, things (identities, pronouns, etc.) are fluid. They are just as fluid as the culture surrounding X and Y.

All these are the reasons why such subjects will be best approached with politeness. Again, PC takes the opposite approach as it ethicizes the matter. The result is not politeness: PC tends to be confrontational. The first example of gender relations in a PC context was that of person X who uses a male pronoun when addressing person Y. Another example is the case in which somebody uses a male pronoun in a text, although *culturally* it is understood that the written "he" can also refer to females. He does not use the words "s/he" or "they" because he thinks that the use of altered pronouns will establish a new, essentialized linguistic reality. The "other" reality, that is, the reality that is not merely a linguistic construct but a reality corresponding to culturally established facts (for example, when somebody writes "he" very well knowing that it can refer to females as well), continues to exist. Again, this is a matter of aestheticization. It makes perfect sense to say that when we write "he" without referring to males only, we look at words from an aesthetic point of view and not an ethical one. The process becomes even more "aesthetic" when we write "she" but mean both males and females. The "she" that does not mean "she" is used in response to the "he" that does not mean "he." This is logically and ethically incorrect but can very well function as an aesthetic conceptual construction that works along the lines of symbolism.

The Dao transcends all distinctions present in particular things and events. Necessarily, the Dao also transcends gender distinctions. The Dao does not split genders up into new essences. The existing (cultural) world is in movement; it undergoes continuous transformation, and no gender rule can grasp this reality. We can thus paraphrase the second sentence of the *Daodejing* and say that "the gender that can be named is not the eternal gender." The eternal gender is a fluid reality of all genders as they interact in culture and that live more or less harmoniously within the entire gender universe. *If* we want to have pronouns, they should rather be like metaphors that constantly refer beyond themselves so that the clear meaning of the metaphor (the pronoun) cannot be determined.

One can also call this a "negative rhetoric approach" because it seems to function like an endlessly circling dialectics, as is most famously employed in Zen Buddhism. Nothing is permanent, and whatever is asserted must be immediately negated and canceled out. It is thus not exaggerated to say that these philosophies apply a perpetual iconoclasm, which, if applied to gender, necessarily leads to a "genderclasm." As long as it can still be specified as a Dao, it will not be a permanent Dao, says the *Daodejing* (§1). The same goes for gender. If the gender can still be specified, it is not the gender as it is lived in culture. For Daoism, the gender must be constantly without name. This is the negative path of thinking nothing, contemplating nothing, and refusing all method, and it is expressed in chapter 22 of the *Zhuangzi* ("Knowledge Rambling in the North"). Such negative paths of cultivation include "forgetting oneself (*wang qi shen* 忘其身)," "being empty" (*xu* 虛), and "fasting of the heart-mind (*xinzhai* 心齋)," which Moeller and D'Ambrosio (2018, 5) see as conditions for "genuine pretending."[6]

Micro and Macro Perspectives

Daoism adopts a macro perspective (or a cosmic perspective), whereas the modern Western mind divides, specializes, and thinks in terms of micro categories. The PC mind in particular, establishes an order of micro-gender elements and attempts to "equalize" them in the sense of gender equality. By contrast, the Daoist "making things into one" does not happen through logical thinking, analysis, or division. Stevenson calls the modern micro mind approach a hyperorder, which can be contrasted with the Daoist macro mind of unity: "To say "all are one" (*yi*) is after all not quite the same as saying "all are the same" (*tong* 同)⁷ the latter suggests an originally heterogeneous mixture now "homogenized," not a logical-mathematical unity or identity; logical "oneness" suggests the unity reached by first cutting holes (as in the story of Hun Dun) and not the initial wholeness of (Dao as) an indeterminate yet continuous thin" (Stevenson 2006, 310). Reality is not made of language but of culture. A complex, chaotic cultural macro reality hides behind a seemingly well-ordered, rational linguistic micro reality, and PC has a very strange relationship with this reality. The African American sociologist Orlando Patterson notes that "it is now incorrect politically even to utter the word *culture*. Indeed, so far has this politically correct position gone that it is not uncommon for people who even tentatively point to social and cultural problems to be labelled and condemned as racist" (1972, 144–45). PC believes that when I say "culture," I necessarily confirm all prejudices and misjudgments of that culture. Male and female standards of appearance are anchored in culture, so if I refer to culture, I simply confirm them. Consequently, all references to culture must be avoided to enable the creation of a "clean" and balanced reality. The same deculturizing process can be observed in feminism. Levet criticizes that neo-feminism⁸ establishes universal norms and disregards the customs, habits, and culturally acquired values of, for example, French culture, which has an "art of gender mixing," or also a "republican ideal of the universal" (1998, 20).⁹ In Levet's model of culture, the republican ideal of the universal is not understood as an abstract rule but rather as a value flowing out of this culture. And it is constantly enacted in various ways within this culture. By contrast, the feminism that Levet criticizes is not an art of living but rather an ideology that believes in norms, rules, pronouns, and all those things that Daoists consider "a dream."

We all know that culture contains prejudices. The *Zhuangzi* does not agree with or confirm the prejudices but wants to chaotify reality by establishing equality. From a Daoist point of view, the prejudices are related to language and not to culture, and the aim must be to liberate the mind instead of crystallizing the mind's fixed positions through language. In the end, this clashes with PC. As mentioned in the introduction, John Lea holds that according to PC, "The purpose of education is to induce correct opinion rather than to search for wisdom and liberate the mind" (2008, 29). Another critic of PC, the Polish philosopher Ryszard Legutko, misses in PC the cultural values of beauty and goodness because these values get crushed under the weight of a formal (linguistic) correctness. Again, we assist the combat of aesthetics against ethics, which is here associated with combat between cultural freedom and (linguistic) constraints. Like many Eastern Europeans, Legutko compares PC with former Eastern European socialism: "Socialists abandoned the criterion of beauty—considered anachronistic and of dubious political value—and replaced it with the criterion of correctness" (2016, 14).

A related way of expressing this state of affairs is to say that PC is always enacted from the point of view of an ego: an ego that man/woman creates for him/herself by taking the ontological center of his/her personality as a point of departure. This is a micro perspective. The *Zhuangzi* criticizes the ego as constant, unchangeable, rigid, and fixed. The ego cannot grasp reality because reality is fluid and moving. From the micro point of view of the ego, our mind tends to stick to an everyday view of reality and essentializes reality through equalizations, instead of overcoming them. As a result, we suffer from the tyranny of the mind. We should therefore recognize that essentialized concepts of men and women as well as the pronouns sticking to them are only dreams produced by our ego. Existence is not the existence of individual things; nor is it the existence of gender terms and pronouns. For Daoism, existence does not take place on a phenomenal level as it did for Aristotle. What exists for the Daoist is not the man or the woman (or something in between) seen by an ego but rather a cultural micro-macro play that can be experienced in different ways and with different shades by equally changeable egos.

For PC, the ego functions as an ontological center, which is why it is so important for PC to establish pronouns. PC strengthens the ego because the "I" (just like other pronouns) has become an ethical and a political notion. The "I," which once was purely personal has become political. Kors and Silverglate paraphrase the moral sentence that "the tip of one's nose defines the limit of a physical assault" into "the tip of one's ego defines the limit of a verbal assault" (1999, 4). This illustrates PC's ego-centered approach, which is diametrically opposed to the Daoist (as well as the Zen Buddhist) approach to the ego. Daoism deconstructs any notion of a constant, unchangeable, rigid, and fixed ego, which becomes clear when looking at the Butterfly Story that has already been quoted in the introduction. Here it is in Giles's translation: "Once upon a time, I dreamt I was a butterfly, fluttering hither and thither, to all intents and purposes a butterfly. I was conscious only of my happiness as a butterfly, unaware that I was myself" (2019, 47). As

The "Equalization of Genders" | 73

a matter of fact, Zhuangzi's dissolution of the "I," the not-knowing who he is, is even more complex and more radical than Giles's translation suggests. The translation is inadequate because it continuously informs us of the narrator's "I" despite the fact that the story's purpose is to show that such an "I" does not exist. Guo Xiang (252–312 CE), in his classic commentary on the Butterfly Story, shows that "there is no continuous substance underlying the different stages of dreaming and being awake" (Moeller 1999, 440). Moeller, who considers these constellations, therefore translates the same passage thus: "Once, Zhuang Zhou fell into a dream-and then there was a butterfly, a fluttering butterfly, self-content in accord with its intentions. Acting happy with himself and with wishes gladly fulfilled" (446). In this translation, the dream is an egoless dream similar to what Buddhist doctrines explain about dreams: it is a reality seen without a seer because dreams are not dreamt by a mind but by a no-mind: "The person of no-mind sees the objects of the world as neither real nor unreal, as neither independent substances nor dreams or illusions." This is how Thomas Kasulis describes the act of subjectless seeing (1985, 44). "Dream" becomes here a metaphorical way of describing the kind of seeing in which the seer and the seen have become one. Dōgen's line "birds fly like birds" from the Genjo Kōan attempts to render this experience. According to Shizuteru Ueda, it evokes a feeling of the real-unreal because it is highly real and at the same time dreamlike (1984, 212). Similarly, the Butterfly Story does not blur the borderlines between dream and waking life, between Zhuangzi and the butterfly, between life and death. Instead, it demonstrates that "the authenticity of each segment of a whole is guaranteed by the very fact that the segments are not connected to each other by any continuous bridge between them" (Moeller 1999, 443). In the end, dream and waking life turn out to be "equally authentic" (441), which is only possible because the pronoun "I" has been consistently deconstructed.

The egoless dream as a "simple presence" is not entirely unknown in Western thought. The French writer and poet Paul Valéry attempted to establish a similarly egoless notion of dreams when writing: "Why does one say 'I dreamt' when it would be better to say 'it has been dreamt?'" (1977, 321). For Valéry, the egoless way of seeing is possible in dreams because dreams contain a "simple presence" in which any "if" as well as the conditional tense disappear. In other words, in dreams, "everything becomes present tense" (1979, 89). Similar to the situation in the Butterfly Story, there is only what Moeller calls a "continuous 'I'" (1999, 440), and which Valéry calls "an element of the system of the instant" ("un élément du système de l'instant"). The "I" in the dream is not based on identification with certain characteristics, but the "I" is "somebody who becomes other, who depends on the actual rest."[10]

Dreaming has some importance for the calibration of the dandy's existence. According to Scaraffia, the dandy "is a dandy in the precise moment in which dream and reality coexist, without losing any of their essence and intensity" (1981, 135). It is appropriate to say that the flâneur produces a "phantasmagoria" of time in which time becomes, according to Benjamin, "a dream-web where the most ancient occurrences are attached to those of today" (1972, 546). The flâneur gives up the fixed position of the "I" from which the experience of flâner can be narrated. Eventually, "life ceases to form itself into epic or narrative, becoming instead a short story, dreamlike, insubstantial or ambiguous," writes Elisabeth Wilson (73). Experience is not backed up by a narrative but remains fragmented and transitory, which shows that the dandy has the Daoist's language skepticism. The experience of flâner is not crystallized in language.

Valéry sees the dream precisely as such: it is not a symbolic language in need of being translated into another language, that is, to be shifted from a language of the nonreal to the language of the real, or from a nonthinking realm to that of thought in order to be real. On the contrary, the dream is "much more comparable with the real than with thought" (1979, 92; from *Cahier* IV, 1910). There is in the dream a primary indistinction ("indistinction première") "where the exchange between things and images is still a groping. [It is] a *real* indetermination, primitive and somehow (. . .) truer than the solution of unique waking life." Jean Levaillant writes this about Valéry's theory of dreams.[11] There is no reason to make the dream more precise by transferring it from nonlanguage to language. Valéry captures the paradox: "The dream wants to be precise, but it does not want to be made precise. And what cannot be made precise will perish when being made precise."[12] Or: "Everything that would be important in this search [for the dream] will be KILLED by language."[13]

The ambition to reify dream through language is due to the desire to find an origin or an original/authentic language. However, any origin would refer to a concrete place and time, whereas the dream just emerges. The dream is not constructed by a dreamer in the way in which one constructs sentences. As a matter of fact, it is not possible to "construct" a dream: "Constructing and dream do not directly agree (ne s'accordent pas directement)" (1979, 136), but the dream develops organically without outside interference of thinking.

Daoism wants to administer a mortal blow to a certain form of intelligence by designing a sort of "absolute existentialism" in which intelligence can no longer cut watertight compartments into the world of being by inventing names, pronouns, and other technical devices. Consequently, it achieves the coexistence of males and females not through division but through cultural enactment. Essences are only potential whereas *in actu* there is only existence. Essences are not real, and to make this obvious, the essentialized reality needs to be chaotified. By inventing new essences (new genders, gender terms for existing genders, and pronouns), the mind makes itself believe that it has attained the ultimate view of things; but the ultimate view is that all things are one. Moeller has a graphic metaphor for this strategy: "The Daoist sage attempts to reach a presexual state of highest sexual latency that precedes the division of sexuality into the sexes" (2006, 32).

Daoism mocks the fact that people are constantly trying to grasp reality through words and arguments created by their own reason. Reason is merely the faculty of setting formal limitations. For the *Zhuangzi*, the mind puts essences in order and thus establishes something solid around us. It merely constructs a fake reality, and PC is doing precisely this. Izutsu warns that this ontological essentialism is dangerous because it makes us "lose our natural flexibility of mind. [It makes us] lose sight of absolute undifferentiation, which is the source of all existing things" (1983, 359). Izutsu's description comes close to the ethicization of society that is happening through PC.

The oneness and equality of things (e.g., of genders) is not an empirical fact. It is not a reality that can be implemented but rather a matter of consciousness. For Daoists, knowing the way means to have grasped an all-pervading metaphysical law of the cosmos. This is a matter of experience, and wisdom or philosophical knowledge fosters this awareness. Philosophical knowledge is not knowledge about the correct use of names. For Daoist philosophers, there is no such correct use of names, and to insist on this nonknowing represents philosophical knowledge. According to Izutsu, philosophizing in the Daoist way is "not reasoning about but experiencing Existence" (1983, 479). Dialecticians, sophists, or all those who acquire petty knowledge through technical reason, enclose the Absolute within the bounds of a number of determinate forms: "They confine the Absolute in an individual form and lose sight of the absoluteness of the Absolute" (33). However, the Absolute cannot be spelled out per se in the form of a rule; it can only be enacted and experienced through culture. Reason weaves around us a veil that develops into an ego, which prevents us from seeing reality.

Seduction and "Chaotification"

What does chaotification signify more concretely in the case of gender relations? Humor, irony, playfulness, and detachment play an important role in gender relations, and it is certainly no coincidence that Bérénice Levet criticizes some major branches of feminism as ideologies lacking humor and detachment. There is a cultural activity where essences are reduced to very little and in which male-female relationships become very much "existential" or "chaotic" in the Daoist sense. This phenomenon is seduction, and it is worthwhile to look at it more closely. The eroticism and playful interaction that emerges from seduction cannot be reduced to correct binary oppositions of yes and no or "this or that." Seduction is *never* correct for the simple reason that it is always transgressive. Levet writes that certain feminists tend to disregard the fact that "the female desire cannot be reduced to a clear alternative of yes and no" (2018, 73). In other words, in seduction, names are no real names. Furthermore, seduction is not—contrary to what some feminists seem to think—about the affirmation of power. It is rather about the ambiguous play with power, that is, the chaotification of power. Daoists would severely reject the objectified linguistic reality of the feminist "no means no." Words have no ultimate meaning and "no" definitely does not mean "no" for a Daoist. For Daoists, such rules could only have been issued by what Daoists call "dialecticians," that is, by those who discuss "that this is right and that is wrong" (*shi-fei* 是非)[14] and believe that everything in the world has a definite, fixed content. In seduction, reality—including the reality of power relations—always remains chaotic and fluid and cannot be reduced to a simple yes or no. Very often, in seduction, the roles of the seducer and the seduced are inverted, which is reminiscent of the Butterfly Story.

The "I" is not a fixed presence. It is enough to think of sexual role plays to find this easily confirmed. Zhuangzi does not know whether he is a butterfly dreaming that he is Zhuangzi or whether Zhuangzi is dreaming that he is a butterfly. Zhuangzi's dream experience, that so many commentators have described and analyzed as such, is not even a "real" dream experience, but it happens in waking life; and I would hold that such a "transformation" happens frequently during the experience of seduction. Seduction is roaming, and roaming has been compared with sleeping and dreaming (see Moeller and D'Ambrosio, 2018, 166). Moeller comments on the Butterfly Story: "The 'Butterfly Dream' story in the *Zhuangzi* paradigmatically illustrates the fluidity of identity. Every night, humans involuntarily slip away from the identity they spend the day maintaining" (2020). Identity is not objectively assumed but pretended—though this does not mean that it is fake. It appears rather that seduction is a matter of "genuine pretending." The problem of "genuine pretending" as presented by Moeller and D'Ambrosio, will be discussed in chapters 5 and 6, which deal with authenticity and sincerity.

Few philosophers have analyzed seduction in more subtle terms than Jean Baudrillard, and he immediately points out that seduction has never been on the program of feminists: "What does the women's movement oppose to the phallocratic structure? (. . .) They are ashamed of seduction, as implying an artificial presentation of the body, or a life of vassalage and prostitution. They do not understand that seduction represents mastery over the symbolic universe, while power represents only mastery of the real universe" (1990, 18). Baudrillard speaks like a Daoist for whom the linguistic universe (or everything that we normally recognize as real) is only a dream, whereas what he calls the "symbolic universe" is real. He also speaks like Eliade, for whom religious language is symbolic and never literally refers to this or that thing (see chapter 1, n. 11 of the present book). The symbolic universe is a chaotic universe of existence where things are fluid and have no essence. In seduction this becomes most obvious, as seduction is basically chaotification: "The capacity immanent to seduction is to deny things their truth and turn it into a game, the pure play of appearances, and thereby to foil all systems of power and meaning with a mere turn of the hand," writes Baudrillard (8).

The dandy, too, foils all systems of power, including his own system, as he has no strategy to maximize profit: "When the dandy seduces, he does it to deceive boredom, and not to gain something," writes Mocchia di Coggiola (2019, 122). Instead, the dandy "always takes care to avoid the contamination of power" (Scaraffia 1981, 53). Of course, this is remarkable for somebody who has the reputation of being a rebel. The problem is not that the dandy *has* no power. This would be a misrepresentation. Brummell had shown that he was able to reverse power systems, when his relationship with Prince George "took place on a level of absolute equality, and, if at times it was a supremacy" (12). But the dandy simply refuses to take advantage of that power.

Furthermore, seduction is not a matter of knowledge. There are manuals of seduction (today, very much for East-Asian teenagers but also, in the past, for French imitative dandies called the *lions*),[15] but they do not seem to be very efficient. In the very end, seduction remains "strange," just like a dream is strange. In dreams, too, we have no knowledge about rules, symbols, or logic while we are dreaming, but the dream just unfolds like a game. Furthermore, seduction is a matter of aesthetics and not of ethics. Against this, PC works toward the ethicization of seduction, just like it works towards the ethicization of everything else.

Daoist-Dandyist "Gender Theory" and Judith Butler's "Gender Performance"

So, what would Zhuangzi have said about gender? My guess is that he would have said the following: since names do not matter, you can call me whatever you want. Call me he, she, or zhe.[16] The real meaning of the pronoun emerges each time anew from the cultural context. Zhuangzi would refer to the cultural chaos that constitutes reality as Nothingness or namelessness. Laozi has a marked preference for this word, too. "Nothing" or the "nameless" are conditioned neither by determination nor by nondetermination. The Daoist sees only Nothingness, which means that he sees neither color, nor race, nor gender. Ecstatic intuition obtained through sitting in oblivion has made the sage "blind" to color, race, and gender. And if there is no gender, there can be no conflict between "true" and "false" genders either. Ordinary people experience the world with the genders, values, and races that it contains as a multiplicity of things that are often arranged in the form of dichotomies. However, this is only the worldly perspective. From the point of view of the Dao, valuations, boundaries, and their accompanying flaws are not real. What is real is the nothingness of genders, values, and races.

Moeller (2009) develops the concept of the "moral fool" that has been previously mentioned, and I believe that the term "gender fool" can be a good description of the Daoist attitude toward gender. The moral fool overcomes the human tendency to look at the world in terms of good and bad. In parallel, the gender fool does not see the world in terms of male, female, trans, or gender fluid. Daoist gender theory rather suggests that there is no theory about genders. For Moeller, morality is not a principle based on an ethical theory, but morality emerges through "the actual social differentiation between those who are deemed good and those who are deemed bad or evil" (25). Gender emerges in the same way: through a *différance* or a differing between various genders. These genders cannot be established theoretically, and consequently, there is no need for gender theory either.

For Zhuangzi, names are only "provisionally" influenced by cultural interpretations. It is tempting to associate this attitude with contemporary gender theories which hold that gender is socially constructed, or more radically, that we should understand gender not as something we *have* but as something we *perform*. The book *Gender Trouble* by gender theorist Judith Butler urged readers in the 1990s to view gender as a mere performance. Butler questions the belief that certain gendered behaviors are natural and emphasizes social and linguistic situations that create conventions. "Because there is neither an 'essence' that gender expresses or externalizes nor an objective ideal to which gender aspires" (1990, 273), for Butler, gender identity remains an illusion. True, Daoism and gender theory (and also PC) have similar starting points: for both, language does not match reality. Daoism clearly holds that any matching of the former with the latter is impossible. The question is to which extent Butler believes in the creation of a new symbolic language that can replace the social as well as the biological natural language about gender. On the one hand, Butler's use of "postmodern" paradigms seems to overcome language or at least any belief that reality can be grasped by language. Necessarily, it also ultimately articulates sex without imposing linguistic norms. In this sense, Butler sounds rather "Daoist" when they[17] write: "'Sex' becomes something like a fiction, perhaps a fantasy, retroactively installed at a prelinguistic site to which there is no direct access" (1993, 5). On the other hand, their critique of normative heterosexuality looks very much like a political program, which moves it several steps away from Daoism. "Daoist gender theory," if there would be one, would suggest that there can be no theory about gender, nor about anything else, whereas Butler clearly suggests a theory. The point is *not* that Daoism is more against rules than Butler is, but that, on the contrary, Daoism (just like dandyism) accepts norms and plays with them.

Butler's militant program, which wants to free us from blatant gender coercions, is not playful in the Daoist sense. Daoism does not care about gender, and Butler cares too much. Butler's purpose is mainly to fight for the rights of marginalized identities, which is a far cry from Daoism. In still other words, despite her gender skepticism, Butler is not a gender fool. As mentioned previously, "Daoist feminism" would strive to attain a reality of gender equality without essential distinctions between men and women, all within a "chaotified" reality. Within that chaotified reality, rules can still be followed but they are not serious. Butler believes in a "right" gender that can be dug out from beneath culture, and for which we must find the correct (and very serious) rules.

The dandy plays with gender too, or at least with his own gender. Dandyist gender bending can go from pseudo-female to asexual (see Fox 2016). It has been noted that dandyism is not a simple male attitude, and challenges, already from the early nineteenth century on, "the rigid separation of the two-sex system" (Feldman 1993, 12). Some interpret dandyism as a form of gender transgression, which is a phenomenon that has often been categorized under the term "queer." For Feldman dandyism exists "in the field of force between two opposing, irreconcilable notions about gender" (6), and David Tacium goes as far as to say that "the inheritors of Baudelaire maintain the hypothesis of castration" (1998). Still, from the previous explanation it emerges that the dandy is not queer. The dandy's gender performative transgressive behavior never strives to be recognized as authentic. In the end, it is only pretended, which is also why its character cannot be grasped by language. All the dandy produces is a personal style.

Before Butler, one of the pioneers of queer theory was Eve Kosofsky Sedgwick, who taught at Duke and New York University. She was a heterosexual woman married to a heterosexual man and called herself queer. For her, "being queer" had nothing to do with sexual orientation but was rather about being part of a subversive intellectual movement. There is something playful in Sedgwick's genderqueer behavior, but it does not entirely overlap with the playfulness of the dandy. Again, the problem is that Sedgwick was a queer *activist*, which the dandy (or Daoist) is not. Sedgwick played, but she played for a purpose, be it only the purpose of being recognized as queer (which had never been on the dandy's mind), or the purpose of bettering society by increasing the number of gender identities (which would be the very last thing a dandy would think of). Dandies are not playing for a purpose, nor do gay people. The merely gay person does not *play* because that person is, in fact, *simply* gay. The dandy does not play for a purpose because such play would quickly turn dandyism into the "busybody" activism that Wilde criticized. Like Daoism, dandyism is always passivism: the dandy is useless and does nothing. Contrary to the activist, the passivist does not search for labels, not even one as ambiguous as "gender fluid." McCormack points to the fact that homosexuality did not even have a consensual name in nineteenth-century England, which means that any "correction of names" was simply impossible: "How exactly did he define his own sexuality in an era when 'being gay' was only just being invented?" (2017, 73). The Marquess of Queensberry misspelled the term "sodomite" as "somdomite" when insulting Oscar Wilde.[18] Obviously, "being gay" had no name. At some point very early on, dandies would receive a special pronoun, but it was more ironic than serious. In 1770, dandies were given the pronoun "it" when the *Oxford Magazine* described the dandy (then called "Macaroni") as gender neutral: "There is indeed a kind of animal, neither male or female, a thing of the neuter gender, lately stated up amongst us. It is called a Maccaroni, it talks without meaning, it smiles without pleasantry, it eats without appetite, it rides without exercise, it wenches without passion" (in Benemann 2006, 53). Dandyism does not engage in a Confucian "correction" of genders but rather follows the Daoist "chaotification" of genders. Camus brings the project to a point. He aptly mentions the "pseudo-correction of language" that the dandy (or, for him, any artist) undertakes, not in view of finding a more correct language but in order to create a fleeting style. The "new law" the dandy finds is not a linguistic definition or a rule about how to use pronouns: "The correction that the artist operates through his language and through the redistribution of elements found in real life is called style and gives to the recreated universe its unity and its limits, to give its law to the world," writes Camus.[19]

Gender Blindness and Color Blindness

"Gender blindness" can also be established in parallel with the American cultural idea of "color blindness." Everything that has been said in this chapter about the Daoist conception of gender can be applied to race, too. In African American thought, the idea of "color blindness" has been developed as a measure against ethicization. It has been found that the ethicization of skin color brings with it a lot of victimization. Most famously, the conservative African American Supreme Court Justice Clarence Thomas supported colorblind policies to forbid preferential treatment such as race-based affirmative action. Thomas believed that race-oriented programs create "a cult of victimization" because they imply that Blacks require "special treatment in order to succeed" (Thomas 2007). The parallel with gender is clear. Gender blindness is an interesting option as it means more than merely ignoring gender when recruiting or enrolling students or employees. It can initiate a peculiar antigender theory based on Daoist "gender foolishness" that could penetrate society.

The opposite of color blindness, which is a seemingly PC-inspired correction of language, has existed in several places. It is very much a matter of creating new words. In the 1930s, Harlem slang knew color gradations such as "high yaller, yaller, high brown, vaseline brown, seal brown, low brown, dark brown."[20] Here one is not blind to color but sees more colors than usual. The project became more complex in Brazil when Brazilians were asked to describe their skin color in a survey and came up with 136 different shades. The survey was done in 1976, and among the 136 terms are *acastanhada* (somewhat chestnut-colored) and *agalegada* (somewhat like a Galician) but also green or red.[21] In earlier centuries, terms defining race have had more serious consequences. It was then not only about color but about genetic makeup. In the slave societies of the Americas, a quadroon (also "quartoon" or "quarteron") was defined as a person with one-quarter African and three-quarters European ancestry. An octoroon was one-eighth black and a hexadecaroon one-sixteenth black. Children from marriages between these groups needed to receive new names, too. In the Caribbean, the offspring of a Black and a white parent was a "mulatto," and a Black person and a "mulatto" produced a "sambo"; a Black and sambo produced a "mungroo"; offspring of a Black and a "mungroo" was Black again. A "mulatto" and a white person generated a "quartoon," a "quartoon" and a white a "mestic," and a "mestic" and a white became "white" again (from Campbell 1851, 176). These language correction projects might be admirable in terms of logic, but they still do not grasp the cultural reality of race. Race, personality, and even the perception of skin color depend on many contingent factors.

There is a human tendency to look at the world in terms of good and bad, black and white, male and female, and many more. However, how serious are these distinctions? Are they not always—or at least more often than we tend to admit—blurred to some extent in cultural contexts? It is obvious that, as Moeller writes, "Good and bad prove to be extremely shaky categories. One changes into the other, they are subject to continuous change and reversal" (2009, 19). This is most obvious for good and bad as well as for skin colors, but it also applies to genders. The gender fool is blind to gender judgments and attempts to grasp the cultural gender reality directly and not through any—not even the most refined—"gender glasses." It is possible to do this, just like it is possible to grasp the reality of a world in which some are deemed good, and some are deemed evil without believing in the essences of good and evil. To do so requires no ethical theory. Ethicists, logicians, language reformers, and gender theorists want to sharpen the focus on the blurred reality so that good and bad, male, female, and dozens of other qualities become more distinct, more differentiated, and more visible. They do this mostly by enforcing linguistic reforms but also through "juridification" and ethicization. Juridification has indeed had a strong impact on gender politics. French philosopher Jean-Claude Michéa suggests that PC leads to an increasing "juridification" of social relations, and thus also of gender relations (Michéa 2008). The Daoist suggests we keep reality blurred and chaotified and accept the meanings that flow out of the cultural play that we usually call "reality."

Chapter 4

Sincerity and Authenticity

Cheng and Zhen

Confucianism has typically been understood as an ethics of the sincere (*cheng* 誠), and the *Zhuangzi* criticizes this philosophy on various levels. Generally, *cheng* is taken to mean both sincerity and authenticity, but, in reality, *cheng* is very difficult to translate; translations go from "perfection" to "realness."[1] It has long been assumed that Daoism wants to replace Confucian sincerity with authenticity (*zhen* 真),[2] but Moeller and D'Ambrosio (2017) have convincingly shown that the *Zhuangzi* does not strive for authenticity but rather toward the kind of nothingness or emptiness that has been described in the preceding chapters. *Zhen* means true, real, factual, genuine, and authentic.[3] Contemporary scholarship sometimes presents *zhen* as analogous to the Western existentialist philosophy of authenticity, which takes as a point of departure the *zhen* person as an authentic and original self. This contradicts much of what has been said above about the self, as well as what will be developed about the self in the following two chapters. As D'Ambrosio points out in his article on *zhen*, though *zhen* "resonates strongly with contemporary Western philosophy and speaks to the existentialist's 'authenticity,' (. . .) it is doubtful that this is an accurate representation of debates in ancient China" (2015, 356).

The *Zhuangzi* finds Confucian moral teachings false and inefficient but does not want to replace sincerity with authenticity.[4] The right way of living is rather to be found by abandoning all ideals of sincerity as well as all socially constructed values and identities, including that of authenticity. According to Moeller, one needs to "let go of *de*," and the *Zhuangzi* thus deconstructs any truth about an authentic self or a sincere way of being.

In contemporary terms, we can indeed call the Daoist project "deconstructive" because it does not turn inauthentic sincerity into authenticity but rather *deconstructs* sincerity, the way Heidegger deconstructs, in *Being and Time*, the concept of Being through time. The German term "Destruktion," which has been translated into English by Stambaugh as "destructuring" and by Macquarrie and Robinson as "destroying," inspired Derrida's deconstruction. Heidegger announces in *Being and Time* (chap. 2, §6) that he wants to "destructure the history of ontology."[5] Derrida (1987) suggests translating the German word *Destruktion* into French as "deconstruction" to avoid the idea of simple annihilation or demolition. Likewise, in Daoism, authenticity is not annihilated because this would simply lead to inauthenticity. Instead, authenticity and sincerity still exist, but they are no longer ideals that can be obsessively pursued. Contrary to existentialists like Sartre, Daoists are not obsessed with authenticity as selfhood.

Confucius puts forward the sincere self that fulfills all obligations generated by one's role or *yi* (義), as the authentic model that we should strive for. *Yi* is the moral disposition to do good; and by practicing *yi*, humans fulfill their way. The *Zhuangzi* deconstructs this idea of selfhood and puts forward a wandering no-self that is constantly subjected to changes.[6] Again, this does not mean that Daoism wants to abolish or destroy the self. Suspect is only the self as an integrated and consistent identity. Daoism rejects the "socialized self" because this self is too much determined by "social usefulness" (Berkson 2005, 307). Just as Heidegger wants to see Being in time or though time, Chinese thought tends to locate the meaning of human life in everyday life. Li Zehou notes that, in general, straightforward striving for an abstract notion of authenticity is alien to the Chinese mindset:

> This kind of religious fervor is vastly different from the psychological structure and thinking based on humaneness that characterizes the Chinese nation (especially the Chinese intelligentsia). This cultural-psychological formation locates the meaning of human life in the everyday interactions of ordered human relationships, whereby the ideals of human life are satisfied by the social nature of ordinary daily interactions

and the human connections within groups. Perhaps in the future this will spare us from the so-called authentic existence of people, whereby the individual is adrift in a uniform and machine-like alienated world, feeling alone and desolate. (Li Zehou 2019, 28)

The purpose of Daoist philosophy and practice is not to find identity in the form of an authentic essence but rather to empty the self of any (social) identity in order to reach freedom. Excelling at "useless arts" is not merely an aesthetic strategy but extends into all domains of life. The *Zhuangzi* deconstructs the utility-self, which does not mean that the self becomes entirely useless. "Of petty uselessness great usefulness is achieved," says the Zhuangzi. Uselessness is a matter of efficient play, just like flâner, as written in the *Grand dictionnaire universel* of 1866, "is the very opposite of doing nothing." And the style it creates is not merely an aesthetic notion, but it also creates human "nature."

It is true that authenticity can be linked to freedom, but this is, again, a very Western approach; and even in the West it is relatively new. It will be shown below that the Enlightenment linked the new value of authenticity to some of its typical, already existing values, such as freedom, individuality, or autonomy. The idea of an original self has been elaborated by Rousseau (in the *Confessions*) *or* Kierkegaard (in various works, especially *Either/Or*) in the form of an "inner self" that is true to itself and able to go against social conventions. However, by doing so, the Enlightenment created an understanding of authenticity that is problematic, especially when seen from a non-Western point of view. For example, striving for authenticity can also have negative consequences as it can lead to selfish individualism. Both the sincerity-oriented Confucianism and Daoism combated selfish individualism, and the same is true for the self. The idea of a reified self as an autonomous inner entity exists neither in Confucianism nor in the *Zhuangzi*. It has been shown above how, in the Butterfly Story, the *Zhuangzi* deconstructs the "I" to the point that the pronoun "I" does not even appear. There is a different idea of personhood that is *neither* a self-conscious "I" *nor* a socialized or useful self. The *Zhuangzi* negates both and puts a general emphasis on "selflessness."

The rejection of the "self" is a complex issue because it functions not through destruction but rather through deconstruction. While Confucianism believes that we can live up to the model of a "perfect person" if we only correct our language and live up to the ideal that this corrected language represents, the *Zhuangzi* holds that we never really have proper control over our social roles. Rejecting the self does not mean that we are completely free, nor that, in order to find an "authentic" self, we have freed ourselves from all "socially fixed goals, values, and commitments that constitute one's identity" (Özbey 2018, 137). Having no self simply because one has decided to live like an outcast is not a solution. Looking for freedom in this sense, will simply make us lose our sense of personhood, which is not desirable either. Daoism does not simply reject the self (as Zen Buddhism often does),[7] but it rather adheres to a more complex, pluralistic, or "deconstructed" conception of the person that cannot be defined through thoughts, actions, habits, or feelings; and even less through names, titles, and pronouns. The Daoist person's self is thus not reduced to nothing but rather deconstructed. It was mentioned in chapter 2 that we should not flee society or reject existing names but rather choose to reside within the rules, follow them in a detached way, and use names sparingly. The Daoist sage will "swim in rivers like fish and turtles" (137), but while he is "swimming" he does not assume an identity and especially not an identity that can be fixed through language. He always has "the ability to assume many roles and positions without committing to any one of them" (137). This is the Daoist definition of having no authentic identity or no self.

The Emergence of Authenticity

Apart from demonstrating the twists of the authenticity-sincerity relationship in the context of Chinese philosophy, I want to show in this chapter that the search for authenticity is also the main driving force of PC. PC unfolds in the context of a typically Western culture of the authentic, though it also partly functions through sincerity. I will then demonstrate how both Daoism and dandyism collide with this culture. The abovementioned false idea that the *Zhuangzi* overcomes sincerity through authenticity fits only too well into the recent Western cultural framework that adulates authenticity and sees sincerity as old-fashioned, bourgeois, and capitalist. Daoism wants freedom, but this freedom is very different from the Enlightenment type of freedom. At the same time, when refusing authenticity, Daoism does not revert to Confucian-style sincerity. Daoism overcomes both authenticity and sincerity, and here it parallels dandyism.

Incidentally, dandyism suffers from the same misconceptions as Daoism. Superficially, dandyism has been described as a search for an authentic and unique style because originality appears to be the dandy's supreme goal. In a world where everything is imitation, the dandy seemingly tries to "be himself." However, this is a misrepresentation because dandyism is neither authentic nor sincere but deconstructs both concepts as well as the notion of the self through mockery, irony, *ennui*, *dédain*, phlegm, and *sprezzatura*.[8] The dandy parodies ranks and positions and does not fully assume any social roles. For example, a dandy would not refuse a high military honor even if his style of receiving it might come close to mockery, as describes Boulenger: "With which grandiloquent dédain the dandy could, for example, accept the officer's rank in one of the first army regiments, a rank that any other smug person of his birth and his age would have considered a dream."[9] The dandy deconstructs sincerity into a playful insincerity, which bars all further approaches attempting to transform sincerity into authenticity. "Is insincerity such a terrible thing? I think not. It is merely a method by which we can multiply our personalities," says Wilde's Dorian Gray (1992, 113).

In Western intellectual history, sincerity and authenticity have often been contrasted though, at the same time, it was also assumed that they are somehow linked. Sincerity, which Lionel Trilling described very well in his *Sincerity and Authenticity* (1972), requires submitting oneself to rules willingly and with devotion. According to Trilling, the idea of sincerity exists in European culture since around 1600 but only became prominent at some point in the early nineteenth century. For Isaiah Berlin, sincerity emerged a little later, as he explains in his conversation with Jahanbegloo: "Sincerity was not (. . .) considered a virtue in the ancient world or in the Middle Ages. Truth, of course, is a cardinal value . . . [but] I doubt if the idea of sincerity as a virtue is much earlier than the late seventeenth century" (2011, 40). Despite this divergence, Berlin is in agreement with Trilling when affirming that sincerity became a virtue during the time of Romanticism. Before Romanticism, sincerity had been neglected to some extent, though not entirely. On the one hand, the Enlightenment was interested in an order imposed by reason and by the human will; and this did not leave much space for sincerity. It was rather Counter-Enlightenment thinkers like Herder and Hamann who would prepare the way for sincerity. On the other hand, sincerity remains an Enlightenment value because authors like Rousseau professed the ideal of transparency as a remedy against the duplicity of the Ancien Regime. Sincerity enabled the solidarity necessary for revolutionary undertakings. It is no coincidence that speculations about parallels between physiognomy and psychological features, or between character and facial features, became prominent around the time of the French Revolution (see de Baecque 1997). One believed that the heart could be read upon the face.

Romanticism shaped and formulated the concept of sincerity until it became a virtue in and of itself. Berlin writes in *The Roots of Romanticism*: "The fact that [somebody] is sincere, that he is prepared to lay down his life for the nonsense in which he believes, is [for the romantics] a morally noble fact. Anyone who is sufficiently a man of integrity, anyone who is prepared to sacrifice himself upon any altar, no matter what, has a moral personality which is worthy of respect, no matter how detestable or how false the ideals to which he bows his knee."[10] This "wholeness" can also be expressed by saying that being sincere means to be "true to oneself." However, this requires valid notions of the self and of individuality beforehand. The conclusion is that the idea of sincerity could not have emerged without the presence of some of those values that are today associated with authenticity. Without an at least vague idea of the "authentic self," no sincerity is possible, which is probably the reason why sincerity appeared so late in Western culture. The self as a sort of inner object that can be shaped by deliberate action until it is "authentic" is the product of a modern mindset that was developed, at the earliest, by Descartes and Locke. The latter describes, in his *Essay Concerning Human Understanding* (1694), the self as a personal identity founded on consciousness, and it can be understood as an "authentic self." Sincerity is thus a modern individualistic notion whose two elements, "truth" and "self," are supposed to overlap, and this concept paved the way for our full-fledged modern idea of authenticity.

It appears thus paradoxical that in the middle of the twentieth century, in Western culture, sincerity would be abandoned to make way for the rule of authenticity. However, this is precisely what happened. According to Trilling, after the nineteenth century, sincerity "lost most of its former high dignity" (6), and the idea of the authentic, which was already subliminally present since the Enlightenment and had emerged from the older concept of sincerity, moved to the foreground. As a matter of fact, it had happened even a little earlier. In the Victorian era, sincerity was still highly regarded, but the authentic as an alternative value had already emerged in parallel. Lynn Voskuil has shown, in her *Acting Naturally: Victorian Theatricality and Authenticity* (2004), that Victorian

Britons saw themselves as "authentically performative," a compound that sounds paradoxical and almost reminiscent of the notion of the Daoist "genuine pretending" that will be examined below. Voskuil finds that, though living up to their reputation of sincerity, Victorians were also fascinated with acting and a social performance that was supposed to look "authentic." In the twentieth century, authenticity and sincerity became clearly distinct until they could finally appear as incompatible entities. Despite these divergences, the terms remained somehow similar: both continued to signify the absence of corruption and a sense of purity. The opposite of both the sincere and the authentic person remained the hypocrite, who is not real but only playing. The sincere person is more authentic than the hypocrite because she is truthful and not fake. She "really" believes in what she is saying. Given these constellations, the authentic can also be characterized as hyper sincere, which is, of course, difficult to reconcile with all other approaches that contrast the authentic with the sincere.

As we approach modernity, an apparently irreconcilable gap between the authentic and the sincere has constantly grown. A major difference between the two would be that sincerity usually requires an effort to come about whereas authenticity can exist "autonomously." The authentic is thus truthful "by nature." Something is authentic without anybody making an effort to render the person or the object authentic whereas sincerity is self- or other-controlled; and control can also mean oppression and lack of freedom. This is one of the paradigms that helped to install the age of authenticity, which—as strangely as this must have sounded to earlier generations—would attempt to overcome the age of sincerity.

The Age of Authenticity

It has been said in the introduction that in the 1980s, during Thatcher and Reagan's heyday, a new individualism became appealing to everyone, even to leftists, and that originality and identity search were no longer the exclusive values of the bourgeois right. It is in this context that authenticity could develop out of an earlier concept of sincerity and eventually replace it. According to Charles Taylor, we are living in an age of authenticity, whose main raison d'être is to overcome sincerity (2007, 473–504), and Lionel Trilling offers similar analyses. Despite this development, the relationships between sincerity and authenticity are more complex than Taylor's and Trilling's formulas suggests. For example, the narrative of authenticity in modern Western culture is both bourgeois and antibourgeois, both capitalistic and anticapitalistic. Authenticity can represent a refuge for the individual who is overwhelmed by the fake "society of the spectacle"; and at the same time, the idea of authenticity has been crucial for the formulation of a modern national identity in politics as well as for the branding of identities in global trade. Taylor demonstrates that the twentieth-century revolt against an ethics of sincerity led to an age of authenticity in culture and politics. So how can the authentic also be, as has been suggested above, a hyper-sincerity? But let us first follow Taylor's analysis, which is pertinent in and of itself. In Western cultures, since the 1960s, an individuating revolution began searching for a more authentic way of living. Such ambitions had already been present in the nineteenth century, where the search for the authentic was also a form of protest but where it used to be much more elitist than it would be in the 1960s. Those nineteenth-century searchers for an authentic lifestyle were called "bohemians," and they will be attended to in chapter 7.

The purpose of the cultural revolutions of the 1960s was to transcend a conformist postwar society steeped in mass production and mass consumption that was believed to crush the creativity of the individual. Governments were authoritarian and families were traditionalist, and both tended to oppress the authenticity of the individual who was in search of freedom of expression. Old societies (Victorian society or the society of the Weimar Republic, for instance) had been societies of sincerity who believed in tradition and efficiency. Their cultures were still very much determined by the values of Romanticism. However, the problem was not just that puritan and authoritarian appeals to sincerity crushed authenticity. Another problem was that this sincerity was actually fake. Helmut Lethen has shown how in the Weimar Republic, which preceded Hitler's Germany, one preached the control of emotions in a way similar to what had been done in English Victorian culture a hundred years earlier (1994, 179). When emotions are controlled and dissimulated, life becomes fake. After World War II, bourgeois behavior, which was now identified with sincerity, would be declared inauthentic because it was fake. This appears strange if one considers that Romanticism had once associated sincerity with truth. Still in the nineteenth century, sincerity signified the "true" overlap of feelings and actions and, as has been explained here, it is precisely these constellations that gave birth to the idea of authenticity. In the mid-twentieth century, many felt that cultures of control and self-control that insist so much on sincerity are fake. One could recognize that this kind of sincerity had enabled modernization and that it had facilitated the immense technological boom through which European culture had been thriving during early modernity. Sincerity creates efficiency and is thus beneficial for development and modernization. However, now it was time to amend lifestyles and to retrieve the authentic. Paradoxically, much of what that newly advertised notion of the authentic was supposed to mean had formerly been represented by the notion of sincerity (that is, by sincerity before it had become "fake"). Georg Simmel explains that in the nineteenth century, (fake) sincerity had killed everything that the Enlightenment had held to be authentic. Simmel's narrative goes like this: in the eighteenth century the individual had liberated itself from the state and from religion and could develop freely without being inhibited by authoritarian or religious constraints. The self had become authentic (which was also called "sincere"), which, in the eighteenth century, had an immensely positive effect because one generally believed humans to be naturally good. It was thought that earlier on, the irrational constraints of pre-Enlightenment cultures had prevented the optimal development of the individual and that the Enlightenment was a liberating force. However, in the nineteenth century, with its industrialization and its economies increasingly driven by technology, the human self was once again leveled, normed, and submitted to outside influences (see Simmel 1995, 116). In this new technological environment, people were again supposed to be nothing more than efficient and sincere. Once again, the authentic was lost. Simmel, who had been an almost forgotten figure in European postwar academia, was rediscovered and translated in the United States in the 1970s and from there eagerly "reintroduced" into Europe.[11] In the post-Fordist work culture that had begun to gain strength in the 1960s, an "authentic lifestyle" with an emphasis on creativity, autonomy, and individuality as new core values, would again become attractive. The "new" ideal was authenticity, which could now be understood as antisincerity.

The cultural revolutions of the 1960s claimed an expressive individualism. The most spectacular episode was certainly the sexual revolution, though many other institutions and ideologies also supported the emergence of the authentic as a relatively new cultural phenomenon. Earlier, Marxist trends had searched for the authentic through their fight against *Entfremdung*,[12] and psychoanalysis had striven toward the knowledge of an authentic self that was perceived as suffering under a heap of "sincere" civilizational prohibitions. When the self is submitted to the discontent of the sincere, it becomes neurotic. Various philosophers supported this trend of the liberation of the authentic self. Heidegger's earlier writings on *Eigentlichkeit* provided supplementary sophistication to this cult of authenticity, and existentialism introduced the idea of "bad faith" that prevents us from living an authentic life.[13] Nietzsche's "God is dead" paradigm created a peculiar background music to this new cultural spectacle. On the one hand, a life in agreement with God was no longer accepted as an authentic life. On the other hand, a world without God, though desired by many in the West, felt uncomfortably "light" because it lacked some sort of authenticity. Consequently, alternative religions or cults providing "authentic spirituality" became a solution for many who sought an authentic lifestyle.

Expressive individualism was also helped by a series of passive factors such as the rise of the "image society" through television (and later the internet) as well as the erosion of smaller communities that had constrained the individual self. Selfies, pictures that people take of themselves in "authentic" real-life contexts, are recent popular expressions of the individualist self. This individualism does not necessarily lead to authenticity (it probably often leads to the opposite), but it can at least lead to an illusion of authenticity. Selfies do not represent much authenticity, but the selfying teenager might indeed believe that social media provides much freedom and helps them escape the sincerity requirements of their immediate environment.

Easier divorces and delayed childbirth facilitated individualist lifestyles, too. All in all, it had become much easier to escape sincerity and to look for one's authentic self. Later, factors like forced job flexibility and the erosion of communal institutions such as workers' unions, contributed as well. Sincerity was no longer required, and authenticity became the new supreme good, or, one is tempted to say, the only remaining good. With the internet and new technical possibilities of copying, the authentic became even more valuable, which was one more reason to defend it. What is the original, and what is the copy? This question became increasingly difficult to answer.

The paragraphs above describe only the first phase of the search for the authentic in postwar culture. The hippie approach can still look distantly "Daoist" because this generation valued feeling and spontaneity and criticized a society of sincerity that had become too mechanical (or perhaps some would say too "Confucian"). What Taylor calls "organic" (as opposed to "mechanic") or also "Dionysian" (477) bears some link with Daoist approaches. James Sellman calls the *Zhuangzi*, with its anecdotes of biological metamorphoses, "organismic" (2016, 164n3), and the organic, as an antiurban and close-to-nature lifestyle, creates a clear connection with this East Asian philosophy. It is certainly no coincidence that since the 1970s, "The Tao of . . ." books have become a common stock in the West. Furthermore, Laozi's suspicion of book learning is in keeping with the values of this counterculture, which resented the head-heaviness of conservative "sincere" cultures. Sincerity-based culture had also become too mechanic in ethical matters, and the relativization of ethics is one reason why Daoism (as well as other East Asian philosophies or religions) became so popular with this generation. One was against the repression of the body by reason and wanted to enjoy a fullness of sensuality, of authentic feelings, and of authentic pleasures. For too long, hypocritical morals had tried to prevent this sensual flourishing.

"Sincere Authenticity"

Despite its initially "Daoist" inspirations, the next step of the 1960s "revolution" would cancel much of its abovementioned libertarian and authenticity-oriented program. The phase that the authentic would undergo now was its ethicization, which took the concept of the authentic in the opposite direction. From the 1980s onward, authenticity would no longer be framed as *beyond* good and evil but *in terms of* good and evil. In other words, the authentic became once again sincere. While individualism, as well as sex and sensuality, were still considered good traits, the former revolutionaries began to pursue individualism and sex "with the kind of earnest concern for self-improvement which is light-years away from the Dionysian spontaneity of the 60s" (Taylor 2007, 477). This is ironic because normally sincerity is ethical, and the overcoming of sincerity through authenticity was very much driven by the will to overcome some of sincerity's ethical aspects. Now authenticity would be relaunched as an ethical program and framed in terms of sincerity. One of the results of this process is PC. Authenticity became a serious business, especially in a time when, as has been described in the introduction, leftist thought had just taken a proindividualist turn.

Individuals needed to be protected, and this approach would especially prioritize those individuals that came from vulnerable minority groups. Still in the 1970s, homosexuals had been a repressed minority; however, in the 1990s, they had made considerable progress in terms of recognition. Now the status of new minorities needed to be improved: that of transgenders, intergenders, and some statuses that perhaps had never been heard of by most people. Everybody needed to be helped. Self-victimization played an important role here. Since there was no "outside" enemy (capitalism) left to fight against, the individual and the authentic became the most valuable goods to defend, and they would be defended with utmost sincerity. In universities, where diversity offices could now employ dozens of administrators, PC rules would not only ban certain kinds of speech and other traditional modes of expression but also looks, body language, and laughter. "HR is going to tell you in a long bullet-pointed list about how you look at people," says Stephen Fry in the Munk Debate (Peterson et al. 2018, 88). The sincerity with which all this was implemented could make one forget that the initial purpose of the procedure had been to celebrate the age of authenticity. And yet, this sincerity would be advertised as "authentic" because it was supposed to help individuals live free, authentic, and autonomous lives, perfectly in agreement with the spirit of the Enlightenment.

Those who were against the new form of the authentic were declared enemies. These enemies were especially those still preaching the old-fashioned sincerity and who insisted on an adherence to (state-sponsored) norms and rules. The state could still be seen as negative because it required conformity; but even more threatening to authenticity was the patriarchy. When rejecting the state and patriarchy, the new authenticity would still follow the old "Dionysian" model of authenticity seen in the hippie years. But beyond this, there are more differences than resemblances. The new culture of authenticity was no longer anarchic but talked much about rules: but not the rules of the state or the patriarch, and not even of the rules of society at large. This new leftist culture had created its own rules, though only within a very limited domain: within the realm of PC, which soon began to focus on language. Much of PC spelled out authenticity in ethico-linguistic terms and implemented authenticity *formally*, often by insisting on language rules. For example, in an ideal society, every member would have the right to receive their own gender term possibly complete with a matching pronoun. This would guarantee everybody a truly authentic existence. As a result, language had to constantly be checked. Authenticity was no longer, as it still used to be during the "Dionysian" phase of leftism, a personal adventure: it had become a human right. The fight for this human right often superseded other typically leftist political causes such as welfare or income inequality that would be conveniently neglected. A generation of "bourgeois bohèmes" (or *bobos*) became economically conservative and consumerist but would still affirm its "leftist" spirit by advertising its fight for the "authenticity for all" and by supporting PC. The human right of authenticity would be particularly strongly defended when it came to minorities. The new leftist priority would now be: (1) the pursuit of self-cultivation, which could mean the use of the right gender terms for everybody, and (2) the support of other peoples' rights to the authentic, which could mean to help them receive the right gender terms.

Despite this clearly sincere spirit, PC conveyers would still see the sincere person as their enemy. Why? Because sincerity would mainly be understood as "fake sincerity." For example, somebody who uses feminine pronouns throughout a text even though the pronoun refers to both male and female subjects, is simply "hypocritically sincere." PC, which basically *is* sincere, claims to be authentic and rejects the sincere. Still, it seems that the main problem with PC is that it is *too* sincere. Stuart Hall sees PC as the "latter-day Puritans [similar to] the Saints of the seventeenth century" who have a "strong strain of moral self-righteousness" (1994, 183), and who were living at a time when, according to Isaiah Berlin, sincerity was forged as a virtue for the first time. Hall depicts these people with "thumbscrews being unpacked, the guillotine sharpened, [and] the pages of the Dictionary of Political Correctness being shuffled" (183).

It remains to be said that the political right has not fared much better and has had similar problems. After 1989, with the disappearance of communism, they too had lost their enemy. However, a new enemy was quickly located: PC. In 1995, John K. Wilson stated that conservatives were framing themselves as victims of PC. In his *The Myth of Political Correctness*, John K. Wilson notes that nobody "except perhaps the conservatives, use[s] the phrase politically correct" (1995, x). A new conservative anticorrectness emerged and was quickly enforced in universities: "While American troops prepared to invade Kuwait, the New Republic found a new Saddam Hussein in the visage of the tenured leftist who controlled American universities" (14). A complete critique of right-wing criticism of PC is beyond the scope of this book, but a "back to the authentic" impulse appears to be central and needs to be highlighted. The right would cast its new enemy by using a familiar pattern, basically declaring that PC's main problem is to be overly sincere, thus killing the authentic. Ironically, this mirrors PC's approach vis-à-vis the right. Right-wing politicians described PC as a distortion of reality that covers up real and "authentic" problems. This anti-PC pattern has remained intact to this day, and it is no less absurd than the aspects of PC described earlier. Right-wing politicians lure their public in with apparently honest and sincere talk, but they always understand sincerity in the "old" way as authentic. Most often they market this "sincerity" by using the age-old link between the authentic and the authoritarian. As Trilling has shown, traditionally, authenticity was linked to masculinity and manly ambition (1972, 95),[14] whereas women were allowed to be "fake" by nature. Baudelaire, for whom the woman is the opposite of the dandy, explains this in his *Mon Coeur mis a nu*. To be authentic meant to be outspoken and brave, which is one more reason why, in the end, for the right, authenticity to this day has remained more important than sincerity. The left is criticized as lacking authenticity, straight talk, and honesty. PC's bigger-than-life sincerity is said to make leftists lose sight of what is authentically real. PC is not authentic, as it simply does not talk about "real" problems, whereas the right wing is believed to have some sort of privileged access to authenticity in all its forms.

Linguist Anna Szilágyi has analyzed how right-wing opponents of PC "picture their agenda and themselves as genuine, sincere, and authentic" (Szilágyi 2017) and declare the left to be fake. While it is true that sincerity still appears on the conservative menu, next to authenticity, the political right still uses sincerity as a traditional value, as it existed prior to the newer wave of authenticity sparked by hippie culture (and which later turned into the sincerity of PC). For the far right, to be "sincere" simply means to be honest and authentic and not to follow the rules of correctness. The far-right most clearly links sincerity to authenticity and uses the authentic in the sense of the hyper-sincere. While liberals want "sincere authenticity" issued by rules and correct terms, the right wants "authentic sincerity" in the sense of the older idea of the authentic, which was an idea that had been subliminally present in the Enlightenment: the authentic-sincere. Things need to be "authentic," meaning they need to be pure and uncorrupted. The others, the liberals, are (according to the right) only playing with—presumably authentic—gender terms and pronouns and are therefore not sincere at all.

One question still needs to be answered: *can* the rules of PC really be played with sincerity? Our age is the age of the authentic, and any sincere rule following has been the red cloth of at least one generation of progressive people. From a PC point of view, rules are not followed because our society ought to be more sincere, or because everyone ought to follow sincere rules; from a PC point of view, that would be oppressive. Rather, rules should be followed because they lead to a more authentic individuality and, finally, to a more authentic society. We hear Confucius speaking. This means that, paradoxically, just like the political right, PC has a much stronger connection to the authentic than to the sincere. The obsession with the authentic here does not become manifest through a display of manliness and authoritarianism but becomes palpable when it develops peculiar reasonings about identity or "identity appropriation." Identity is a complex term and cannot be reduced to authenticity, but PC vigorously defends minorities' rights to assume their identities to the point of saying that minorities' identities cannot be appropriated by dominant groups. Here PC speaks the language of the authentic, and it speaks this language with utmost sincerity.

The phenomenon of identity appropriation does not only concern minorities. For example, when, in 2016, model Kendall Jenner did a photoshoot for *Vogue* magazine dressed as a ballerina, there were complaints that the photoshoot "appropriated" ballerina culture (Waterton 2016). The quest for authenticity made any kind of roleplay or playful pretending inappropriate. The reasons were ethical: ballerinas work hard to have a ballerina identity, and Jenner was stealing what these women had been working toward. The problem was thus not the search for authenticity in the first place but rather the ethical sincerity with which authenticity would be defended. This reasoning has created the peculiar culture of PC that has spread into all domains of life in Western societies.

The hippie movement of the 1960s adopted Zhuangzi's Daoism as an alternative way of life that promoted the freedom and the autonomy of the individual over the constraints of society and government. Later, through PC, this became a new form of constraint. Neo-conservatives respond to a left totalitarianism represented by PC, which they feel threatens traditional values. Only a "moral fool" like a Daoist or a dandy can handle the PC controversy through playfulness without being fooled by morals. Both left and right ethicize freedom and the autonomy of the individual and submit it to rules. However, rambling is not about rules, ethics, authenticity, and sincerity, but it is an aesthetic activity in the first place. Gender, race, and all PC matters can be more easily handled by leaving ethics out of the equation.

Chapter 5

The Authentic and the Sincere in Daoism

In Chinese, the concept of sincerity (*cheng* 誠, see footnotes 1 and 3 of the last chapter) roughly overlaps with the Confucian idea that our actions must involve our inner mental and emotional self. Simply playing one's role is not enough, but a person's heart-mind (*xin* 心) must be involved as well. Nor should roles be assumed to deceive others or ourselves merely for the sake of personal gain. In order to count as real virtues, virtues must be *sincerely* assumed. The new Western quest for gender correctness talks much about rules and is therefore kindred with Confucianism.

Daoism depicts sincerity as "overly sincere" and as something that one should cleanse oneself of. The *Zhuangzi* (chap. 32, *Lie Yu-kou*) mentions a story about the Daoist sage Liezi (Lie Yukou), who went to the province of Qi to offer his services to the ruler. But having almost arrived, he turned back home without meeting the ruler. When asked what made him return, he gave the following explanation: "I had eaten in ten soup-shops and in five of them they attentively served me first." "But if that's how they treated you," asked Uncle Obscure Dimbody, "why were you startled?" "If one's inner sincerity is not released, the physical form will divulge a realized light. When one subdues others' minds with one's external appearance, causing them to belittle the honored and the elderly, various troubles will ensue."[1] Jean François Billeter interprets this story as suggesting that Liezi "has not yet gotten rid of his sincerity (*cheng*), that is, the will to do good, to be useful, to help others by giving advises. His manner had betrayed him, and he felt trapped: if the people saw in him the wise man, they would submit themselves under his authority and ask him to solve all their problems" (Billeter 2013,

17). Liezi really was sincere. A move toward a more authentic attitude would not have solved his problem but would have made it even worse.

It has been shown in the previous chapter that sincerity is closely linked to authenticity and therefore also—indirectly—to a sense of the self. Daoism has difficulties with both sincerity and authenticity, which has to do with Daoism's peculiar assumptions about the self. The *Zhuangzi* recommends having no sense of the self (*ji* 己) or "I" (*wo* 我),[2] but the *Zhuangzi* seems to be more affirmative when it comes to *shen* (身), which is translated as body or person. *Shen* is a way of expressing personhood[3] (as are *wo*, *ji*, or *xin*), and *shen* can also mean "myself." One could thus suspect that *shen* will point toward a strong idea of authenticity because the body is natural and not social. However, this is not the case. The body might be the core of the being, but it too is given to transformations, as the Butterfly Story demonstrates. Thus, Daoism does not assume that the self as a social identity is fake and that the body or the person is authentic or even natural. Sonya Özbey explains that the *shen* is not an embodied or natural self and that "there is also no categorical suggestion that we should preserve our *shen* in the *Zhuangzi*" (2018, 137). However, because the *Zhuangzi* recommends "avoid[ing] things that reduce the person to a limited set of roles, commitments, and functions" (135–36), the *Zhuangzi* also rejects the relational aspect of the *shen*. Özbey cites various interpretations that see the *Zhuangzi* favoring the *shen* as a "natural/inner/authentic core of a person" and that reject the *shen* as a "social/constructed/external identity" (124). For example, Berkson (2005) translates *shen* as "embodied self" and contrasts it with the "social self." Slingerland (2004) describes the *shen* as one's "true self," which he classifies under those things that belong to one's inner/essential core and that he subsequently contrasts with what is external to that core (such as cultural standards). Jochim (2016) leaves *shen* untranslated but still uses the adjective "authentic." All three authors claim that "the *Zhuangzi* presents losing one's *shen* as a bad idea in general and tells us to preserve, nourish, and cultivate it." Özbey does not agree with these interpretations. According to her, there is nothing authentic or natural about the *shen*. The *shen* is not "an artifice-free and inner aspect of one's person but appears as simply the organic body that can be modified by socially significant patterns (which pertain to artifice)" (136).

It has been shown above that the search for the authentic is a revolt against the ethics of sincerity, against an ethics that demands individuals play their role sincerely. Roles—especially gender roles—are always imposed by society. When society forces us to play certain roles, such as that of the male or the female, it might prevent us from finding our true and authentic self. Consequently, new roles, such as "gender fluid," will be officialized and sanctioned. What would be the Daoist response to this? The Daoist would not insist on the male or female role but would rather claim no real knowledge of what the "authentic male and female" means *in culture*. The Daoist has no knowledge of the authentic self but considers such knowledge to be, as all knowledge required by sincere persons, petty knowledge. When asked about the "authentic gender" the Daoist would most probably act like the "moral fool" defined by Moeller and claim to be blind to the authentic because: how can anybody pretend to know what is authentic (or what is an authentic gender) in societies as complex as ours? Modern societies are rife with slogans aggressively pushing for authenticity, such as "Be yourself" or "Just do it." They promise, in an Enlightenment fashion, utmost freedom and independence through authenticity. However, such slogans merely illustrate that the Daoist position is correct. "Be yourself" presupposes that we *know* what the self is, when in reality we don't. Similarly, Confucius preached the duty of correct performance, but how can we know what that performance is? We strive for authenticity without knowing what it is. When it comes to authenticity, we are all fools, but few are ready to admit it. The only thing we know for sure is, perhaps, that in a world full of copies we adore "the authentic." Daoism shows us that our knowledge is nonknowledge because when we admit that we do not know what authenticity is, *this* makes us authentic. The *Zhuangzi* says that

> to him who does not dwell in himself
> the forms of things show themselves as they are.
> His movement is like that of water;
> his stillness is like that of a mirror;
> his response is like that of the echo.
> His tenuity makes him seem to be disappearing altogether;
> he is still as a clear (lake),
> harmonious in his association with others, and he counts
>   gain as loss.
> He does not take precedence of others but follows them.[4]

Authenticity is here, paradoxically, reached by abandoning any idea of authenticity or sincerity. This is the "mindless mind" or the "no-mind."

It is not reached by following, in an only apparently Daoist act of spontaneity and forgetting, the slogan of "Just do it." On the contrary, the sage follows others, but he is not sincere when doing so. He gets rid of all fixed opinions (about authenticity) until things present themselves to him as they really are. Things always remain fluid and are not fixed because the mind does not establish categories such as genders or ethical categories. Gain can be loss, and loss can be gain. Important is the idea of moving—which is here expressed through water—which Daoism emphasizes through its discourse on *you* or rambling.

The slogan "Just do it" does not live up to the ethical potential that it pretends to provide.[5] Today, many imperatives to "be authentic" are even cynical because they arise against a background of economic precarity in which sincerity is no longer possible, and authenticity is advertised as a new value. A new capitalism that only provides part-time jobs and short-term contracts puts forward the idea of the "creative job" in which everything is fluid and flexible instead of secure, stable, and sincere. In this fluid world, modern humans are supposed to find a fixed position by desperately clinging to something authentic. Life coaches support this pattern and make us more "effective" by telling us that stability (and thus sincerity) is fake and that only a fluid lifestyle leads to authentic self-realization. The *Zhuangzi* renounces this option. It renounces both the sincere and the authentic, thus becoming a new viable philosophical option.

The Authentic Gender

What role does sincerity play in gender politics? Let us take the case of a biological male who wants to be addressed as a woman. One could say that s/he has chosen this option because s/he cannot play her role as a man with sincerity and so steps out of this social game and adopts the self that is considered more authentic: the self of a woman. In PC terms, this man/woman discards sincerity in favor of authenticity. Though some members of her environment might not see her as an "authentic woman," she is clearly striving *exclusively* for authenticity. She does not *choose the role* of a woman; she is not trying to play the role of the woman with more sincerity than she can play the role of a man. For PC, gender change is not a matter of playing roles, but it is a matter of what one *is*. One does not receive a new gender term for simply playing a role.

However, in the case of this man/woman, the same degree of authenticity can rarely be obtained. Normally this would create a dilemma.

I must clarify that I am writing about the *PC perception* of trans culture and not necessarily about how trans people themselves would define their position. I take trans culture as an example to elucidate the relationship between language and culture as defined by PC. Though PC and trans culture can these days appear to be tightly linked, it is worth insisting that trans individuals and cultures associated with them have always existed, long before the recent phenomenon of PC. Indeed, one might even argue that in most cases throughout history, the views on gender of trans individuals come closer to the Daoist position that I am trying to define here, whereas the PC interpretation insists on authenticity.

The impulse of freely choosing a gender derives from the modern search of "oneself," for one's true Me. It is embedded in the culture of authenticity described by Taylor and others, and in a PC society, everybody is supposed to go along with it. As mentioned, the Canadian court decided to penalize anybody who refuses to use the modified gender terms and pronouns. One will not be punished for refusing to believe in the trans person's sincerity, but one will be punished for doubting the gender's authenticity. To be on the safe side, the State of New York has adopted thirty-one gender terms, each of which is supposed to be authentic. Theoretically, one could invent a unique gender term for every inhabitant of the world so that everybody's authenticity is/would be guaranteed. Still, the man who wants to be addressed as a woman will not be "authentic" in the way in which society used to see biologically female individuals.

PC gender politics believes it has solved this dilemma, but it is obvious that this approach to authenticity is flawed, which is why Daoism would have approached the problem differently from the beginning. The Daoist attitude that I am trying to describe here would hold that in culture, *any* gender is played to some extent and that everybody has his/her own way of playing that gender. This does not mean that some play it well and others badly, because how could such standards be established? A Daoist way of seeing gender would not be grounded in authenticity at all, but it would have nothing to do with sincerity either. There would be no ethical input, only functionality within a social game. Furthermore, Daoists will accept the contingencies of social roles and know that roles are not permanent. In contrast, an official gender term attempts to sanction a role by conferring (permanent) authenticity. The key idea of a Daoist gender theory would therefore be to say that gender emerges through cultural play, and a priori, this play has nothing to do with sincerity or authenticity.

There is another problem with sincerity that needs to be addressed in this context. Any question about sincerity can only arise on the condition that one *can* also be insincere. Moeller and D'Ambrosio (2017, 23) point to this paradox in Confucianism, and it has strange repercussions when applied to gender. Sincerity is about the proper correspondence between names and actualities: one must live up to what one is. Consequently, it only makes sense to speak about sincerity when there *is* a gap between names and actualities. Here we perceive a problem with gender because gender is not supposed to have that gap. Does a woman who *is* a woman (and who is not just called "woman" by name) need to *sincerely* be woman in order to be a woman? No, a woman is a woman. Only a woman who is "somehow" not an authentic woman can be asked to sincerely be "woman" in order to achieve her womanhood. Originally, gender is an *authentic* attribute, and the question of sincerity does not arise. She might deviate from the cultural expectations of how a woman should behave, dress, and so on. But nobody would take away her gender for that reason. If she dresses like a man, one might say that she is not *sincerely* woman and that she should be more sincere when playing her female role in society. But she will still be an authentic woman. In no way is her gender affected by insincerity. Gender is what one is, and not what one plays. One can sincerely or insincerely play certain gender *roles*, but the gender itself is not affected by that role play. Therefore, the "real" woman is not trying to be a woman, but she is always an authentic woman no matter how she behaves. Anybody who tries too hard to be male or female demonstrates that there is a gap between the name and the actuality and is thus not authentic.

The Daoist-minded stance on this problem can be made clear by looking at virtue. What happens to gender in the case of the man who wants to be addressed as a woman is similar to what happened to virtue as seen from a Daoist point of view, which Slingerland summarizes in this way:

> Once upon a time, people were genuinely virtuous—they had real Virtue with a capital "V" (*de*), precisely because they didn't try. Things then got progressively worse. First, we had the "benevolent" person, who was relatively sincere but still felt the need to act in the world, to "do good." That's where

the trouble started. Then we had the dreaded "righteous" person, a sanctimonious poseur who couldn't stop dwelling on how wonderful he was and felt the need to stick his nose into everyone's business. Even worse were those who knew nothing but rigid adherence to ritual guidelines, driven by an insatiable urge to see their sense of what was right imposed on everyone around them. This, in turn, forced people to become hypocritical. (Slingerland 2014, 95)

The world would obviously be an easier place to live in if everything had remained genuine, including gender. No striving, no posing, no hiding: "Once upon a time, people were genuinely male or female—they had real Gender with a capital 'G,' precisely because they didn't try. Things then got progressively worse." Today, even gender can be played, and PC attempts to solve this paradox. The paradox is that for gender, a gap between name and actuality should not exist, but obviously it does exist, and it even *has* to exist because otherwise it would be impossible to be sincere about gender. But for PC, gender cannot be conceived as a matter of role playing and always needs to be authentic. To solve this paradox, PC discards the possibility that having a gender can ever be a matter of playing a role. For women who are not "authentic" women, PC simply invents new genders to maintain its politics of authenticity. For PC, the gender-fluid person *is* gender fluid, s/he is not switching between two authenticities, the male and the female. The already quoted website Healthline.com describes a gender-fluid person as someone who "might identify as a woman one day and a man the next," and very much insists that "gender fluid" is different from "non-binary." S/he is not playing. Switching is not acceptable because it denotes a lack of sincerity, and "authentic fluidity" is considered the only viable option. In this way, PC re-creates the "once upon a time where people were genuinely virtuous" in the realm of gender. Once a range of new pronouns has been invented, the strenuous Confucian question "do I play my role properly?" can conveniently be discarded. Everybody can join the age of authenticity because I *am* what I decide to be, and the existence of a gender term proves that I am authentic.

For Confucius, name and role must match, and in principle, this has not changed. But now the perfect match is not achieved through sincerity but through the invention of a new "authentic" gender term. The case of the gender-fluid person illustrates the absurdity of this approach.

Many people would criticize this man/woman's lack of sincerity because his/her identity seems to be determined too much by contingencies. However, s/he claims to have an essence (the essence of gender fluid) and can refer to this essence by pointing to a matching gender term.

The Daoist Politics of the Person

The Daoist idea of the genuine, which will be amply discussed in Chapter 6 through an evaluation of Moeller and D'Ambrosio's term "genuine pretending," avoids such absurdities because it replaces, and thus deconstructs, both the sincere and the authentic. In Chinese, genuine is *zhen* (真), and the *zhenren* (真人) is the genuine person. The term *zhenren* appears first in the *Zhuangzi*, and it is also used in Chinese Buddhism as a translation of the Sanskrit *arhat* (see Funayama 2019, 92).[6] The *Zhuangzi* contrasts "heavenly" genuineness with the Confucian following of *li*, which it considers artificial and ossified. Roaming within Confucian guidelines can lead to some degree of authenticity and sincerity, but it does not create the *zhenren* or the Sage who follows "the path of pure simplicity [純素之道] which guards and preserves the Spirit" as the *Zhuangzi* says in chapter 15 (*Ingrained Ideas* 3, trans. Legge). The genuine person is "not a state one reaches but a broadening of perspective" (Coyle 2016, 201). For Coyle, *zhen* is thus "used in counterculture fashion to criticize Confucius" (198).

What does this mean for gender? Real gender freedom in the Daoist sense would drop both sincerity and authenticity because only this can solve the above dilemma: the dilemma that arises because sincerity can only exist when name (gender) and person do not entirely overlap. Of course, transcending both sincerity and authenticity in gender politics is a difficult undertaking because gender identities—or any identity, for that matter—tend to be established in terms of either authenticity (one simply *is* male or female) or sincerity. To deconstruct this paradigm requires a lot of chaotification: chaotification of the conventional identity reality until *it no longer matters* whether this man/woman is sincere, authentic, or neither. S/he is simply what s/he is in culture. Any application of fixed gender terms and pronouns can only hamper this fluid process.

Sincerity means "being true to one's own self." Actions must be backed up by feelings and convictions. Authenticity does not require this, which becomes crucial when the relation between the private and the public persona is not submitted to scrutiny in terms of sincerity but when the public persona is accepted—for reasons of PC—as an authentic private persona. Now sincerity no longer matters. He feels like a man, therefore he must be accepted as an authentic man. This way of thinking has become common in times when social media can create public images, not just for actors and famous people (as it used to be the case in old media) but for everybody else as well. We are used to accepting peoples' avatars that communicate with unlimited self-assurance (and apparent sincerity) an identity that does not represent the "real," private self but is merely a public image we find in social media. Anything is perceived as authentic once it has received a name or a public image.

Daoism accepts the mismatch between form (name) and content and does not require a correction of names in terms of authenticity or sincerity. What we need is rather a humorous and paradoxical engagement with gender and its terms and pronouns (as well as with avatars and public images) so we can depict gender politics as a cultural play without constantly looking for deeper meanings in terms of sincerity and/or authenticity. Much humor can emerge when name and behavior do not match. The subversive is indeed a deep fount of creativity. Rather than *correcting* gender terms, these terms can be dissolved and deconstructed. At present, Western culture is too much rooted in the politics and ethics of authenticity to do this. The problem is that anybody who is not authentic is believed to be pretending, which is judged ethically. Pretending is fake, and even though "sincere pretending" (the sincere playing of a role) can sometimes attract some sympathy, it is not accepted as *real*. Current gender politics is determined by this ethical philosophy of the authentic.

A Daoist way of thinking offers an entirely different solution. It does not pretend to be anything, but he is not striving for authenticity either. Moeller and D'Ambrosio, in their book on the *Zhuangzi*, call the Daoist's playful, distanced, and ironic way of pretending that is constantly aware of the "chaotic" cultural situation around them, "genuine pretending." Genuine pretending means to play without too much engagement. It has been suggested in chapter 3 that seduction is a matter of such "genuine pretending." Like the dandy, the Daoist has "an ability to roam around in the world without an intentional concern for authenticity or real greatness" (Moeller 2015, 80). Moeller also calls this behavior "childlike sanity." The genuine pretender takes the social game sufficiently seriously, but he always knows that, to some extent, he is only pretending. He will play the game *as if* it were real, but he will not play it with utmost sincerity. Nor does he believe in the reality of this game as if it were authentic. Unlike the *simple* pretender, the *genuine* pretender does not strive toward authenticity. His game (which is not just a role) includes, like any game, contingency, improvisation, as well as distancing and indifference toward the real world. As a result, the Daoist will approach gender in the same fashion and see the man who wants to be a woman, or any other person, as a genuine pretender. No ethical judgment will be emitted. According to Moeller and D'Ambrosio, genuine pretending permits people to "operate smoothly in the midst of a social environment full of hypocrisies" (2017, 181). Genuine pretending is not just fake sincerity because ethics has not been entirely abandoned. The concept of genuine pretending will be more closely analyzed in the next chapter.

This section mentioned many concepts that a Daoist gender politics would attempt to implement: seduction, genuine pretending, chaotification, indifference, and playfulness, for example. These concepts are aesthetic but also dependent on the (anti)ethical idea of the "moral fool" from which the "gender fool" is derived. In any Daoism-PC discussion, PC would have to confront these aesthetic-ethical views of the *Zhuangzi*. Daoism would not suggest abolishing PC but rather try to make it less sincere and less authentic. If PC refrains from essentialist thinking, authenticity politics, and the overpoliticization of family life, marriage, sexual relations, and religion, PC will automatically move back to the ironical state of nonsincerity that it had embodied at the very beginning.

Antikitsch: Daoist and Dandyist Aesthetics

The *Zhuangzi* suggests freedom in the sense of "emptiness." Gender, gender terms, pronouns, and gender relations can become play. They should not be fixed through rules and definitions but rather be determined by the emptiness of seduction. As has been shown in chapter 3, seduction does not use real names and is not about affirmation, fixed presences, and identities but rather about chaotification. The Daoist accepts the gap between form and content, between names and phenomena, and between gender and person—holding that such gaps will always exist. We remember that Confucianism struggled with the paradox of sincerity: we can only speak of sincerity when there is a gap between name and actuality. When everything is one—when the name *is* the thing, and when the form *is* the content—logically, there can be no sincerity.

In art, the gap between form and content can be most intriguing. As a matter of fact, a major quality of genuine art is to be insincere, whereas the complete overlap of form and content, or of expression and intention, is called "kitsch." When everything is spelled out and when everything matches, art becomes kitsch in the form of an overly perfect aesthetic expression. It becomes too sincere in the sense that it is naïve. Too much sincerity is always kitsch. Or perhaps kitsch is naïve because naivety is a simplistic form of sincerity. Kitsch is also fake, but kitsch lovers accept this fakeness as authentic art.

Genuine art always needs a gap (a leeway, in German *Spielraum*, which literally means a "play space") in order to play freely with form and content.[7] Without this leeway, aesthetic perception becomes too direct, which is precisely what happens in kitsch. What Moeller and D'Ambrosio call "genuine pretending," which is supposed to function as an alternative to both sincere roleplay and authentic being, applies to art in the form of "genuine art." Genuine art can only emerge when the requirements of both the sincere and the authentic are temporarily abandoned because art plays with mismatches. For art, to be genuine does not imply sincerity but rather insincerity, be it only because one does not want to end up as "overly sincere," that is, as kitsch. In Daoist terms one can say that instead of the fullness of authentic feeling, art always also needs some *wuqing* (無情) or nonfeeling.[8]

"All bad poetry springs from genuine feeling," says Oscar Wilde's Gilbert in *The Critic as Artist* (2005, 186), a text that Wilde published just a few months after his review of the *Zhuangzi*. Aesthetic expressions are not authentic, and the artist is always wearing a mask. Genuine feeling without any pretending or without a mask, that is, without that necessary gap between form and emotional content, will produce kitsch. Looking for authenticity is useless because truth is not authentic but rather transcends the naïve striving for authenticity; and this applies not only to art but to everything. The "gap of pretending" tends to be missing whenever we talk about ourselves, which is why Wilde's Gilbert in "The Critic as Artist" suggests giving the person who talks about himself a mask. Only when he is wearing a mask will he tell the truth. Gilbert says, "Yes, the objective form is the most subjective in matter. Man is least himself when he talks in his own person. Give him a mask, and he will tell you the truth" (Wilde 2007a, 185).⁹ Trilling comments on this suggestion: "The direct conscious confrontation of experience and the direct public expression of it do not necessarily yield the truth and indeed (. . .) they are likely to pervert it. 'Man is least himself'" (1972, 119). Talking about yourself is very likely to become kitsch because the distance (or the *Spielraum*) is lacking. We risk becoming too sincere and thus embarrassing ourselves. Only a mask, and not more authenticity, can help here. This does not mean that the genuine has been suppressed. On the contrary, the genuine is there, but it needs to be pretended in order to emerge. In other words, you are allowed to be genuine, but you should have enough distance from your genuine self to make sure that your speech is never entirely sincere. You must always know that—to some extent—you are only pretending. Similarly, and equally paradoxically, authentic art emerges through a combination of pretending with the genuine, and Moeller's and D'Ambrosio's concept of genuine pretending, which they find crystallized in the *Zhuangzi*, confirms this.

The remedy against kitsch is not sincerity but genuine pretending. Too much sincerity or, even worse, being proud of one's sincerity, creates kitsch. Alceste, a character in Moliere's *Le Misanthrope*, says that his "chief talent is to be frank and sincere." Trilling comments: "The whole energy of his being is directed towards perfecting the trait upon which he prides himself. (. . .) Alceste's point of pride is his sincerity, his remorseless outspokenness on behalf of truth" (1972, 17). Alceste is a kitsch character. Similarly, in "The Critic as Artist," Oscar Wilde creates the moralist Earnest who defends (as his name suggests, in a rare case of the matching of name and role) strong values of sincerity. For Earnest, arguments based on naturalism or common sense do also fall into the category of sincerity. These are arguments also most typically put forward by defenders of kitsch. Earnest's opponent Gilbert deconstructs all these values in a way that echoes, as finds McCormack, "the principles of Zhuangzi" (2017, 87). The name "Earnest" reappears in Wilde's final play, "The Importance of Being Earnest" (1894), which deals with the theme of switched identities in the form of a farcical comedy in which the protagonists maintain fictitious personae to escape burdensome social obligations. Earnest is here not the character's real name, but Jack (Earnest) leads a double life. Truth is deconstructed in a typically Wildean way when Jack says: "Gwendolen, it is a terrible thing for a man to find out suddenly that all his life he has been speaking nothing but the truth. Can you forgive me?" (Wilde 1899, 151) While other dramatists of the period (for instance Bernard Shaw) used their characters to draw audiences to grander ideals and tried to tackle serious social and political issues, Wilde deconstructs ideals. Russell Jackson concludes that "Earnest is superficially about nothing at all" (1997, 172).

Gwendolen, too, is a kitsch character, because she insists that she can only love a man named Earnest. However, in the end, Jack's pretense turns out to be "genuine pretending" because he discovers, when examining old army lists, that his father's real name—and hence his own real name—was in fact Earnest. Pretense was reality all along.

Daoism is an antikitsch philosophy. From an aesthetic point of view, the Dao is the opposite of kitsch, be it only because the Dao has no specific taste: "In order to be able to taste the tasteless, one has to overcome—or to reduce—individual sensual preferences," writes Moeller (2006, 89). At best, in art, kitsch can be played with, which turns it into camp or "kitsch art."

Susan Sontag has delivered some important reflections on dandyism and camp, which are worth considering here. The dandy can be called "camp" if we look at Sontag's classical definition: "Camp art is often decorative art, emphasizing texture, sensuous surface, and style at the expense of content. (. . .) To perceive Camp in objects and persons is to understand Being-as-Playing-a-Role. (. . .) It is the farthest extension, in sensibility, of the metaphor of life as theater" (1982, 278, 280). The aesthetics of camp suggests a concept of the self that is always performative and transient. It is only constituted through repetitions and stylized actions. Daoist aesthetics can be called "camp" for the same reasons. Gender identities as seen through Daoism are camp, too, because they are neither authentic nor fake but performative and pretended, which means that even queer gender identities circumvent kitsch and can end up as camp. According to Sontag, camp is one of the main aesthetics of gender transgression or of the androgynous: "Allied to the Camp taste for the androgynous is something that seems quite different but isn't: a relish for the exaggeration of sexual characteristics and personality mannerisms" (1982, 279). Camp-dandyism, Sontag points out, is never "exaggerated he-man-ness" but "what is most beautiful in virile men is something feminine; what is most beautiful in feminine women is something masculine" (279). Sontag clearly classifies camp as a homosexual sensibility. All this does not mean that the "camp-gender" should be recognized as a new gender to be added (complete with its special pronoun) to the City of New York's gender list. This gender performative, transient, transgressive behavior is not authentic but only pretended. It is genuinely pretended, which means that its genuine character cannot be grasped by language. The only positive element that the dandy will ever produce is a personal style.

Echoing Daoist aesthetics, Sontag also describes camp as "the consistently aesthetic experience of the world" because it "incarnates a victory of 'style' over 'content' [and of] 'aesthetic' over 'morality'" (287). When dandyism and Daoism describe life as style, they do not create a simulated kitsch reality. According to Gillo Dorfles's classical definition, kitsch invents a reality "that is essentially the falsification of sentiments and the substitution of spurious sentiments for real ones" (1968, 221). In kitsch, the authentic becomes fake whereas in camp authenticity no longer matters. Strangely, Sontag does not follow this reasoning to the end. Instead, she *questions* the compatibility of camp aesthetic with dandyism. Her main reason for this is that the dandy's fervent antimass elitism would be incompatible with camp's populist demands. This is an undue polarization, and it is due to the fact that Sontag deals mainly with the decadent and overly elitist aspect of dandyism personified by Huysmans's Des Esseintes in *A Rebours* (*Against the Grain*). The antipopulist, elitist strain is also present in the British Aesthetic movement (which Sontag does not mention), especially after it had been condensed into a pose in the late nineteenth century. Like those aestheticists, Huysmans's dandy seeks only "rare sensations, undefiled by mass appreciation" (289). However, other dandies, and especially flâneurs, were not living completely outside mainstream society. Even Brummell could speak spontaneously and naturally with simple people. And for Baudelaire, the dandy is always in *la foule*, in the crowd, though he resists becoming part of it, which is very precisely the secret of Poe's Man in the Crowd. Des Esseintes simply turns his back on the outside world and embraces an immobilized, automatized, luxurious self-enclosure, reveling in nostalgic cravings for the past. By contrast, the active flâneur is the counterpart to the passive Des Esseintes, and it is odd that Sontag does not make use of this classical model of dandyism. Instead, she defines dandyism in the age of mass culture solely in terms of camp aesthetics, which is for her no "real" dandyism: "The connoisseur of Camp has found more ingenious pleasures. Not in Latin poetry and rare wines and velvet jackets, but in the coarsest commonest pleasures, in the arts of the masses" (289). However, this camp-dandy *is* the flâneur, and he is not decadent but even acts as a social critic experimenting with avant-gardist expressions.[10]

For example, both camp and the flâneur contest "functional, utilitarian culture" (Sternberg 1972, 8).

Des Esseintes approaches kitsch much more consistently than the flâneur or the original dandy conceived by Brummell. One needs to keep in mind that dandies originally eschewed all arbitrary ornamentation as bad taste and emphasized rightness of cut and total perfection of fit instead. Basically, dandyism started as an antikitsch movement, as Brummell's main achievement might have been to prevent Prince George from wearing ridiculously exuberant outfits and to have convinced the regent that true elegance is refinement hidden under the veil of simplicity (see Scaraffia 1981, 19). Later, when exuberance had sneaked into dandyism through French dandies such as Count d'Orsay, Balzac (1799–1850) would reinstate Brummell's original principles by drawing a clear line between the dandy and what today would be kitsch. Balzac, himself an adept of dandyism, was perhaps not well versed in its practice but still remains one of its most brilliant theoreticians. In *The Treatise of Elegant Living*, which is a cornerstone of dandyism, *Balzac* insists on the simplicity and naturalness of outfits when putting down the following two maxims: "XXIV. The man of taste must always be able to reduce his needs to a simple level; XXVIII. In everything, the multiplicity of colors is bad taste. The prodigality of ornaments harms the effect."[11] Twenty years later, Baudelaire would utter the famous sentence that "perfection in dress consists in absolute simplicity, which is, indeed, the best way of being distinguished" (1986, 27). Des Esseintes clearly oversteps all these antikitsch guidelines.

PC and Kitsch

The authenticity wave of the 1960s, which in the 1980s morphed into the "ethical authenticity wave" called PC, is kitsch in the above-explained understanding. Taylor describes how "in this newly individuated space [of authenticity], the customer was encouraged more and more to express her taste, furnishing her space according to her own needs and affinities, as only the rich had been able to do in previous eras" (2007, 474). This is paralleled by what happened in the nineteenth century when the new and aesthetically misguided bourgeoisie purchased fake items of the upper classes, which led to the birth of kitsch. The instantaneous gratification achieved by the neat overlap of form and content (the beautiful flower that is simply beautiful and nothing else), or of feeling and action, which is supposed to create authentic expressions, leads to the kind of aesthetic death that the twentieth century would later call kitsch. Art always needs some chaotic background noise, some rugged cultural reality, or some "gaps": gaps of "pretending" that are installed between representation and presence, names and actualities, action and emotion, as well as gender and person. Those gaps can cause a mismatch of form and content. I previously mentioned Frank Stevenson's concept of "background noise" that he uses in his study of Daoism, and I want to employ it here again as a component of a special aesthetic theory. Earlier, it was said that culture is a sort of "background noise" that will never entirely overlap with distinct language because the Dao is chaos and not a "rational discourse." It is only a noise "out of which 'language' or 'meaningful sounds' emerge" (2006, 308). In his article, Stevenson derives these thoughts from Michel Serres's communication theory in which the French epistemologist explains that "a too-efficient communication between two parties (A and B) becomes redundant (A = A = A . . .)" (304).[12] Such communication causes "information death," which, in art, leads to the aesthetic death called kitsch. Stevenson applies this model to the *Dao*: "For once it reaches the point of taking itself too seriously as 'logic' [or] a 'truthful' form of demarcation (. . .), it becomes excessively self-repetitive and redundant; now its own chaotic background appears to it as what is most 'real'" (317). We reach an "extreme limit of hyper-rational redundancy" (307). In other words, our philosophical reflection reaches kitsch. In art we always need a "roughness" from which "real" expression can emerge, and in philosophy things are similar. Only when there is some cultural chaotic roughness will we have the "possibility of actual meaning rather than the death or 'burning out' of meaning" (310).

Kant's famous metaphor in the *Critique of Pure Reason* of "the light dove cleaving in free flight the thin air, whose resistance it feels, might imagine that her movements would be far more free and rapid in airless space" (1900, 19; 1911, 6) describes precisely this phenomenon. The dove believes that it is not necessary to exercise its wings against something that is empirically given: some air, some noise, or some cultural reality. This dove has reached the level of kitsch philosophy and is therefore bound to crash. Its thinking is so efficient and pure that it no longer thinks anything. Kant's criticism was directed at Platonist thought that had lost its experientially grounded roots. Plato "met with no resistance which might serve him for a support" (19; 6). PC risks the same kind of Platonic burnout. It risks running out of meaning because its only raison d'être is to *perfectly* match form with reality, or to match name or pronoun with an ethical rule. Daoism tries to prevent this "reality burnout" through the chaotification of forms. The overlap of ethics and aesthetics becomes here most obvious. Ethical truth cannot be found in a straightforward fashion, but it emerges through a social game. The straightforward implementation of behavioral rules or the correction of language can be called, in a Daoist anti-Confucian mode, ethical kitsch. Kitsch is not just aesthetics but also a political notion. Kitsch can be found in politics, education, as well as in business. Most dictators have attempted to reinforce their authority with the help of kitsch propaganda. Liberal capitalism produces an aesthetics of the "too much" in all domains of life. There is communicative kitsch and administrative kitsch. Contemporary culture with its exaggerated belief in the individual, its humanitarian appeals to pity, the sentimental defense of the weak, and its simultaneous exaltation of social Darwinism, can well be grasped using the concept of kitsch.

Chapter 6

The Authenticity of the Dandy

The Dandy Has No Skills

Daoism resists definition. Graham (2001) writes that Daoism cannot be defined but is perhaps best *described* as a sort of rambling, roaming, or sauntering (*you*). Dandyism resists definition in a similarly adamant way. The dandy is subversive to the point of constantly transcending his own definition and exists only through a stroboscopic there and not-there effect that is difficult to stabilize. Dandyism shifts back and forth between apparently contradictory items: conservatism and progressivism, simplicity and splashing exuberance, rule-following and anarchy: the dandy decries the superficial materialist spirit of the modern age but is firmly part of it to the point that, for Walter Benjamin for example, he even becomes its symbol. A further contradiction is that the dandy refuses to be defined by others because he does not want to become an object of public consumption and yet advertises himself lavishly as if he invites imitation.

Though the dandy's actions are couched in perfectionism, he cannot be defined through his actions either. The dandy is perfectionist only in a Daoist sense. Regular perfectionists try to approach an ideal, but for the Daoist, "The moment man *does* something, his very consciousness of doing it renders his action unnatural. Instead, the Perfect Man leaves all things (. . .) to their own natures" (Izutsu 1983, 437). The dandy just *is*, and everything he does emerges "naturally" from his being. Therefore, he cannot be defined in terms of excellence. Excellence is a moral notion and a virtue describing a right action, but the sage's virtue "should be passive, not active. He should be rather than do," says the *Zhuangzi*.[1]

However, his actions can still be described. Both dandyism and Daoism adhere to fluid movement in society, both literally and metaphorically. The strong link between walking and aesthetics turns Daoism into a dandyist flâneur. In England and France, literally moving around became the new activity of the flâneur while in Daoism, travel was a key concept to a good human life. Similar to flâner, rambling (*you*) is not an ethical activity in the first place but rather an aesthetic concept, be it only because it is so closely linked to contemplation. Daoist roaming depicts the highest state of being, and through roaming one can obtain the utmost beauty. Rambling also cultivates spontaneity because it creates an interaction between virtuosity (*de* 德) and the paths (*dao*) on which the rambler is roaming (see Fraser 2012, 1). The identity of the rambler remains equally fluid because it "is constituted in multiple respects by our relation to the landscape" (11). Moeller and D'Ambrosio describe *you* as the "itinerant, aimless, and attentive way of moving around in life" (2018, 164) or as "a rambling mode of being that allows one to take on whatever task or attitude that the hand you are dealt with requires" (166). Rambling is an "aimless motion" and has "no provenance and no destination (. . .). It meanders through places and positions that it provisionally occupies" (167). *You* can also be written with the water radical (游), which emphasizes its sense of fluidity even more. The water metaphor also evokes the idea of "going with the current" or of spontaneous action (Zhang 2019, 81). Both *you* characters (遊 and 游) appear more than a hundred times in the *Zhuangzi*.

Sometimes the dandy sits down and has a break. We see him quietly installed in the window of a London coffee house, but something is not normal: he displays a strange "animally ecstatic gaze." This is how Edgar Allan Poe describes the "Man in the Crowd" in the short story bearing the same name (1840). For Baudelaire, who translated this story, the Man in the Crowd is the typical example of a dandy. The Man in the Crowd sits at his table, cigar in his mouth and newspaper on his lap, and peers out the window watching the "innumerable varieties of figure, dress, air, gait, visage, and expression of countenance" of all those who are walking by. According to Poe, he is in "happy moods, which are so precisely the converse of *ennui*moods" (Baudelaire 1986a, 1). Baudelaire, in his commentary, exalts this character and suggests that he seems to have just "returned from the valley of the shadow of death," which is to say that he has been "on the brink of oblivion." Having just returned from this state of forgetfulness, he now has a heightened consciousness, which means that he "remembers, and fervently desires to remember, everything" (7). The Man in the Crowd seems to come out of some Daoist key meditation practice session called "sitting in oblivion" (*zuowang*), which leads from oblivion to heightened perception.

In his essay "The Painter of Modern Life" (1863), Baudelaire depicts the dandy as a man stoically devoted to "cultivat[ing] the idea of beauty" in himself (27), thus assiduously crafting his existence into a work of art. This is another useless skill. Because the dandy's skills are useless, he takes no pride in them. Vanity would be the end of dandyism. Similarly, the man in the *Zhuangzi* who falls off carts without hurting himself has no vanity: after all, what could he be proud of? There is neither an ideal of falling nor rules about it, so how *could* anybody claim to be good at it? Many people have talents but no skills simply because they have never developed their talents. The Dao hero and the dandy have skills but no talent because "talents are a hindrance," as says the *Zhuangzi*.[2] This constellation most efficiently prevents conceit. A person who has talent *and* skills will feel superior to whoever has neither talent nor skills, or whoever has just talent and no skills. What will the person who has skills but no talent feel? Although he is excellent, the cart-jumping drunkard never attempts to construe his activity in terms of excellence. He simply falls when he falls and does not even feel like he is *doing* anything, let alone doing something excellent. Only egos do *something*, but this man has given up his ego. Only egos strive to achieve excellence, and only egos will be proud once they have achieved it. Egos do things in view of ideals or rules based on ideals, whereas this man is just falling without investing his person into this activity. He has no identity as a "faller."

The dandy cultivates the same kind of nonidentity. He also rejects identities for another reason: identities tend to be ranked. Like the Daoist cart faller or the other protagonists of knack stories, the dandy wants to exist beyond rankings. Similarly, Brummell was not a "better" dandy or the "best" dandy. He was a real or genuine dandy, but he did not attain this status by following an ideal of dandyism. Therefore, it is impossible to say that he was the best. Brummell might be considered the only authentic dandy, but then again, he never strove to be authentic but was only playing/pretending. Authenticity is another of those ideals that many people strive for, possibly by engaging in competitions of who is the most authentic. Brummell did not have this ambition. If Brummell *is* the authentic dandy, it was only because his authenticity emerged while he was rambling. He did not *create* it by following rules or by aspiring to an ideal. Any striving for dandyist authenticity would lead to self-idolization in terms of essence, virtue, and excellence. The result would not be a genuine dandy but rather a parody of a dandy. Brummell consciously avoided creating an ideal person with which the dandy could be identified. Such an ideal might have existed for his imitators but not for Brummell himself.

Bruce Bashford, in his article on Wilde, refers to Charles Taylor's text on authenticity, which says that "for both Taylor and Wilde, persons do not have direct access to their distinctive identities; rather, they discover themselves through an engagement with others" (2007, 57). Similar to the Daoist sage, the dandy tries to "reflect his situation like a mirror and respond[s] to it with the immediacy of an echo to a sound or shadow to a shape" (Graham 2001, 6). This is a comment Graham makes in his introduction to his translation of the *Zhuangzi*. Ellen Zhang sees this as a condition of Zhuangzuist *you*, or of the particular art of Daoist rambling because it is just "skillful spontaneity that serves as a reference point of an intrinsic satisfaction [that] one experiences [and which is] not conditioned by external factors (e.g. honor and wealth)" (2019, 81). Among the ideals to be avoided are also excellence and authenticity.

There is no essence of dandyism, though many people have tried to establish such an essence. Baudelaire insists that even though the dandy aspired to have money, he did "not aspire [to have] money to do something essential" (1986a, 27). Dandyism has no essence either, and those who believe to have located the essence of dandyism confine, in Daoist terms, "the Absolute in an individual form and lose sight of the absoluteness of the Absolute" (Izutsu 1983, 33). This is how a Daoist describes the seeing of an essence when there is no essence. There might be something absolute in dandyism/Daoism, but this absolute cannot be spelled out in the form of a rule, ideal, image, or essence. It only emerges while enacted and experienced. Emergence rather than creation is an important Daoist concept and is also most essential to all Chinese "creation" myths.[3]

Both the Daoist and the dandy are aware of the danger posed by idealizing excellence. Should they give in to it, they would become parodies of themselves. To prevent this, they try to merely play without playing "something" because any "something" would already contain an ideal. Strictly speaking, the Daoist is not playing the role of the Daoist (in the way in which Sedgwick played the role of the queer), and the dandy is not playing the role of the dandy; however, both engage in what Jacques

Derrida has called "miming." In a pertinent passage in *Dissemination* Derrida writes: "The mime imitates nothing. And to begin with, he doesn't imitate. There is nothing prior to the writing of his gestures. Nothing is prescribed for him" (1972, 208).[4] Derrida locates this constellation in Mallarmé's poem "Mimique." Similarly, the dandy is miming something that does not yet exist, and eventually his being emerges through this mimicry. In other words, the dandy is not playing the role of the dandy but is "just playing." Playing a role requires knowledge about the role and about its ideals, but the dandy is in the mode of "non-knowledge." Judith Butler and even the more playful Eve Kosofsky Sedgwick are in the mode of "knowledge." Ideals are always seen from the point of view of an ego, even in play, but the mime's action is egoless. It is obvious that contemporary adherents to new genders such as the "genderfluid" or the "gender gifted" are not miming but rather reinforcing their ego though their play.

Given the observations about egoless dreams that have been presented in chapter 3, one can also say that all three—the mime, the dandy, and the Daoist—act or play as though in a dream. It is again Paul Valéry who provides interesting insights. Valéry has established a link between the mime and the dreamer (in a text that seems to have been unknown to Derrida) when suggesting that the dreamer "simulates without knowing" (simule sans le savoir; 1979: 239; from *Cahier* V, 538) and that "the dreams are truth but expressed like the pantomime expresses them" (1979, 52).[5] As has already been explained, Valéry establishes the dream as an egoless simple presence (1979, 89) and finds that, in order to appreciate these expressions, we need to first of all "stop looking for the dream's possible meanings" (1986, 527). As a result, "Truths about the dream are not obtained through interpretations but are expressed by the dream in the same way in which a pantomime expresses something," as writes Jullien Rouart about Valéry's philosophy of dreams (1979, 242). In parallel with what Moeller says about the Butterfly Story, play and dream are here "simple presences" (1999, 440). In the *Zhuangzi*, dreams are not the products of thought but simply expressive realities. The dream is not an appearance or an imitation of images or something meaningful that preexisted in waking life. On the contrary, in the dream, the distinction between dream and reality entirely disappears. Valéry very much insists on a similar procedure suggesting that "the dream gobbles everything" because "in the dream everything is dreamt, that is, nothing is dreamt" (1979, 35; Cahiers 1907–8, IV, my trans.).

It is interesting to note that in another area of East-Asian aesthetics, in Japanese Kabuki theater, actions are not seen as expressions of "something" either. I point this out because the aesthetic strategy of Kabuki can be efficiently linked to the above questions of gender. Kabuki is not a theater of expressions but of signs; yet contrary to what Saussure might have expected, these signs do not refer to a certain meaning. When an ideal woman is signified (and not represented) by a male actor, the actor is not imitating a "real" woman. There is nothing authentic to be looked for in these signs, but the actor is only "genuinely pretending" what he sees as a woman. He does not put forward the essence of the woman because this would be an imitation or a representation. The dandyist and Daoist actions can be grasped through this notion of "genuine pretending" that is important in much of East Asian art, whereas "postmodern" notions like Baudrillard's "simulation" express this idea only partially. The Kabuki woman is not "simulated" in the sense of imitated, which is the only reason why the Kabuki signification never produces a kitsch reality of a woman. Signification is not *mere* pretending: in Kabuki the pretense becomes genuine. Baudrillard's notion of simulation, which suggests that social and personal interaction is nowadays mostly artificial, does not retrieve this concept of genuine pretending. It is true that simulacra are copies depicting things that no longer have an original (or had no original to begin with) and thus seem to come close to Derrida's mime miming "nothing." However, it cannot go unnoticed that Baudrillard's entire system exposed in *Simulacres et simulation* (1981) is still based on the distinction between the real and the unreal and that the loss of the real is presented as negative—or that sometimes its disappearance is celebrated as a nihilistic postmodern fad. From a Daoist or dandyist perspective, the distinction between the real and the simulated simply does not matter. The dandy is not anti-real, whereas postmodern simulation still smacks too much of either utopia or dystopia. There is no place for utopias in the non-dichotomous world of the dandy or the *Zhuangzi*. When Paul Valéry writes that "the dreamer "simulates without knowing," he establishes a clear difference with Baudrillard's *simulacre*, because the latter is still due to a conscious act of simulation.

According to Moeller, genuine pretending counters a Confucian role ethics that attempts to achieve identity through a sincere commitment to social roles, "for instance by being a dutiful son or a benevolent ruler" (Moeller 2020). Genuine pretending is not *simple* pretending: the former is miming while the latter is just imitating. One might say that

Brummell (who had no aristocratic background) imitated an aristocratic lifestyle. However, had he *only done* that, he would have become a good fake aristocrat at best and not a dandy. At the same time, Brummell was not "creating" the dandy either because this would have required an ideal, or at least an idea of what an authentic dandy should look like. It would have required knowledge about what a dandy is. Both the dandy and the Daoist sage are what Moeller calls "idiotic" because their actions are not based on knowledge: "[The Daoist sage] does not know how he would know anything in the first place. The Daoist sage simply does not operate in a mode of knowing and also not [in a mode] of 'critical' knowing in a relativist or skeptical form. Rather than a skeptic or a relativist, the sage is simply someone who has not yet been exposed to intellectual knowledge; he is an ultimate simpleton, a perfect idiot" (Moeller 2006, 118). Even the Daoist ruler is "a human 'desert,' an 'idiot,' an infant that does not yet smile" (267).

Oscar Wilde's aversion to knowledge had a similar argumentative basis. Not knowledge but idiotic nonknowledge leads to the emergence of the dandy. In the *Pall Mall Gazette*, Wilde published a piece called "To Read, Or Not to Read," which is basically a list of books. The list of "not to be read" books is very long and ends with these two items: "All argumentative books, and all books that try to prove anything" (Bashford 2017, 54).

The Authentic and the Genuine

What is the difference between the authentic and the genuine in more formal terms? Authentic means "real" in the sense of being made in a traditional or original way. For example, "authentic Korean food" is food prepared the way Koreans prepare food in Korea; but the food does not have to come directly from Korea. It could even have been made by a non-Korean who learned from a Korean how to make authentic Korean food. What matters is following the right rules. *Genuine* Korean food would have to come from Korea. For originals there are no degrees: either it comes from there or not, whereas food (or anything else, for that matter) can be *more or less authentic*. A document that is authentic is "known to be true," it is reliable or trustworthy, which means that it is *supposed to be* the original. But in the end, the authenticity remains a matter of trust, that is, of the sincerity of those by whom it has been authenticated. Authenticity has the same root as "authority": it depends on the strength of the authority whereas the genuine does not need an authority in order to exist. Arguments from authority are inductive whereas the genuine is a matter of definition and thus deductive. Things can be authenticated but not be "genuinized." The genuine simply *is*. Strictly speaking, the authentic document does not *need to be* the original document. Once the "authority" is sincere enough, the document will be generally recognized as authentic. For the genuine, sincerity does not matter. This means that in the authentic, there is always some space (which has in the preceding chapter been called "*Spielraum*" or leeway in reference to Gadamer) for imitation or pretending, even if this space is minimal. In the genuine no such space exists. Theoretically, Korean food can be *not* genuine but still authentic if it follows—more or less—the rules of authentic Korean food.

What matters for the correct definition of "genuine Korean" food are not rules but rather space and time in the sense of duration. If Koreans have prepared a certain food in a certain way in Korea over a certain period, then this has to be accepted as "genuinely Korean," even if it contradicts some of those rules that stipulate what is commonly known as authentic Korean food. And just as Korean food can be not genuine but still authentic, the converse is also possible: it can be genuine but not authentic. In some extreme cases, the food can even be genuine despite the fact that "authorities" refuse to authenticate it. It will then be genuine but not authentic. The gist of the difference between authentic and genuine is reflected by the difference between creation and emergence that has been sketched above when defining the dandy and the mime. If a Korean *creates* a new food instantaneously, we can object that what he is doing is not really authentic and not genuine either. But if the Korean food *emerges* within the confines of a certain space and during a certain period, then it becomes genuine simply by that fact.

A Daoist conclusion would be that "genuine Korean food" should ideally be made by an "idiot," that is by somebody who does not follow instructions from cooking books (which could be wrong) but whose cooking emerges within a Korean cultural context without any conscious input from the self. The idiot does not proceed scientifically, he does not necessarily "know" what he is doing. Logically, the idiot would not take pride in his cooking skills either because he would simply act "naturally" within a certain culture.

Genuine Pretending

Given the above, it would normally follow that for the genuine, pretending is impossible. The genuine cannot be pretended, nor can anything pretended be genuine. So, what do Moeller and D'Ambrosio mean by "genuine pretending"? The twist is brought about by the notion of sincerity. Despite the frequent contrasting of authenticity with sincerity (most obvious in Trilling's book), authenticity always depends on some amount of sincerity (as has been shown in chapter 4) whereas the genuine does not need sincerity. The hypocrite or the pretender, that is, the nonsincere person, is not "real," but he can move toward a more authentic behavior if he pretends well. But he can never become genuine. The genuinely honest person simply *is* honest, she does not need to make an effort and pretend to be honest. Once again this confirms that the authentic and the sincere are intimately linked: the authentic is a sort of hyper-sincerity that exists because any pretending has been reduced to zero. The genuine, by contrast, does not have this relationship with the sincere.

So, once again, how can one pretend and still be genuine? The answer is: by simply *being* without caring about either authenticity or sincerity. One can pretend genuinely only because genuine pretending does not imitate *something*. Just like the Daoist or dandyist actions, genuine pretending is not about doing (something) but about being. Only when *not something* is imitated, only when there is pure imitation (as it happens in dream, play, or in Derrida's example of Mallarmé's mime), the question of sincerity will not occur. Can a mime mimic "sincerely?" No, one can only sincerely imitate *something*, but one cannot sincerely just imitate. One cannot *play* sincerely or *dream* sincerely either. One can play *something* sincerely or imagine *something* sincerely. The dandy's actions look more like pretending than like "real," purposeful actions. And the purpose is not even to pretend *something*, which is precisely what makes these actions genuine.

Genuine pretending is not as unusual as it sounds: to some degree, we all practice it daily, though mostly without noticing it. The defenders of authenticity urge us to—in a more or less Confucian fashion—play our roles genuinely: our roles as son, employee, manager, etc. "Genuinely" means here to do only what is *necessary* to fulfill these roles without letting any contingency slip in. However, how much is the fact that I am playing this or that role due to necessity and how much is it due to contingency? Is every aspect of these roles really necessary? How can I be sure that *this role* (for example the role of the teacher) is my authentic way of life? Am I not just playing it for better or for worse? If we think about our roles in this way, we recognize that we are more often genuinely pretending than we tend to assume. Moeller supports this view by writing: "On the one hand, such roles are constitutive of what one "is," for instance in the family (e.g., a "son") or in political context (e.g., a "ruler"). In this sense, these roles are "genuine." On the other hand, these roles are also, in contemporary vocabulary, "social constructs." They are temporary, contingent, and incongruent, or, using Daoist vocabulary, they are subject to the "transformation of things" (*wu hua* 物化). In this sense, they are played, or 'pretended'" (Moeller 2020). Since I can never be sure that *this* is my authentic way of life, all modern calls to "be yourself" are flagrant manifestations of a fallacy. Skepticism toward authenticity is one of the foundations of Daoism as well as of dandyism. Bashford sees this skepticism at the root of Oscar Wilde's negative view of any argument that pretends to provide information about the authentic. He refers to Taylor's text on authenticity that reflects precisely this position when Taylor writes: "There is a certain way of being human that is my way. I am called upon to live my life in this way, and not in imitation of anyone else's. But this gives a new importance to being true to myself. If I am not, I miss the point of my life, I miss what being human is for me" (2007, 28). Here, like in the slogan "Just do it," the main question remains unanswered: How can I know what my own originality is? I only discover this originality, that is, my potential, while I am playing or rambling. Eventually, my original being might emerge, but consciously trying to be "true to oneself" is a logical impossibility. The problem is that any solicitation to "be yourself" or "be authentic" is an ethical appeal that asks us to be honest and not hypocritical. To "be yourself" is an appeal to sincerity based on the moral belief that an ethical way of acting does actually exist and that eventually all actions—including the idea of "being myself"—can be evaluated with the help of ethical standards.

However, first, as has been shown above, it is logically impossible to "be oneself." Second, the link between authenticity and ethics remains fallacious. It is a very shaky premise to believe that "the more I am authentic and true to myself the more I am ethical." The drive for authenticity combined with a sort of positivistic idea of "truth" makes people blind to the most obvious fact that "being yourself" can also be very unethical. Criminals can claim that they are just being themselves. We hear in this "be authentic!" appeal the echoes of sincerity and naturalism that Oscar Wilde's character Earnest in "The Critic as Artist" puts forward and that Gilbert deconstructs by using the most "dazzling paradoxes, many of which echo the principles of Zhuangzi" (McCormack 2017, 87). Gilbert says that "it is very much more difficult to talk about a thing than to do it" and "to do nothing at all is the most difficult thing in the world, the most difficult and the most intellectual" (Wilde 2007a, 158). To the "Just do it" appeal, the Daoist and dandy oppose "do nothing." Do nothing, but let things emerge while you are rambling. Ellen Moers describes precisely this constellation when writing: the dandy is "a Hero so evidently at the center of the stage that he need do nothing to prove his heroism—need never, in fact, do anything at all" (1960, 13).

It follows that neither the dandy nor the heroes of the *Zhuangzi* can or want to be role models. The dandy has imitators, but he does not actively promote a mass following. It is appropriate to say that the dandy has no followers but only admires and imitates because, in the end, few people understand the gist of his philosophy. The reason is that his ideas were (and still are) unable to create collective identities, which distinguishes him from the contemporary hipster, yuppie, or the—less contemporary—hippie, all of whom claim to be individualist (all three can also occasionally claim dandyist credentials). The dandy's lack of "identity mass-appeal," which is partly due to his elitism, also distinguishes his dandyism from PC. PC creates a new political language based on criteria such as gender or race and therefore *can* create a social movement. More reflections on the dandy as an "anti-role model" will follow in the next chapter in connection with the snob and the revolutionary.

Role models must be either authentic or sincere, but can we imagine a sincere dandy? Sincerity means to be honest to oneself, but the dandy has given up his self or his ego. Sincerity requires submitting oneself to rules willingly and with devotion. Is the dandy "devoted" to dandyism? No, he simply *is* a dandy without being sincere or devoted. One cannot be "sincerely dandy" because the dandy has neither a well-defined self nor a role that he could play sincerely. The dandy is too evasive and elusive to be sincere. The only honest thing about Brummell is that he "honestly" does not care about what it means to be a dandy, which is similar to Daoist forgetfulness. In this sense, the dandy resembles the handicapped man in the *Zhuangzi* who simply does not care about his handicap. At the root is a lack of knowledge: both the dandy and the Dao-hero honestly do not understand why they should worry about such things. How *could* the handicapped man define himself? He could define himself as a victim and require that the PC standards be applied to him. Both dandyism and Daoism avoid this strategy. "Men forget each other in the arts of the Way," says the *Zhuangzi* (Watson 2013, 87). The dandy forgets himself in style and flows with his style like fish flow with water, never thinking and never knowing: "Fishes breed and grow in the water; man develops in the Dao," says the *Zhuangzi*.[6] The master swimmer in the *Zhuangzi* explains that he can navigate waters so turbulent that even fish, turtles, and crocodiles avoid them because he does not impose his selfishness on the water. He has forgotten himself and the water. The dandy's Dao is the style in which he swims.

Chapter 7

The Dandy and the Snob

Dandy, Snob, Careerist, Bohemian

A well-known imitator of the dandy is the snob. But contrary to the dandy, the snob is not *just* imitating. He is imitating "something," namely the dandy. The snob is the dandy's nemesis. He pretends to be something that he is not (a dandy), and when he thinks he is imitating well, he takes pride in his dandyist excellence. The dandy's approach is diametrically opposed: first, the dandy is not pretending to be what he is not, and second, he is not trying to be an authentic dandy. We should not be opposed to the snobbish imitation of the dandy because an authentic dandy has never existed.

The word "snob" is said to have arisen from the custom of writing "s. nob.," that is, "sine nobilitate," after the names of children of untitled parents in certain English schools. Like the dandy, the snob can thus be contrasted with the aristocrat. In literature, the snob is exemplified by characters such as Mr. Placid from Robert Plumer Ward's 1825 novel *Tremaine*, "who after attempting a seat higher up the table than he had a right to, was regularly giving way to everyone who claimed a chair above him, until he had reached the bottom" (Ward 1826, 38). Usually, the snob is unable to sustain his pretensions. Aesthetically, the snob is very much on the side of the kitsch-man, that is, rather conservative and most probably a lover of traditional images and icons. Both kitsch-man and snob want the world to be predictable: kitsch takes no risks, avoids genuine novelty, and abhors cognitive, social, or ethical challenges. All this also characterizes the snob. By contrast, the dandy is avant-garde because he likes surprises and improvisation.[1] Both the dandy and the snob were born at a time when kitsch came into being in European civilization (yet without having received the label "kitsch"). The old aristocracy could still simply "be" without having to constantly visually manifest their social superiority. In this new society, the rising bourgeoisie had to *appear* in order to be recognized as superior.

Both the dandy's and the snob's striving toward appearance are thus symptomatic of their time. However, each has a different approach to the problem of "being" and appearance. As mentioned in chapter 5, Balzac drew a clear line between the dandy and what today would be called a "kitsch person." Despite these differences, it remains relatively easy to confuse the dandy with the snob simply because somebody like Brummell clearly indulged in snobbish behavior. Moreover, the dandy's trademark is being blasé. The difference is that the dandy does not have the *essence* of the blasé but simply plays the role of the blasé dandy. Furthermore, he does not play it sincerely, nor is his blasé-ness authentic. First of all, it *can't* be authentic because it is impossible to be authentically blasé: authenticity is always spontaneous and, according to Georg Simmel, "Blasé is the contrary of spontaneous" (1995, 121). To be "sincerely snobbish" is equally impossible.

Balzac established the dandy as a thinking being who is incapable of "authentic" spontaneity. The dandy always thinks, and his thinking creates a critical distance between his own person and the world. Most people think that "in making himself a dandy, a man becomes a piece of boudoir furniture, an extremely ingenious mannequin, who can sit upon a horse or a sofa, who obsessively bites or sucks the end of his cane, but a thinking being . . . never. [But] man who sees only fashion in fashion is a fool. Elegant life excludes neither thought nor science."[2] The first part of Balzac's statement is often quoted and used in literature to summarize Balzac's criticism of dandyism. However, the second part shows that Balzac's point is, quite to the contrary, to conjure the intellectual and critical powers of the dandy. Despite this, spontaneity is not inexistant; it is even important in dandyism (as well as in Daoism), but it should never become an ideal. There are even many instances where dandies appear spontaneous with the purpose of distinguishing themselves from the snob. Mocchia di Coggiola mentions the poet Lord Alfred Douglas who "despised Oscar Wilde because, at table, Wilde loudly praised the food. Douglas held that a gentleman should never point out when the food he had on his plate was good because he was used to good food"

(Mocchia 2019, 131). Douglas represents the blasé snob whereas the dandy Wilde insists on spontaneity. The situation also shows that the blasé, though important for dandyism, should not be an ideal; it rather functions as a regulator of spontaneity. Authentic people react spontaneously to stimuli, but the blasé person has delayed reactions. Simmel explains that the modern urban world is a world of overstimulation that necessarily produces dandies who use the blasé as a sort of protection. What he has in mind is of course the flâneur. The dandy is blasé because he is constantly submitted to an overstimulation of the senses and can no longer react "normally." Either he cannot or he pretends that he cannot. Baudelaire holds that "the dandy is blasé or pretends to be so, for reasons of policy and caste" (Baudelaire 1986, 9).

The blasé signifies mental boredom, *ennui*, existentialist anguish and, to some extent, the illness of English aristocrats. Lord Byron uses the word "spleen" as a quasi-synonym when introducing, in a poetic fashion, *ennui* and boredom in the image of Childe Harold. Not noticing things on purpose, appearing to have forgotten names—this is the attitude of the blasé dandy. A similar mode of protection in a world of overstimulation is anonymity, which becomes important for the flâneur. The flâneur protects himself from the temptations and vulgarities of mass culture by being anonymous and "invisible."

The dandy and the snob are thus similar in many respects, but the snob has a sincerity and ideological conviction that the dandy lacks. Brummell's snobbism is invariably parodic and ironic. By contrast, according to Jacques Boulenger, the snob claims to be a dandy, which makes him even more of a snob whereas Brummell "flattens himself being a snob, but because he flattens himself, he stops being one."[3] Anecdotes narrating Brummell's comical snobbism abound (most of them can be found in Captain Jesse's voluminous biography): he once refused a marriage proposal because he heard that the lady had eaten cabbage (Jesse 1844, 1:119). He himself never touched vegetables and once replied to a lady who asked him if he is really that serious about his diet: "I once ate a pea" (1:111). This is a *parody* of snobbish behavior. About his personal situation he once made a statement that can appear snobbish, but then again, it is too exaggerated to be sincere: "Imagine a position more wretched than mine—they have put me with all the common people. I am surrounded by the greatest villains, and have nothing but prison fare" (2:186–87). In reality, Brummell did not have much patience with snobs and made fun of them. One day, when Lord Bedford asked

Brummell to evaluate his new coat, "Brummell examined him from head to foot with as much attention as an adjutant of the Life Guards would the sentries on a drawing-room day. 'Turn round,' said the Beau: his Grace did so, and the examination was continued in front. When it was concluded Brummell stepped forward, and feeling the lapel delicately with his thumb and finger, said, in a most earnest and amusing manner, 'Bedford, do you call this thing a coat?'" (1: 64).

The snob cherishes sincerity. His sincerity might be fake, but still he cherishes it. The snob can even be proud of his sincerity, like the already-mentioned Alceste in Molière's *Le Misanthrope*, who has one chief talent, which is to be sincere. According to Trilling, Alceste's entire energy is "directed towards perfecting the trait upon which he prides himself (. . .). Alceste's point of pride is his sincerity, his remorseless outspokenness on behalf of truth" (1972, 17). Alceste is a fake dandy, that is, a dandy of sincerity, which is just another word for a snob who tries to survive amidst people who are almost as snobbish as himself: "Every ridiculous person in the play has his point of pride; for Oronte it is his sonnets, for Clitandre his waistcoats, for Acaste his noble blood, his wealth, and his infallible charm. Alceste's point of pride is his sincerity" (17).

To fully clarify the differences between the dandy and the snob, it is necessary to consider a third person: the careerist. The nineteenth century was invaded by two characters under which dandies like Oscar Wilde would suffer: the snob and the careerist. Once the premodern aristocrat had been confined to a less important role, the snob and the careerist began monopolizing a large part of the modern cultural environment. The dandy is not a snob, and it is clear that he is no careerist either because he strives neither for money nor for honors. Rather, the dandy represents an alternative that remains unreachable for both the snob and the careerist.

There is, in the nineteenth century, a dandy-snob-careerist triangle, which Emile Carassus summarized like this: "The careerist sought power whereas the snob and the dandy sought a mirror. But in that mirror the dandy created his own reflection with the images that were already inscribed on it. Both placed the utmost importance on appearing, but the dandy sought to appear 'differently' [autre] whereas the snob sought to appear 'similarly' [parmi]" (71, my translation). The outward-directed will to power is reserved for the careerist, whereas a narcissistic mirror is reserved for both the snob and the dandy. However, snob and dandy use this mirror differently.

Despite these differences, the snob and the careerist have one thing in common: both believe with an utmost sincerity in the rules of the game that is played by high society and do their best to play a good part in it. True, the careerist is more pragmatic and follows rules more single-mindedly than the snob. The snob follows the rules but forces himself to be relaxed because he wants to appear as a dandy. He is "trying not to try," to use Slingerland's formulation, but he is not very successful in doing so. His "dandyism" remains pretentious because he attempts to radiate the lightness of the dandy though, in reality, he follows the rules with the same unimaginative seriousness as the careerist. The snob despises the careerist rule-follower because he believes to have a certain aesthetic surplus that can be called "style" or "coolness." The problem is that he still cares too much about his career and is not ready to take risks whereas the dandy is a true risk taker. The snob sees dandyism merely as a career option, which is why snobbery can be scheduled as "dandyism by hypocrisy."

The snob might look and act like a dandy, but this is merely a part of his career plan. The snob's problem is that he cannot "do nothing" and will rather do too much; he lacks *wuwei* or the kind of coolness that will be examined in the next chapter. The snob finds the life of the careerist too mundane, but in the end, he will not abandon his careerist agenda for the simple reason that he is too sincere. One can also say that the snob and the careerist do not zigzag as the dandy does but that they follow the straight line of a preconceived plan. The dandy resembles Zhuangzi's madman who has a crooked style of walking (see above chapter 2) whereas the snob *pretends* to zigzag though, in reality, he is taking utmost care not to veer from the straight line that is leading to success.

Dandyism arises as a curious alternative lifestyle surviving within the triangle of careerism, snobbism, and authentic aristocracy. Though the dandy opposes the ambitious careerist, it would be wrong to assume that the dandy has no ambition. The relationships are fairly complex. Young Brummell in Oxford certainly was a careerist and a "relentless social climber" who was constantly planning to "make intimacies with men of high rank and connexions" (Kelly 2006, 116). His family was even an extreme example of upward mobility. Brummell's grandfather had been a valet and a servant to a Lincolnshire politician and later bought a boarding house in London in an area that was famous for high-class brothels.[4] However, Brummell must have noticed very early, when looking at his own capacities, that being merely a careerist cannot be a career. Since he did not produce any surplus value (such as being a good administrator or a good investor, like his father), he added to careerism the *ennui*, the tedium, or the *dédain* that would later become the trademark of dandyism. In this way, he created for himself a career, or rather an anticareer. This "career" went along the most meandering of paths possible. Among other things, Brummell developed the art of doing nothing, which is certainly the opposite of a career plan.

"Snobbism consists of (. . .) accepting only those who submit to the rites of integration," notes Jean d'Ormesson (1964, 450). Such sincere criteria of authenticity are alien to the dandy. Like the careerist, the snob is a formalist, an ideologist, and a technocrat who constantly measures the social network within which he is moving. He can only be horrified by the nihilistic and anarchic tendencies that are part and parcel of dandyism. The snob cannot make fun of himself because he aspires to what he considers to be a sort of dandyist authenticity, which is precisely what Brummell avoided.

To the above three characters, one might want to add a fourth who is, according to Daniel Schiffer, the cousin of the dandy: the bohemian (2010, 45). The concept of the bohemian appeared in England and France at a time when dandyism was going through its more advanced phases. In France, the word "bohème" became popular through Balzac's 1844 novella *Un prince de la bohème*. A little earlier, Balzac had invented the literary figure of the dandy in the form of the perfectly unmoved Henri de Marsay in his novel *La fille aux yeux d'or* (1835). The bohemian is a dandy who refuses to pretend, and as he does not want to play along the rules of society but simply drops out. He rejects bourgeois culture and the rationality that he sees as the trademarks of industrial society and decides to follow a romantic artistic ideal clearly separate from normal society. Bohemian culture thus bears much resemblance to the above-described counterculture that Taylor had called "Dionysian." The bohemian shares with the dandy an apparent adherence to a "religion of the aesthetic" with the difference that in bohemianism there is no mockery, irony, or *dédain*. The bohemian can also quickly adhere to some utopian idealism, which remains antithetical to any dandyist project. The bohemian is more Romantic in his spiritual orientation and tends to follow a quest for a mysterious absolute closely related to what was preached at that time by German and English Romanticism. Seen from this perspective, dandy and bohemian live in parallel universes: the former in an emerging modernity; the latter in nostalgic and emotional retro-Romanticism. However, these two worlds can fuse. The dandy is anti-Romantic but is also antirealist. Dandyism, too, was a response to a prevailing state of fashion that was rooted in the values of Romanticism. Consequently, a few protagonists brought these two forces, which normally contradict each other, together. Lord Byron is the foremost example and can be called a "Romanticism dandy." French examples of "bohemian dandies" are Alfred de Musset and Eugene Delacroix. They were less blasé, less distanced, and not merely spectators like the flâneur. Though both the Romantic and the dandy rebel against "classicist" traditional society and plead for a more "populist" and individualist culture (dandyism does so at least in the case of the flâneur), their approaches remain different, which becomes most obvious in Romanticism's veneration of nature. The Romantic bohemian is the ancestor of the modern antiurban hippie, who will be characterized in the next chapter as an outspoken antidandy. Another difference is that the bohemian, contrary to the dandy, is willing to accept poverty and frugality. The dandy does not drop out of society but aestheticizes society's ethical rules through his ironical behavior. Both dandy and bohemian oppose the careerist, but while the bohemian simply pursues no career at all, the dandy manages to design for himself an ironical "anti-career." Both dandy and bohemian tend to be wanderers, adventurers, and risk takers, but the bohemian does not flow in the social crowd as freely as the dandy and the flâneur do. Both dandy and bohemian despise the snob, who is a careerist who imitates the dandy and sometimes even the bohemian.

To make the list complete, one could add a fifth character, the *gagà*, who is just as unique as the others: the *gagà* is a failed dandy, a failed snob, as well as a failed careerist. On top of it, he is no bohemian either. The *gagà* is a character occurring in Italy, in the land of *sprezzatura*, though it is safe to assume that the phenomenon exists everywhere without necessarily having received a name. Adolf Loos, in his famous text "Men's Fashion" (1898), speaks of the "gigerl" (1962, 21–22), which has been translated into Italian as *"gagà."* Originally, the *gagà* dates from around 1900, but there are antecedents. Mocchia di Coggiola (2016) cites the French *"lions,"* and typical *gagà* are, for Mocchia, Gabriele D'Annunzio (62), as well as Disraeli and Eugène Sue (52). Like the snob, the *gagà* looks for security but, most of the time, he is unable to obtain it. He also is a womanizer; though here, again, most often he is a failure. Most importantly, the *gagà* does not actively look for an alternative lifestyle, as do the dandy and the bohemian, but he merely attempts to add his personal note to the latest fashion, which can be a pretentious approach. Nor is he a flâneur because he lacks the distance and coolness. The *lions* and the *gagàs* might have been the nineteenth-century yuppies who tried to create a certain code, race, or style that enabled them to attract followers. This is alien to the dandy. Also, as has been mentioned in the last chapter, the elitist dandy has neither followers nor mass appeal.

The dandy exalts the gentleman's *aesthetic* perfection but rejects the *ethical* image of the perfect gentleman. This lack of sincerity provides the dandy with a unique leeway or *Spielraum* in which he can practice his play. Brummell's friend Prince George (and eventually King George IV) was called "the first gentleman of England";[5] Brummell never had the ambition to be the first or the best. Though his perfect manners could perhaps have earned him such a title, he always remained too incorrect. Also, in order to become "the best" one needs enthusiasm, but the dandy plays the game of being a gentleman without enthusiasm, which confers upon his actions a peculiarly cool and smooth attitude. In the end, he seems to be more comfortable in this society than anybody else, which is a proof of his genuineness. The dandy Lord Goring in Wilde's play *An Ideal Husband* says that as the dandy plays with life, he "is on perfectly good terms with the world." Marc Le Bot concludes that "the dandy benefits from a sort of grace": Activities like being a "perfect gentleman" or making revolutions are ethically inspired activities, but since the dandy is fundamentally disinterested in such ethical activities, this provides him a comfort or "grace" that the rest of society does not have (1990, 6).

Utilitarianism and the scientification of ethics would lead to a twofold death of dandyism. In the Victorian era, Bentham's and Mill's utilitarianism propagated an extreme form of businesslike efficiency. Furthermore, these philosophers made ethics scientific. The beginning of the Victorian era is often given to be as early as 1832, thus overlapping with part of a broad definition of the Regency period.[6] However, the influence of evangelical moralizers began as early as the 1790s, most prominently with the antislavery movement. During this time, moral sensibilities were strongly enhanced, and talk about responsibility, self-examination, and self-improvement became increasingly important (see Young 1936, 1–5). An ethicized society began to revere the "moral self." All of this was incompatible with dandyism.

The dandy does not turn the "politically correct" into the "politically incorrect," but rather deletes the "political" in order to stick to what is "correct"—although it is only correct *for him* and only correct in an aesthetic sense. Therefore, he can appear as an example of hypercorrect incorrectness. By replacing ethics with aesthetics, the dandy invents his own correctness, which he exercises to perfection. The dandy does not politicize but depoliticizes his struggle against snobbish correctness. Political correctness is about being a perfect gentleman. The dandy supplements this concept by inventing a language of cynicism and mockery. The refusal of ethics is important because in the end, the dandy can only survive in the sphere of amorality. Ethics is a sincere business, and if the dandy can get away with what he does, it is only because people understand that he is not sincere. In a way, he joins an earlier, more original form of PC.

The dandy stands out from this modernizing society for two reasons: he is neither the old-fashioned perfect aristocratic gentleman, nor the more progressive and ethically minded bourgeois. His place is nowhere but on the aesthetic playground called "dandyism" that he has built for himself. And this playground is getting increasingly narrower. The dandy does not comply with Georgian rationalism but cannot pass as a Victorian romantic fighting for humanist values either. There is nothing mystical or religious about Brummell or the young Oscar Wilde. The dandy's moral neutrality strives for an absolute aestheticism for which these societies no longer have a place. Already during the Regency era, ethics was on the rise because middle-class modernizers began emphasizing business and puritanical religious values. The ascent of the middle class became more pronounced in the adjacent Victorian era. Here ethics killed aesthetics. Oscar Wilde did his best to survive as a dandy but landed in prison.

Daoist Dandy versus Confucian Snob?

Can the previously described "dandy versus careerist/snob" scheme provide insights into the realm of ancient Chinese philosophy? The attitude of the blasé dandy, his tendency not to notice things on purpose and to forget names, has parallels in Daoism. Daoism recommends forgetting, especially the forgetting of names and titles, in order to perceive the world's events more spontaneously. By contrast, the Confucian remembers everything. So do the careerist and the snob. Some stories in the

Zhuangzi do indeed echo the dandy versus careerist theme. For example, in "External Things" (What Comes from Without) in the "Miscellaneous" chapters, Lao Lai-zi (also named Chenopod or Wildweed in other translations) castigates Qiu (Hillock), who represents Confucius, for his arrogance, dedication to self-promotion, calculated behavior, and tendency to judge and stereotype others. Confucius's careerist behavior is depicted many other times, as John Makeham shows in his article "Between *Chen* and *Cai*: Zhuangzi and the Analects": "The impression Mencius gives is that Confucius was regularly 'job hunting' and regularly being frustrated. Similarly, in Xunzi, it is a politically ambitious Confucius" that is put forward (2016, 89). Zhuangzi, the "free-wheeling scamp," is a dandy, and Confucius can easily appear as a careerist. However, this antagonism needs to be nuanced. In reality, Confucius mastered rituals in a quasi-dandyist fashion, too, because he was not a mere formalist but aspired to have *wuwei*. It would be a mistake to reproach Confucius to be mindlessly insisting on duties and rule-following. Confucian rule-following is always meant to create a second nature, that is, to instill in the person a new character until the "doing" finally appears as "non-doing." "For someone like Confucius at age seventy, all that uptight ancient cultural stuff has become like the water in which a fish swims, completely unnoticed and yet perfectly comfortable," writes Slingerland (2014, 77), and Sigurdsson finds that "this crucial feature of the Confucian philosophy has been largely ignored by later interpreters, not least by those who tend to cling to an image of Confucianism as dogmatic and reactionary" (2020, 33). There are therefore some Confucian resemblances with the dandy that make Zhuangzi appear, by contrast, quite bohemian. However, this needs to be explained, too. Confucius *does* want effortless *wuwei*, but the problem is that he obtains it through conscious doing. Taste, for example, must be slowly refined over time by following rules until it is no longer dependent upon rule-following but has become automatic. Xunzi, a Confucian, explains how Confucian learning enters the aspiring Confucian and changes his very physiological makeup. In "Encouragement to Learning" (which I quote here from Slingerland), Xunzi says that "the learning of the gentleman enters his ear, becomes firm in his heart-mind, spreads out through his four limbs, and manifests itself in both activity and repose. In his merest word, in his slightest movement, the gentleman can always be taken as an example and a model" (2014, 77). Just like in *wuwei*, action is free and easygoing. However, at the same time, it is morally correct because, as Xunzi explains, it "has been regulated [so] they accord with civilized norms."

The *Analects* (Book 10) contain detailed descriptions of Confucius's behavior not only in formal contexts but also when eating, sleeping, or mounting his carriage. This might look formalistic, but it brings Confucius close to the dandy's aesthetic perfectionism and obsession with behavioral details. Confucius was not only a master of ceremonies and perfect behavior, but he also was well dressed. Descriptions of his appearance can be found in the *Analects*. Confucius

> did not use reddish-black or maroon for the trim of his garment, nor did he use red or purple for his informal dress. In summer, he wore a single layer of linen or hemp, but always put on an outer garment before going out. With a black upper garment, he would wear a lambskin robe; with a white upper garment he would wear a fawnskin robe; and with a yellow upper garment he would wear a fox-fur robe. His informal fur robe was long, but the right sleeve was short. He required that his nightgown be knee-length. He wore thick fox and badger furs when at home. Except when he was in mourning, he never went anywhere without having all of his sash ornaments properly displayed. With the exception of his one-piece ceremonial skirts, his lower garments were always cut and hemmed. He did not wear [black] lamb skin robes or dark caps on condolence visits. On the day of the "Auspicious Moon," he would always put on his [black] court attire and present himself at court. (10.6) (. . .) He would not sit unless his mat was straight. (10.12). (. . .) When mounting his carriage, he would always stand facing it directly while grasping the mounting strap. Once in his carriage, he would not let his gaze wander past the crossbar in front of him or to either side, he would not speak rapidly, nor would he point with his hand. (10.26, trans. Slingerland 2003).

We might find such an insistence on dress rules exaggerated or even bizarre, but unlike Zhuangzi's hobolike attire, we also will find this side of Confucius reminiscent of the dandy. There is, however, a difference in the approach toward *wuwei*. Despite his aspirations toward freewheeling *wuwei*, Confucius remains a careerist. Confucius "does" a lot in order to create a second nature, which creates a contrast with the dandy. Confucius's actions always have a purpose: mostly that of creating a second nature, which means that his actions are useful, whereas the dandy's behavior is useless throughout. And, paradoxically, it is this uselessness that creates his "nature." Confucius will always have a reasonable explanation as to why rituals need to be enacted, whereas the Zhuangzist dandy will engage in absurdities. In Daoism during the Wei-Jin period (220–420) there was even a metaphysical "study of the abstruse" (*xuan xue*) (Li Zehou 2009, 89).

Confucius's paradox is that he wants to achieve nondoing through the rigid strategies of doing. His striving, learning, and self-reflections remain part of a rational career plan supposed to lead to the creation of the perfect gentleman: "Do not look unless it is in accordance with ritual; do not listen unless it is in accordance with ritual; do not speak unless it is in accordance with ritual; do not move unless it is in accordance with ritual" (*Analects* 12.1). *Wuwei* is part of this career plan, which must look odd because normally, in a career plan, there is no place for "doing nothing." Many a snob has struggled with this problem. For Confucius, *wuwei* is a matter of "carving-and-polishing" the self in view of the gentleman career. Confucians want to "let go," and they are trying very hard to do so, which is the problem. The Confucian "letting go" is real work, rigorously structured and executed over decades. The dandy and Zhuangzi are more consistent because they distance themselves from any career in the first place, and they do so through nondoing. They practice *wuwei* in a way that comes much closer to its literal meaning. In the end, Confucius remains a careerist who wants to be a dandy, which is precisely the definition of the snob. For Zhuangzi, Confucians and Mohists have only a "petty understanding" of their place in the world, which they perceive in terms of a career. They have a "narrow, rigid view of the world, [which] sets the tone for society as a whole, giving rise to a society composed of arrogant know-it-alls, publicly prosperous and confident but secretly miserable, feverishly pursuing a false vision of happiness" (Slingerland 2014, 140). It gives rise to a society of careerists and snobs.

We can say that Confucius himself might not have been a snob but that his method can easily produce snobs. "For every effortlessly graceful and sincere Confucius, the hard grind of self-cultivation produces a dozen wannabes, counterfeits of virtue who talk the talk, and even walk the walk, but lack the inner commitment of the true gentleman" (Slingerland 2014, 78). The snob is not against spontaneity but aspires to it; however, he does not understand how spontaneity comes about. He thinks it can be learned through doing and by following techniques. Spontaneity is on his career training program, and it will be taught by spontaneity coaches. While Confucianism cultivates social ambitions in the sense of careerism, the *Zhuangzi* and dandyism offer existential-sociopolitical critiques that show that ambitions directed toward careers or superior roles are likely to be disappointed. Nondoing must lead to a noncareer.

The *Laozi* finds that "the Confucian scheme—with its emphasis on striving and learning and endless self-reflection—is incapable of producing anything other than village poseurs" (Slingerland 2014, 96). The village poseur is yet another snob imitating the dandy. Confucius also criticizes the village poseur but for entirely different reasons. Confucius finds that the village poseur studies the Way without being sincere. And the Confucian Mencius describes him as one who "follows along with all the popular trends," practices all the rituals, learns the Odes by heart, and so on—but ends up as "a counterfeit of a good person: someone who looks like a good person on the outside but has no real virtue on the inside" (194). Confucius calls the village poseur the "thief of *de*" (the village poseur represents one of the first cases of identity appropriation). The problem for the Confucian is that the poseur is not sincere or authentic and that he appropriates an authority and a career that he does not deserve.

The Daoist paints the case of the village poseur differently. For him, *de* is rather the dandyist "je ne sais quoi" that will be identified in chapter 8 as coolness. For the Daoist, the village poseur is politically correct because he always "seems dutiful, trustworthy, honest and pure" (194). His problem is not that he is not authentic and only pretending but rather that he is a "non-genuine" pretender. This is another way of saying that he lacks style. In the nineteenth century, the word "poseur" was, in both England and America, another word for dandy, and it was always used in a negative sense. (The insult that Oscar Wilde had suffered from the Marquess of Queensberry consisted of calling him a "*posing* sodomite.") English culture produced "beaus, flops, dandies, flâneurs, [and] poseurs," write Pountain and Robins (2000, 55). However, this poseur is not so much a wannabee careerist (as Confucians classified the village poseur) but a wannabe dandy. His lack of style is not a lack of some authentic "good person substance," but it is rather a lack of *wuwei*. This means that, for the Daoist, the village poseur commits no ethical mistake but "only" an aesthetic mistake. He is no failed careerist but rather a failed dandy.

When it comes to careerism, the scientifically minded Mohists fare much better. On the one hand, the Mohists were perhaps the sincerest careerists of all Warring States philosophers, as they raced from one end of China to the other, offering their services to rulers whose states were under attack. Mohists were like the busybodies seriously working for the public good whom Wilde repeatedly criticizes. On the other hand, Mohists were skilled engineers and were never tempted by dandyism of any sort, which prevented them from becoming snobs. Mohists might have been misguided in their belief that logic and calculation can establish right behavior, but at least they never pretended to retrieve spontaneity with the help of some method. They rather ignored spontaneity altogether. Nor did they ever pretend to be authentic but were simply correct. They might have looked silly at worst but never snobbish. Zhuangzi depicts Huizi, who was close to Mohist thought, as somebody who simply cannot understand *wuwei*. However, what saves Huizi is that he was never looking for it anyway, which is probably why Zhuangzi got along so well with him.

Though the dandy is always wearing a mask, he never turns into a poseur. The reason for this is that his mask is not fake but part of his genuine existence. The dandy is acting and playing, and, in principle, these activities are *always* carried out while wearing a mask. Without a mask, the dandy would end up being sincere, which would signify the end of dandyism. Paradoxically, the dandy becomes real only through a lack of authentic grounding, whereas his imitators strive for authenticity by sincerely following certain doctrines. It is Baudelaire who very aptly describes this situation when writing about fake dandies: "What then is this passion, which, having become a doctrine, has produced such a school of tyrants as well as an unwritten code that could deliver such a haughty and exclusive sect? It is, above all, the burning desire to create a personal form of originality, within the external limits of social conventions" (1986a, 27; 1885, 93, trans. modified).[7] The passion that Baudelaire describes is the fake dandies' desire to be original or authentic. It concerns only the poseurs but not the dandy himself. Brummell is not passionate about being a dandy let alone about being an authentic dandy. Passions lead to doctrines, but Brummell is what he is, without any ideological or emotional support. "Never have something like passion—it will make you too real to be a dandy," explains Brummell to all future dandies (Barbey 1926–27, 30–31). Humor, distance, and self-ridicule are the safety valves that prevent the dandy from becoming too sincere, too real, or snobbish. Accordingly, Sartre saw that Baudelaire's most striking particularity was "the fundamental impossibility of taking oneself completely seriously" (1947, 94; 1967, 82). Brummell did not need spontaneity training either because, according to Barbey, he was already against all seriousness. Brummell could also speak spontaneously and naturally with simple people, which, given his alleged elitism and his expressed desire to distance himself from the ordinary herd of men (let alone his "blasé-ness"), is surprising. His relationship with "the people" remains determined by this important ambiguity.

In summary, it can be said that the dandy joins the Dao-heroes described in the *Zhuangzi*, such as the "cart faller," a waterfall diver, a ferryman, a woodworker, or the butcher Ding who carves an ox. There is also a cicada-catching hunchback and the carpenter Shi who slices mud off his friend's nose with a whirling hatchet without hurting him. These professions (if they are professions at all) are not noble but modest, or even decadent, and certainly not highly recognized by society. Though some of these heroes are regular craftsmen, many of the most grotesque protagonists of these "knack stories" are excellent at what they do, although society would hesitate to reward them for their excellence. Nor do these people expect such a reward. There is not much content in these activities if we define "content" as having ethical or utilitarian purpose. The dandy, too, has often been reproached with being all style and no content, a reproach that misses the point of dandyism. The Dao-heroes might appear superficial, but everybody must agree that their childlike honesty and their directness are disarming. There is no trace of pride or snobbism in their actions.

It is thus no coincidence that Baudelaire attributes even to Poe's slightly eerie "Man in the Crowd" (who is Baudelaire's model of the dandy) a "childlike perceptiveness," which is "acute and magical by reason of innocence" because "the child sees everything in a state of newness" (Baudelaire 1986a, 12). Playing children are not snobs. As pointed out above, the Man in the Crowd emerges from an oblivious state of meditation and enters the state of "convalescence, [which] is like a return towards childhood. Like the child, [he is] keenly interesting himself in things, be they apparently of the most trivial" (1986, 12). The point is that dandies and Dao-heroes do not pretend to be *not* superficial, nor do they impress us with the sincerity proper to adults who are passionate about their professions and feel obliged to constantly manifest sincere devotion. Dao-heroes and dandies play like children, and they do so in the mode of serious play, which is distinct from the devotion proper to adults when they exercise a profession. The latter attitude is too much dependent on the ethical notion of sincerity, which is alien to the masters of serious play. Masters of serious play focus on their activity and have no time for pride, questions about usefulness, or pretentions of any kind. By contrast, people who are ethically devoted to their work often expect a reward or some social recognition. In such cases, snobbism is always lurking around the corner.

Acting "Naturally"

The countercultures of the 1960s, with their exuberant celebrations of a simplified lifestyle, were submitted to a romantic or bohemian "back to nature" impulse that was often combined with the desire to be removed from the unnatural city as far as possible. For the hippies, to follow one's spontaneous inclinations, tendencies, desires, preferences, and capacities meant to be "natural," as opposed to artificial. We will see below that this lifestyle philosophy would even find the urban dandy suspicious because urbanites were found blasé. Nature is always straightforward, honest, and free, and thus opposed to the hypocrisy of civilization. This idea of nature is determined by a strong belief in the authentic, and its idea of nature is therefore fundamentally different from Daoism's and dandyism's idea of nature. *Wuwei* or "doing nothing" do indeed enable "natural action," and the dandy and the Dao-hero are supposed to act "naturally." However, this does not mean that they follow the ideal of nature. Neither dandies nor Daoists are ecologists. Ecologists tend to be sincere people, whereas Baudelaire insisted that "nature teaches us nothing, or practically nothing" (1986a, 31). Baudelaire was basically opposed to nature, and once even explained, when walking through a natural setting, that natural, freely flowing water was unbearable for him. He aspired to imprison the freely flowing water "in a straitjacket between the geometrical walls of a dock."[8] Brummell, too, grew quickly tired of the romantic raving about the outstanding natural beauty of the Lake District, leading him to make infamously dismissive remarks when asked about the lakes' beauty (see chapter 8). Later, in a premodernist vein, British aestheticists would consider nature as crude and lacking in design when compared to art. Life should copy art and not nature. Vivian, in Wilde's *Decay of Lying*, clearly says that "the more we study Art, the less we care for Nature. What Art really reveals to us is Nature's lack of design, her curious crudities, her extraordinary monotony, her absolutely unfinished condition" (1895, 73).

The antinature feeling has deep roots. After Kant, it had become fashionable to mock the neoclassical idea that art imitates nature. In his *Critique of Judgment* (1790) Kant had postulated that the artist should not imitate "natural beauty" but draw from their own "fertile spirit." The artist should not replicate natural forms because this reduces the creative act to conforming with observable natural laws (1908, 399). Over the next hundred years, aesthetics would develop an explicit culture of the artificial. The culture of dandyism, in particular, would elevate the artificial to a primeval aesthetic category similar to the Kantian sublime, and by the end of the nineteenth century, Oscar Wilde could write in his "Phrases and Philosophies for the Use of the Young" (1894) that "the first duty in life is to be as artificial as possible," adding that "what the second duty is no one has yet discovered" (2005, 305). Still there is a search for the natural because the dandy strives to act naturally: "The dandy intends to understand the voice of nature, without giving in to its calls crippled by the logic of domination. He aspires to be a human being and not to be reduced to an animal dependent on the mechanism of jouissance postulated by society," writes Scaraffia (1981, 55). In Italy, *sprezzatura* had a paradoxical ring of "artificial naturalness" since the Renaissance (Paulicelli 2019, 103). All this is key to this peculiar relationship with the nature of aestheticists. It can always be assumed that there is "underneath the crust of an induced second nature, a buried naturalness," believes Scaraffia (1981, 53). But this naturalness will not be discovered like an essence but rather be enacted, as paradoxical as it sounds, by being artificial.

Wilde's attraction to East Asian culture can also partly be explained by this peculiar relationship with nature. In a key passage of *The Decay of Lying*, Wilde extols Oriental art for its rejection of naturalism: "The whole history of these arts in Europe is the record of the struggle between Orientalism, with its frank rejection of imitation, its love of artistic convention, its dislike to the actual representation of any object in Nature, and our own imitative spirit" (2007b: 80). Trilling, when commenting on this phrase about the artificial versus the natural, highlights the link between the natural and the sincere and points out that Wilde teases the idea of sincerity as one of the cherished attributes of philistine respectability. This perfectly summarizes the idea that there is no being "naturally dandy"; just as there is no being "sincerely dandy." Not only is playing never sincere, but it is never a natural activity either.

The paradoxical concept that one must act naturally but without seeing nature as an ideal, and that one must even act naturally by being "artificial," is indeed prominent in Chinese aesthetics. Chinese art rejects not nature but naturalism. Neither nature nor the artificial are ideals or anti-ideals. Thus, nature is not overcome by being turned into the artificial: it is rather left intact so the artificial can coexist with nature. In other words, the artificial is not an "anti-nature," but nature must exist in order to enable the existence of the artificial. Li Zehou (2009) explains this peculiar constellation: "Nature [i.e., human nature] is the unhewn, plain wood; artifice is its ornamental carving. Without nature, artifice would have nothing to add to; without artifice, nature could not beautify itself" (66).[9] There is no artifice without nature, which is why for Li "Chinese art lacks the artificial, material demonstration of human resistance to or conquest of nature. On the contrary, it has always sought harmony with nature, subordination and submission to nature, and finally unity with nature" (96). Art can reach harmony with nature only by being distinct from nature, that is, first of all, by refraining from naturalism. In no case does art imitate nature. Nor should nature either be idealized or seen as an "evil temptress," two attitudes that Li correctly attributes to Western art (2009, 97). According to Li, Chinese literati not only had more contact with nature than Western artists in general (Li thinks of feudal Lords of the Middle Ages) but, more importantly, when it came to aesthetic questions, they saw nature neither as a problem nor as a solution. It is thus, paradoxically, a certain indifference to nature that produces a "natural" attitude. Nature is not worshiped and spiritualized, which even enables its extension into the realm of the divine: "In China, because of the absence of such a religious, spiritual pillar and the lack of abstract, metaphysical speculation, nature comes to encompass all things, including God, so that one can simply allow the spirit to rest" (101). Nature is not declared to be God, but God is declared to be nature.

Wilde speaks in his *The Critic as Artist* also of Aristotle, who wants nature to be spiritualized and purified by catharsis, and he insists that this process is merely aesthetic (as Goethe saw it) and not ethical (as Lessing believed) (see Wilde 2007a, 140). This, again, is similar to the Chinese model, which does not engage in an ethical struggle to transcend nature but rather believes that "nature is just another part of the human world" (Li Zehou 2009, 101). One does not seek solace in a (more ethical) "beyond" but *in* nature. As explained in chapter 2, both the dandy and Zhuangzi transform the world by implementing their own lifestyle. Aestheticization is better than the ethical options of revolution or reclusion. Aestheticization has no rules. The man who falls off carts as described in the *Zhuangzi* and the dandy have skills, but these skills appear only in the moment these people act. They do not know about rules leading to these skills; they do not even know that they have these skills. Then these perfect actions come about "naturally."

Chinese philosophy is dedicated to nature, though not the nature of wilderness but rather a cultivated kind of naturalness, and here we see a link with dandyism and aestheticism. For both Confucians and Daoists, being natural does not refer to nature "out there" but, paradoxically, to culture. Zhuangzi does not want to be confined by the standards of civilization, but the solution is not a "return to nature." Similarly, Confucius achieves the state of being natural only through a process of acculturation. As mentioned, even for Confucians, it is possible to achieve *wuwei* through training in civilization; in the end, our actions are supposed to become natural. Daoism is more consistent because here artisans, butchers, ferrymen, and draftsmen act naturally, in the sense of effortlessly. But naturalness is not achieved through work: it is rather attained by doing nothing.

Zhuangzi becomes "natural" by letting go, by submitting himself to forgetting and "natural" roaming. However, contrary to what many hippies of the 1960s believed, following the body and forgetting the mind does not mean renouncing civilization. Like the dandy and the flâneur, the natural person may well decide to live in urbanity and in civilization. A natural state can be reached simply by rejecting the eternal search for sincerity. The latter is a negative aspect of civilization, and the dandy attempts to overcome it by acting "naturally" within a hypocritical and corrupted society. Effortless ease includes responsiveness to civilization whereas escaping from civilization does not provide that ease. Zhuangzi does not venture into an idyllic nature either but meets "strange" people such as hunchbacks, cripples, lowlifes, freaks, madmen, and criminals, all of whom have been produced by civilization and live *in* civilization. Zhuangzi wants to show how these people manage to live "naturally" in civilization.

Baudelaire designs in his *Fusées* a long list of aesthetic concepts that are supposed to transcend the "natural" idea of beauty and can thus be associated with an artificial beauty. He calls these concepts the "charming looks that bring about beauty" ("les airs charmants [. . .] qui font la beauté," Baudelaire 1986b, 76). Beauty is not an essence "out there"; it can only be brought about through certain behaviors. In other words, beauty is not an ideal but emerges through play. Apart from those concepts that are immediately linked to dandyism such as the blasé and the bored (ennuyé), Baudelaire lists many others, among which are: the imprudent, empty-headed (l'air evaporé), the ailing (le malade), the imperious (l'air de domination), the capricious (l'air de volonté), the naughty (le méchant), the frigid (l'air froid), the introspective (l'air de regarder dedans), and the feline. The latter is a blend of childishness with nonchalance (76). Baudelaire glorifies the artificial, but all these qualities must be enacted naturally. Baudelaire's aversion to nature pushes him toward the artificial, but at the root of this aversion is the mistrust of the authentic and the sincere. None of the above expressions evoke sincerity.

The fact that the dandy does not follow the authentic model of nature is also demonstrated by his gender-bending tendency. In Baudelaire's short story *La Fanfarlo* (1847), a female admirer of Samuel Cramer, who is Baudelaire's alter ego, says: "I wanted to be like him, to be even more beautiful than him, that is to say, coquettish, coquettish for him, like he was for the world."[10] Samuel Cramer's female beauty is highly unnatural; still, he acts "naturally" through play.

Later, a new generation of dandies would push the cult of the artificial to the extreme. Breaking in a very self-conscious fashion with naturalism, Huysmans's *A Rebours* (1884) becomes the ultimate example of decadent literature, as Des Esseintes prefers artificial flowers to natural ones. This dandyism has moved away from the earlier paradoxical "naturally artificial" principle that could so conveniently be linked to Chinese aesthetics. Des Esseintes simply *is* artificial; this artificiality becomes almost neurotic when he muses about tastes, literature, painting, religion, and sensory experiences. Oscar Wilde's *Picture of Dorian Gray* inflates this aestheticism, which is then depicted, rather surprisingly, as unethical.

The Daoist sage's perfect actions come about "naturally." No moral input is possible in such actions. Since nothing is known, nothing is aspired to, and nothing has even been "done" in the sense of rational doing, these actions are necessarily beyond good and evil. Paradoxically, the "beyond good and evil" aspect makes these actions, which follow no ideal of nature, natural. Moral people often like to support their ethics with arguments about nature, insisting that their ethical behavior follows the rules of nature (arguments against abortion or homosexuality most clearly employ this pattern). As an ethical principle, this is weak simply because following nature *can* also lead to unethical behavior. As a matter of fact, many ethical theories have been created to strengthen the values of civilization *against* nature. The Daoist-dandy takes the opposite approach: in order to act "naturally," he rejects the ideal of nature. Only in that way can he act "naturally," that is, without being blinded by ethical ideals. Ethical people are sincere, and nature tends to be the fetish of the sincere. The snob is the foremost example of such ethical beings because he does not act "naturally" in the dandyist sense.

Daoism formulates such views in opposition to Confucianism, holding that "the Confucians' mistake is the labeling of an act as "morally good" instead of just natural or instinctive. We also do not ascribe morality to animals that protect their offspring. Why is one then forced to declare something that is merely natural and instinctive as 'good' or 'bad'?" (Moeller 2006, 109). In his 2009 book on amorality, Moeller calls Daoist sages "moral fools," and dandies are "moral fools," too. They are moral fools in the same way an artist can be called an "aesthetic fool." Most artists do not deem it necessary to study Aristotle's or Kant's aesthetic theories to become good artists. An artist does not need to know why he is painting the way he does—he simply does it, and any theories would most probably only block his creativity.

It is therefore no coincidence that dandyism effectuates such a strong shift from ethics to aesthetics. Both dandies and Daoists are artists. The dandyist impulse to place style over substance, or manners over morals, is not due to a desire to be superficial. The dandy prefers to act in terms of aesthetics because in aesthetics it is much more common to act "naturally." Furthermore, aesthetic fools are more commonly accepted than moral fools. Mair calls those people "morosophos" or "foolosophical" (1983a, 88), and their existence is due to a childlike spirit of genuine pretending. They know that they are fools, and "he who knows he is a fool is not the biggest fool" (trans. Watson 2013, 139).

Negativity in Dandyism and Daoism

Both the dandy's ethics and aesthetics are negative, which is another reason why they must be opposed to the more naïve and literal understanding of the natural in philosophy. Much of Daoism and Zen Buddhism follows what is called "negative ethics," and the dandy does the same. Negative ethics does not say what is "good," and it does not create an ideal to be followed: it only states what should be avoided. It has been said that the definition of Daoism is best established by defining it in terms of what it is not (see McCormack 2017, 75), and dandyism is built on a similar principle. According to Albert Camus, "These mad dandies could define themselves only with regard to their enemies, take shape in relentless combat,"[11] and for Baudelaire, dandyism puts "distinction above all things" (1986a, 27), which is a sort of negative aesthetics. The good and beautiful are only defined through their distinction from what is not good and not beautiful. All ideals or essences that could positively establish the right dandyist action are avoided. This negativity and lack of definition lets the dandy appear to lack an ontological, ethical, or aesthetic grounding.

Saying what it is not is still a statement. More negativity is produced when the statement is neither affirmative nor negative but simply open-ended. Barbey points out that Brummell was not from an aristocratic background and that his greatness was based on nothing at all: he simply projected "an image of mysterious superiority based on nothing at all and that nobody can define" (1897, 26). Sartre found something similar in Baudelaire who "neither can nor wants to live the being or the existence to the end" (1947, 90). According to Sartre, Baudelaire's existence was "restraint, fleeting, and similar to a scent" (204) as he was "never completely there but not entirely invisible either, he remains suspended between nothingness and being" (200).[12] Brummell refrains from clear statements and expresses his opinion through nonparticipation and abstinence rather than through dissent; which means that he does not express it but always remains "in between." Several of the dandy's features demonstrate this both/and, which avoids any statement. The dandy does not work but is not a libertine either. Some would describe Brummell as an extravagant and excessive figure, but he also has something akin to an ascetic. He is at home in Epicurean hedonism as much as in Stoic ascesis. Dandyism's "monastic rule (. . .) borders on the spiritual and the stoical," according to Baudelaire (1986a, 28), adding that it is a "gymnastics designed to fortify the will and discipline the soul" and that "the penalty for drunkenness was enforced suicide" (28). Dandyism might be a sort of religion, but it is not the evangelical, puritan religion of the Victorian era.

There is a further contradiction: Brummell's dandyism is linked to a pronounced restraint toward women as Brummell was no Don Juan and has even been described as entirely "useless" for women. However, he does not seem to have been homosexual either, which creates a sort of male bodily self-denial. The dandy's image is not that of a transgender person either. He is effeminate but feels no solidarity with women. Women like the courtesan Henriette Wilson were rather jealous of Brummell because "the qualities that made the power of the dandy would have made the fortune of the courtesan" (Barbey 1897, 62). Barbey stated that "women will never forgive him for having been graceful as they" (65).

Brummell himself clearly saw that his existence was grounded on nothing other than his absurdities and provocations, as he confessed to Lady Hester Stanhope:[13] "It is my folly that is the making of me. If I did not impertinently stare duchesses out of countenance, and nod over my shoulder to a prince, I should be forgotten in a week: and, if the world is so silly as to admire my absurdities, you and I may know better, but what does that signify?" (1845, 281) Sartre described the dandies as a "suicide club," suggesting that these people play a game where winning needs to be avoided at any cost: "In this game of 'the loser wins,' the winner claims victory because he has been defeated."[14] The idea of the "negative game" (in which the loser wins) is interesting and will be analyzed below.

Sartre's "club de suicidés" echoes Daoist ideas of emptiness and the deconstruction of the ego. The "negative" attitude becomes manifest through the dandy's refusal to identify with social positions and ranks, which is, once again, similar to the Daoist critique of titles and names: "While [in Confucianism] the 'root' of filial piety symbolizes the solid and healthy beginning of what is perceived to be a process of growth, the root image in the *Laozi* is more associated with qualities of invisibility, shapelessness, darkness, and being unmoved," writes Moeller (2006, 89). Laozi uses the words "nothing" or "the nameless" for such constellations, and the dandy expresses the same nothingness through an air of boredom or *ennui*. Baudelaire summarized this importance of nothingness better than anybody else when describing the dandy's cosmetics that always aims at simplicity: "Nothing embellishes something" (1986, 31). Since there is no definition of dandyism, and dandyism must be reinvented each time anew, as a result, anything can be dandyism. Brummell insisted that dandyism is not a matter of clothes and that "one can be a dandy in ragged clothes" (Barbey 1897, 13), and Baudelaire confirmed this: "Contrary to what a lot of thoughtless people seem to believe, dandyism is not (. . .) an excessive delight in clothes and material elegance" (1986, 27).

The Anti–Role Model

It has already been said that neither the dandy nor the heroes of the *Zhuangzi* can or want to be role models. Dandyism is basically individualism and can never become a collective identity. Above, I mentioned yuppies and hippies; now the analysis will be directed to snobs and revolutionaries. Role models must be authentic or sincere, which is impossible for the dandy. Brummell was much imitated, but this does not mean that he was seen as a role model. Being a role model bears an ethical input whereas being merely imitated does not. In general, ethical people like to be role models. Correspondingly, the snob is flattered when people see him as a role model, but the Daoist and the dandy find that any following of a role is too similar to following a rule. Especially as "aestheticists," they are necessarily skeptical of role models, because in art, role models are less highly regarded than in the realm of ethics. Did Picasso want to be imitated? It might have flattered his ego, but he must have clearly seen that it would not have led to better artistic productions. Insistence on roles, rules, and names can quickly become self-righteous and create snobbish behaviors. Playing roles also creates false sincerity, and Daoism saw this tendency in Confucianism. Commitment to one's own excellence can be "reverted into a violent and moral frenzy," write Moeller and D'Ambrosio (2017, 182). However, the Daoist criticism of Confucian role models does not imply that the Confucian roles should be replaced with Daoist ones; it rather suggests "the abandonment of narrative and ideological idolizations altogether" (Moeller 2020b, 8), which Bulwer-Lytton's character Pelham perfectly well summarizes: "Life is a comedy and its rules need to be followed, but one should avoid enthusiasm" (1840, 14). Second, being a role model implies that one has a role to play. Next, one needs to be *entitled* to play a certain role and then also be committed to the role.

A typical representative of a role model is the revolutionary. Brummell was what would today be called a "fashionista," that is, somebody who was revolutionizing fashion; yet he did not seem to be committed to a fashion revolution. He had imitators, but this is not enough for the instigation of a revolution. Revolutions need ideals, leaders, and role models embodying these ideals. Revolutions are not pushed through by imitating certain people. The dandy has no ideal but is simply "against" and never in favor of something. Like Zhuangzi, who, according to Victor Mair, "does not proffer answers to unasked questions nor offer solutions to hypothetical problems" (1983a, 98), the dandy does not make any suggestions about what should be done. By acting this way, he avoids the snobbism typical of revolutionaries. Many revolutionaries are snobs, even though the revolutionary snob tends to advertise himself as an antisnob whose aim is the inversion of all existing structures.[15] For Barbey, dandyism is therefore "a peculiar tyranny that never asked for a revolution" ("singuliere tyrannie qui ne revoltait pas," 1897, 53). In other words, dandyism is the state of being in revolt without having an ideal on which to base a real revolution. Camus brought this to a point saying that "the dandy is a man who is permanently *revolté* but who does not ask for a revolution" (1965, 672). Being in revolt becomes an end in itself, and especially with Baudelaire, dandyism enters the stage of "rebellious dandyism." It contains irony, which is contrary to the revolutionary spirit, as Van Norden points out in his discussion of the *Zhuangzi*: there is probably no one "who played a significant role in any major progressive social movement who was an ironist" (2016, 17).

Some want to see in dandyism a conservative revolution protesting against the leveling effect of egalitarian principles. England in the eighteenth century did indeed see such public resentment (see Ribeiro 2002). The Regency era was a renaissance of high culture, and the Restoration that took place in France at the same time *could* be seen as a sort of counter-revolution. However, we do not find the dandy occupying any well-defined position in any of these political landscapes; these revolutions or counter-revolutions would, at least, have required the ideal of "the perfect gentleman," which Brummell never incorporated. He was too provocative, which makes him progressive and even anti–high culture. Dandyism symbolizes a clear break with the old aesthetics. Though Brummell *somehow* embodies the ideals of the upper class, he directs his mockery precisely at this class. Later dandyism brought art into the streets, cafes, and malls through the culture of the flâneur; but then again, as a bourgeois parvenu, Brummell *could* symbolize the decline of aristocratic culture, but he is also seen as the symbol of its last flourishing.

The dandy does not preach feudal or preindustrial values because such commitments would only lead to the idolization of excellence.

Nor is he entirely against it. The dandy is thus the real revolutionary without enthusiasm, which brings him close to the Daoist spirit. He has what the *Zhuangzi* calls a "mind without fixed opinions" (6, 229–231).

The Way to go (the Dao) should not be impaired by a fixed mind, although revolutionaries tend to do precisely this. Commitments lead to the idolization of excellence. Therefore, the dandy's and the Daoist's alternative is "genuine pretending." The dandy's convictions are never rigid. The skepticism of Ward's Tremaine is said to be "solely of the head, while genuine religion and natural piety, had, at least, originally possessed his heart" (1825, 286). Count d'Orsay, the famous French dandy and artist, had a charm that his contemporaries described as "smooth and adaptable" rather than rigid (Moers 1960, 206). In parallel, according to Moeller and D'Ambrosio, only genuine pretending allows one to "operate smoothly in the midst of a social environment full of hypocrisies" (2017, 181). Brummell does not even play a role but lets his dandylike existence emerge through miming or genuine pretending, which is why he did not become an (ideologically and ethically inspired) role model but a model of imitation at best. His "role"—if there was one—could only be spelled out in negative terms by distinguishing his behavior from that of others. Irony plays an important part here, as will be shown in the next section.

Homo Ludens

The dandy has no essence but is only skillful play. He plays himself, and he plays it without ever being a dandy, that is, without ever manifesting something like the essence of a dandy. The dandy hates uniforms because only decadent imitators and snobs wear the dandylike uniform. Some snobs believe they have discovered the essence of dandyism and disregard the fact that dandyism merely exists as a style without rules. They do not understand that in order to join this pure existence, all essences and rules need to be forgotten. Barbey summed up this process of forgetting: "If he wants to, a dandy can spend ten hours to prepare his outfit, but when it's finished, he forgets about it" (1895, 311n22).[16] This comes close to the ecstatic intuition that the Daoist sage obtains when sitting in oblivion. Forgetfulness (*wang* 忘) is a recurring theme in the *Zhuangzi* and is often used to challenge conventional moral norms. In the *Qiwulun* (chap. 12) there is an account of a master who practices the meditation of forgetfulness.[17] The Daoist simply forgets about norms. The forgetfulness goes even further as it concerns the forgetting of the self. Daoist and dandyist agencies most clearly overlap. Real flow of action can only be achieved through forgetting about one's own person, just as shoes only really fit when one forgets about them: "To be unthought of by the foot that wears it is the fitness of a shoe; to be unthought of by the waist is the fitness of a girdle" (*Zhuangzi*, "The Full Understanding of Life," chap. 19).

The action of flow is dependent on forgetting. Several game theorists could be cited testifying that this paradoxical fusion of knowing and forgetting, of consciousness and unconsciousness, of seriousness and nonseriousness, is essential for the existence of such a peculiar phenomenon like play. In other words, play is always genuine pretending. Johan Huizinga, the classic writer on play, notes in his *Homo Ludens* that the player of the game "knows perfectly well that he is only pretending" (1970, 18). However, contrary to the *simple* pretender, the genuine pretender does not want to turn the game into something authentic. He will take the game as seriously *as if* it were real but never believes that it could be real and has no desire to make it real. Huizinga explains this double consciousness, which simultaneously affirms seriousness and nonseriousness and thus circumvents any sincerity, through the example of a four-year old boy "sitting at the front of a row of chairs, playing 'trains.' As [his father] hugged him the boy said; 'Don't kiss the engine, Daddy, or the carriages won't think it's real'" (27). The child is seriously playing but he is not sincere. He is genuinely pretending in the Daoist-dandyist sense. Precisely by signaling that he does not believe in the illusion, he *pretends* to believe in the illusion. In the moment he declares he is not aware that he is playing a game, he shows he is aware of it. Were he really not aware of it, he could not have said he was not. For these reasons, Victor Mair calls Zhuangzi a *homo ludens*, a "man the player," and believes that *homo ludens* freely and joyously engages in *you* because a "playful man is ever shifting and roaming" (1983a, 86).

The dandy founds his existence on such a play, too. Melissa Knox (2017) finds that *Homo ludens* is the philosophy of Oscar Wilde because the idea of serious play is the guiding force of Wilde's life. Serious play is nothing other than genuine pretending. *Homo ludens* "refuses to be pegged down by any given stereotype. We may say that the *raison d'être* of *Homo ludens* is to stand in a perpetually antithetical relationship to fixed categories" (Mair 1983a, 86) or—and this has become the trademark of dandyism—to be "playful and without transcendence" (Aman 2015, 8). Playing is not a religious ritual evoking a transcendent god but is self-sufficient, though also constantly representing—in a symbolic fashion—more than merely itself. This feature is prominent in dandyism, and it is also present in various branches of Eastern thought. Theodor and Yao describe the Zhuangzi and the Gaudiya Vaisnava, a Hindu devotional tradition, in precisely such terms: "In both traditions, play and experience of play have the following features: naturalness, transformative aspect, risky nature, freedom that it offers, being lost within it, its effortlessness, and its self-representative nature. As such, play embodies an irrational nature, suggesting that humans are more than rational creatures. It connects humans to the cosmic while simultaneously subsuming and transcending wisdom and folly" (2013, xvi).

Chapter 8

The "Ethics" of Coolness

Balance and Indifference

The kindred positions of Daoism and dandyism can be further clarified by referring to the concept of "coolness." Coolness, as it is known and appreciated across the world today, emerged in African American culture and is linked to peculiar forms of ethics and aesthetics. In principle, to be cool means to remain calm even under stress (see Botz-Bornstein 2011). Initially, coolness had been developed as a behavioral attitude practiced by Black men in the United States during slavery. Slavery necessitated the cultivation of special defense mechanisms, which employed emotional detachment and irony. After slavery, during segregation, these mechanisms were reinforced.

Like dandyism and Daoism, American cool culture arose in conditions of rapid social change. The slavery-supporting Confederate system of the American South disintegrated, and the loosening of traditional structures produced a value crisis. In this situation, a cool attitude helped former slaves cope with exploitation—or even just made it possible to walk the streets at night. In coolness we thus find both the emotional restraint and the free-flowing playfulness that we have observed in *wuwei*. Slingerland, in his book on *wuwei*, cites the jazz saxophonist Charlie Parker who was said to have advised aspiring musicians, "Don't play the saxophone. Let it play you" (2014, 1). Charlie Parker is a popular symbol of African American coolness, and the *Zhuangzi*'s recommendations to having a successful life by according it with *de*, concords to a large extent with a definition of coolness that African American jazz musicians or other protagonists of cool would have agreed with: "Complete relaxation and freedom from external concerns perfect your *de* and make you formidable, conveying a confidence and ease that makes others think twice before messing with you" (155). The idea that you are not actively playing the saxophone but are passive and "let[ting] the saxophone play you," seems to be paralleled by the once pronounced perception that a dandy does not tie his tie but that he is "tied by the tie" (Scaraffia 1981, 78).

According to Pountain and Robins, the driving force of cool is a "passive resistance to the work ethic through personal style" and a "defense mechanism against the depression and anxiety induced by a highly competitive society" (Pountain and Robins 2000, 41, 158). Dandyism is founded on similar premises. African American coolness has been compared with Stoicism, Epicureanism, and Cynicism (see Shusterman 2003, 425), and Barbey declared that dandyism introduces "antique calm among our modern agitations" (1897, 43n†; 1879, 28n1), which may as well be another description of "staying cool." Charles Stanhope, father of the abovementioned Lady Hester Stanhope and Brummell's friend, used the word "coolness" already in 1844 when writing that Brummell "had wit as well as humor and drollery, and the most perfect coolness and self-possession" (Brown 2006). In the same year, that is, four years after Brummell's death, the anonymous author of an article in *Blackwood's Edinburgh Magazine*, identified as the key to dandyism the capacity of being "chill as the poles to the indulgences of others" (Anonymous 1844). Brummell has repeatedly been described as cool in a way that comes amazingly close to present aesthetic codes of coolness: "The gray ray that transpired from his languidly half-closed eyelids knew how to wonderfully express superiority, such as irony, hostility or indifference" (Scaraffia 1981, 12). The dandy wanted to "create surprise by remaining impassive" ("produire la surprise en gardant l'impassibilité" (Barbey, 1897, 43; 1879, 28), and both Barbey and Baudelaire stress that the dandy must *astonish* without ever being astonished himself. The emotional detachment and irony necessary for this behavior are also the cornerstones of cool behavior. Kelly reports that "Brummell's notorious 'coolness' allowed his early formidable success as a gambler" (2006, 284).

American coolness also comes close to the dandyist pose as it fights bourgeois work ethics and a drab, tedious, and mediocre mainstream culture by inventing a strong personal style. There is, in coolness, a rebellion; yet the result is not a straightforward and formal ethics but rather a complex mode of aestheticism that remains based on the principle of seduction and transgression, or, perhaps more precisely, of seduction *through* transgression. In all this, ambiguity and emotional balance remain important: cool behavior should never be *too* cool.

Chris Fraser (2011) explains that the Daoist must be "free from strong, disruptive emotions, whether pleasant, positive ones such as joy, or unpleasant, negative ones such as sorrow" (99). What Fraser calls the "Zhuangist 'Virtuoso View' of emotion" (99), is in full agreement with the idea of coolness. Like the cool person, the Daoist has the phlegm necessary for balanced play. For example, a tennis player "who has just scored a point or committed an error does not dwell on it and may experience only a weak emotional response, if any" (100). Cool behavior leads to *de*, which has been translated as "virtuosity, power, potency, virtue, vitality, charisma, adroitness, proficiency, and capacity" (100). For Slingerland, "*De* is the attractive vibe—a combination of body language, microemotions, tone of voice, general appearance—kicked off by people who are honest, sincere, self-confident, and relaxed. It's attractive because it's a relatively hard-to-fake signal of a trustworthy cooperator" (2014, 192).

Dandyism has often been depicted as cool in the sense of cold, which is related to the above-described blasé attitude: "A dandy (. . .) may even suffer pain, but in the latter case he will keep smiling, like the Spartan under the bite of the fox," writes Baudelaire.[1] Dandyism is most often "provocative in its very coldness" (1986a, 28; 1885, 94), but this coldness, or this state of being blasé, is rather complex, which becomes clear in Baudelaire's further descriptions. First, Baudelaire renders the blasé attitude of the dandy as an aesthetic quality, which brings it close to the modern notion of coolness. Being blasé is not an ethical statement but a matter of aesthetic play. Second, Baudelaire relates coolness to fire, which crystallizes an ambiguity: "The distinguishing characteristic of the dandy's beauty consists, above all, in an air of coldness (*l'air froid*), which comes from an unshakable determination not to be moved; you might call it a latent fire which hints at itself (*qui se fait deviner*), and which could, but chooses not to burst into flame" (1986a, 29; 1885, 96). Baudelaire goes even further by attributing a strong amount of empathy to the dandy and even accredits him with a degree of empathy toward social and moral problems. The dandy has an "understanding of the entire moral mechanism of this world; with another part of his nature, however, the dandy aspires to insensitivity" (1986a, 27; 1885, 93). This means that he *does have* empathy but that he forces himself to observe the world from a distance. Baudelaire's life is the proof that dandyism does not avoid suffering. Consequently, for Scaraffia, there is "nothing more sensitive than the insensitivity that the dandy intends to achieve" (1981, 53; my trans.).

Such an attitude comes close to a Daoist understanding of the cosmos as a phenomenon with transcendental appeal. In Daoism, "understanding of the entire moral mechanism of this world" leads to a distanced, aesthetic perception. According to Fraser, the Daoist virtuoso "sees everything, including his own life, as part of 'the same' unified cosmic process and will hold no preferences regarding the outcome of changing circumstances. Such an agent will thus be emotionally unperturbed by any change whatsoever" (Fraser 2011, 104). The cosmos is the Great Dao, and it is perceived from a distance with the help of a "wandering" view. It recognizes particularities as contingencies that are subordinated to the flow of a broader totality. In a similar vein, Baudelaire states that the dandy is the "lover of universal life" and that he is "the artist, man of the world, man of the crowd, and child" (1986a, 5). This means that his existence is defined by universality, which permits him to view details from a distance.

The *Daodejing* recommends one not use weapons, suggesting instead that staying calm is best (see Moeller 2006, 78). However, this does not imply a simple decrease of "heated" emotions. Nor is this stance identical to the Confucian harmonization of emotions that societies are expected to cultivate by encouraging every individual to play their role properly. The Daoist sage-ruler is emotionally "cool," but this coolness has a peculiar philosophical grounding. Much of what Moeller says about "genuine pretending" is contained in the idea of coolness that we have in mind when we say that somebody is "a cool person." Though rarely analyzed in everyday life, the qualities attributed to such a "cool person" are complex. Coolness is not about Aristotle's Golden Mean: the cool person is in a state of mind in which the felt emotions do simply not affect their actions or their way of being. Moeller and D'Ambrosio express precisely this quality as a primordial Daoist principle: "*Immunity to emotional afflictions does not mean being immune to feelings altogether but being immune to getting hurt by what one feels*" (2018, 175, the authors' italics).

McCormack detects the same pattern in Oscar Wilde's dandyism, which he explains through the Daoist principle of *wuqing* (無情) or nonfeeling.[2] Nonfeeling in dandyism "is not necessarily a lack of feeling, but the ability to step aside from conventional emotional reactions into a larger, arguably an aesthetic, view of things" (McCormack 2017, 93).

There is no identification with emotions but not because emotions would not exist but rather because there is no identity. Nor are the emotions considered authentic. They are not fake either, but they appear within a game of genuine pretending, which changes their status. Coolness restrains emotions, but a maximum of emotionlessness does not bring about a maximum of coolness. On the contrary, coldness leads to extremism and is thus "uncool." Both hot-headedness and coldness try to express authentic feelings and seek to engender authentic actions. In other words, they are too sincere to be pure play. In this game of coolness, nothing should be taken personally. Fraser, too, insists that "the Daoist 'virtuoso,' though having an empty heart-mind, is not 'utterly emotionless'" (Fraser 2011, 100). Again, this does not mean that he should have "just the right amount of emotions." Coolness is possible only because there is no identity that would be willing to identify with certain emotions. Coolness presupposes an emptying of the I or of the self.

Cool Idiocy

One could also say that what is necessary for coolness is a certain amount of "idiotization." The person who has too much knowledge about his own coolness and about how it can be attained, and who possibly supports these convictions with various theories or statistics, is not cool. The skills of the Dao-hero (who *is* cool) cannot be expressed through algorithms. The snob exemplifies such a self-consciously "cool" person. Those who think too much (about themselves) while playing the game of coolness (or any game) is pretentious. In order to avoid snobbism, coolness calls for what Moeller names "idiotic irony." For Moeller, the Daoist sage is neither a skeptic nor a relativist but rather "the ultimate simpleton, a perfect idiot. (. . .) The cultivation process of the sage is supposed to (re)turn him into a complete idiot, someone who does not have any particular mental contents, no plans, no agenda, no volition, no personal interests or inclinations" (2008, 118). This perfectly reflects the dandyist phlegm and indifference just as it does the proper functioning of the cool person. As soon as the cool person is too aware of their own coolness, the effect turns into ridicule. The conclusion is that acting cool without knowing what coolness is brings the best results.

All this has further consequences. The cool person should never be authentic in the sense of having the perfect mastery of coolness. Some lack of perfection—due to idiocy—is always cooler. Authenticity in coolness is impossible anyway because, by definition, coolness is *always* about pretending. Any striving for the authentically cool is "uncool." Nor is coolness sincere, not even in the sense of believing in the authenticity of one's own coolness. Coolness should avoid what Ervin Goffman has called the deceptive nature of "false fronts." In self-presentations, "the performer can be fully taken in by his own act; he can be sincerely convinced that the impression of reality which he staffs is the real reality" (1959, 17). By contrast, coolness is not a reality to be believed in; it would be uncool to believe that one is "really" cool. Yet, at the same time, self-presenters do not perceive their own acting as fake; and only this ambiguity lets their acting appear natural. In other words, the "natural" act comes about through the temporary forgetting of what is real and what is pretended. To obtain this, it is necessary to not care whether one's cool behavior is authentic or not. The flow, or what Fraser calls the "virtuoso view" in Daoism, depends on this act of forgetting, too. There is, in Daoism, the idea that one should not be "all-too Daoist," which suggests, according to Moeller and D'Ambrosio, "paradoxical models of skillfulness through disowning skills" (2018, 162). This perfectly echoes the idea that it is "uncool" to be too cool or that it is uncool to openly strive for coolness. "Deliberately striving for quietude and freeing oneself from vain thoughts would necessitate affirming and clinging to quietude and vain thoughts, which is the opposite of 'no thought,'" writes Li Zehou (2019, 211).

It goes without saying that it would be vain to look for any "correctness" in coolness. The dandy pays attention to etiquette but pays even more attention to improvisation and surprise. It is uncool to follow any supposed rules of dandyism (see Botz-Bornstein 1995). It is also uncool to follow any supposed rules of cool because that presupposes that an authentic cool exists. Any authentic, that is, "non-pretended" cool, is uncool. Authentic cool is the forced and "trying too hard" cool, which is often obtained by enthusiastically following rules. In art this formulaic and naively idealist quality is called kitsch, and both dandyism and Daoism destroy kitsch. Balzac's explicit antikitsch principles have been mentioned in chapter 5, and according to Baudelaire, dandyism's purpose is to "destroy triviality" (1986a, 28; 1885, 94). Kitsch is also incompatible with Daoist principles as it is the exaggeration of certain properties, or the insistence on certain qualities for their own sake. As mentioned, the Dao is empty and shapeless and therefore opposed to kitsch by definition.

Being *too* cool and trying too hard will necessarily end up as kitsch. Kitsch is fake, but this does not mean that cool is authentic. Cool overcomes the authentic-fake dichotomy through genuine pretending. The "medicinal effect" that Moeller mentions for genuine pretending is due to the insight that identity or authenticity cannot be reached and that genuine pretending is the best option available for having a good life: "Ultimately, an insight into the fact that identity is genuinely pretended is supposed to have a medicinal effect and allow for social and individual 'ease' (*you*)" (2020). At the same time, cool is not pretending to be cool; it is *being* cool but in play mode, which is genuine pretending. Saying that the cool person is not self-conscious about his or her coolness while acting does not mean that person has no awareness of his or her actions; that person simply does not have an awareness of them *as cool actions*. The cool man is the Daoist Perfect Man who *does* nothing but leaves his actions to nature. Cool actions are flowing, and any knowledge or self-awareness would only harm the flow.

All three, the dandy, the Daoist sage, and the cool person, switch off the "knowing mode." There is, of course, some irony in this "non-knowing." Coolness means to remain calm under stress. However, the person who stays cool in face of an imminent danger and rescues others from a burning building is probably "actually" scared; she simply does not show it and manages to stay calm. Were she really not scared, we would *not* say that she is cool. This is a further illustration of the idea of "idiotic irony." Cool people force themselves to ignore the disasters that *could* happen in this dangerous situation, and only for this reason can they act in a cool fashion. Still, these cool people only *act* cool. They know about the danger but pretend not to know while they are acting. Should they really not know about it, they would not be cool but a real idiot. Only idiotic *irony* produces coolness.

The pattern becomes even clearer when we look at the initial context of coolness. During slavery, overt provocation of white people by Black people was punishable by death. Provocation had to remain inoffensive, and any level of serious intent had to be disguised or suppressed. A Black person venturing into an area off limits at night could be approached and threatened by a white person. Overt resistance would have been dangerous, whereas mere submission would have signified a loss of dignity. In this context, neither sincerity nor authenticity but "idiotic irony" represented the most viable alternative; and it created the now famous ethics and aesthetics of coolness. For example, the Black person could say: "I did not know that this area is off limits." This idiotic—and ironic—claim could have been a cool way out of the dangerous situation, especially when enacted calmly. Coolness is the paradoxical fusion of submission and subversion, which always requires irony, and it functions particularly well through idiotic irony. Cool irony is to not insist, in this particular moment, on the ethical "I know that am right and that you are wrong" position. By switching off the knowing mode, cool irony (or cool idiocy) refrains from solving the conflict but keeps the contradictions intact. However, momentarily, the situation has been brought under control. Insisting on correctness would probably have yielded the worst outcome. Cool behavior also perfectly overlaps with what has been said in chapter 2 about the dandy's state of being *revolté* and that I have called "polite incorrectness." The dandy, too, develops a playful "rule following attitude" that combines the contradictory forces of submission and transgression, and Daoism perfectly duplicates this behavior. Similar to the abovementioned cool slave, Zhuangzi's strategy "not only aims at ensuring safety in potentially dangerous encounters with authority, but also the avoidance of 'authenticating' authority," write Moeller and D'Ambrosio (2018, 1).

Most important for cool behavior is that nothing is authentic or sincere, neither one's own self nor the self of the other. We are in revolt but within a playful context. Only this guarantees survival. Tyranny and oppression are self-centered attitudes, and genuine pretending deflates them by emptying the action of any connotations of authenticity and sincerity. To confront sincerity with sincerity would lead to the opposite result. In chapter 4 of the *Zhuangzi* (Man in the world), Yan Hui plans to meet the dangerous tyrant Wei. It turns out that when facing violent, destructive, and dangerous social powers or evils, genuine pretending is more efficient than moral sincerity. To wit, Moeller and D'Ambrosio write: "Genuine pretending helps to build immunity against these powers, which are, in various degrees, found everywhere. This immunity is twofold. On the one hand, one becomes less vulnerable by avoiding direct confrontations with these powers—one has a better chance of eschewing execution" (2017, 146–47). Identical recommendations follow from the abovementioned slavery situation.

From a Daoist point of view, cool irony undertakes a "chaotification" of what, from an ethicist perspective, appears to be a right/wrong situation and relaxes the tension, albeit without entirely canceling the conflict. This temporary equalization of things does not lead to relativism. On the contrary, insistence on relativism could invite a new conflict. Relativism is never a cool option be it only because it leaves little room for irony and play. Relativism is very much related to PC, whereas coolness deals with contradictions through play.

Both submission and revolt tend to end up as kitsch. In the Deep South situation that has been described, any striving for moral excellence or correctness and any self-righteous insistence on right and wrong would most probably have led to a tragic and pathetic end. Therefore, drama had to be avoided at any cost, and it was best avoided through play. Ethics, right and wrong, true and false, or correct and incorrect should never be used as transcendental, otherworldly categories. Instead, one should accept that such categories only emerge in concrete contexts where they must be dealt with playfully. In real life, that is, the life that we play, everything (including these categories) is transmitted to a transformative process, which is also why many of life's "dramas" are not as dramatic as they appear to be. Looking at life this way does mean one is being relativistic. Self-transformation (*tu hua* 獨化) has already been mentioned in chapter 1. In Daoism, transformation is *hua*, and "Zhuangzi conceives of the world playfully because its *hua* has the lightness of the everyday for him, rather than the heaviness of 'fate'" (Crandell 1983, 108). The lightness creates an aesthetics and ethics of coolness with dedramatized and ironic qualities. The opposite, the reproduction of the drama of life with "real" feelings and the pretension to be authentic and sincere, leads to kitsch dramas. One problem is that real and authentic feelings quickly become sentimental, which increases the effect of the dramatic.

It has been said above that the dandy is camp because, according to Susan Sontag, "to perceive Camp in objects and persons is to understand Being-as-Playing-a-Role" (1982, 280). According to Sontag, the aesthetics of camp suggests a concept of the self that is always performative and transforming. In other words, camp dedramatizes kitsch through irony, and this is precisely what also happens in dandyism, in coolness, as well as in Daoism. For Sontag, camp and tragedy are antithetical because camp puts "irony over tragedy" (287). Camp-dandyism might maintain an awareness of the tragic sense of all human proceedings, but it transforms the tragedy of life into play. It deconstructs true and false as well as authentic and fake. As a result, real drama is no longer possible, which has an effect on the perception of rules and norms. The dandy's life never gains a dramatic dimension because he has decided that rules or norms do not matter. It is not that he has decided to break these rules: they simply do not matter.

Ethics and Authenticity

What does it mean that one should be cool but not "too cool?" Does it mean that one should be moderately cool? No, coolness is more complex. A cool person should never act as if coolness is an ideal or a virtue that can be straightforwardly aspired to. If coolness were an ideal, we would probably have more cool idealists, but reality suggests otherwise. Very few of the coolest rappers are idealists, and it even appears that idealism can be very uncool. Idealists are more like Wilde's philanthropist busybodies, whom he depicts as uncool. Idealism is predominantly ethics-based and therefore has no role to play in enactments of coolness. Most self-righteous people (religious fanatics, neo-Darwinists, creationists, but also convinced atheists) would not pass the coolness test, and Daoists and Zen Buddhists would probably have bashed all four. Li Zehou quotes the story of Chan Master Kesong who was asked by a student about the right path in life. The Master said: "Be a killer and an arsonist" (Li 2019: 107). He did not say "become a philanthropist."

The acquisition of cool should not lead to an *authentic* form of cool since that would simply be *too* cool. Cool *cannot* be authentic, and it is therefore surprising that coolness could so often be seen as a form of identity therapy, enabling suppressed populations to escape from the fakeness of their existence. Norman Mailer depicts, in his celebrated *The White Negro* (1957), coolness as a higher form of authenticity offered to oppressed Black people as well as to all those who are socially misled. For Mailer's young males and rebellious criminals, coolness is the authentic surplus added to their otherwise boring existences. They look for authenticity and find it in coolness. However, Mailer's world of purely masculine coolness is not what the dandy or the Daoist aspire to: even if it is only because his concept of cool is too "revolutionary." Still there is, even in Mailer's text, a perhaps unexpected insight into the ambiguous nature of coolness when he writes: "Therefore, men are not seen as good or bad (that they are good-and-bad is taken for granted) but rather each man is glimpsed as a collection of possibilities (. . .) and this is the dynamic, provided the particular character can swing at the right time" (14). Here Mailer recognizes that coolness transcends all ethical appeals.

People who see coolness as a value tend to understand cool as an ethical or moral concept, which is a misunderstanding because coolness is basically amoral. The most unethical person can be cool, whereas the most ethical person can be uncool. Coolness is simply the right action at the right time. The *Zhuangzi*'s charismatic criminals like Robber Zhi, outlaws, or those people who wear marks of previous legal punishment, are most often cool. Coolness does not care about ethics simply because it is spontaneously enacted and not fully rationally controlled. As it is instantaneously created, coolness cannot even be called a habit (an ethos). It is for this reason that it also necessarily transgresses ethical categories such as authenticity and sincerity. One cannot be "sincerely cool" or "authentically cool" but only be genuinely cool. Using coolness as an ideology or an ethical guideline spoils the concept of coolness simply because in certain situations, it is cooler not to be cool and better to proceed to nonaction rather than action. Any concept of the "authentic cool" is bound to become a parody of cool sooner or later; or, in the realm of aesthetics, it will become kitsch.

Ziporyn describes this same mechanics of avoidance of ethical values in Daoism when writing that "the deliberate commitment to a set of values ironically obstructs the actual emergence of the valued things. To produce a desired value, one renounces all deliberate values and allows the spontaneous preevaluative process at the basis of all action, virtues and things: "nonaction" (Ziporyn 2012, 183). Normal actions are utilitarian or ethically (and sometimes aesthetically) motivated whereas coolness must emerge "naturally" through play. Within this play it is not supposed to have any ethical connotations and not even—though this is difficult to understand—outspoken aesthetic connotations. The straightforward ambition to beautify leads to kitsch. Beauty, like coolness, must emerge naturally. Also, whenever we "do something," there is the danger of idealizing our actions in terms of excellence. Even when we "only" pretend, the dangers of pride and arrogance do not disappear and might become even more imminent. The *Zhuangzi* argues that "over-commitment to (. . .) roles typically results in conceit in the case of privileged roles (such as ruler) or in despair in the case of subordinated roles (such as wife)" (Moeller 2020). Contrary to the snob, the dandy—or the Zhuangzist man who falls off carts—will never be conceited, proud, or "over the top" (kitsch). Similarly, the style of jazz musician Lester Young was credible mostly because, as Dinerstein writes, "Young was neither proud nor ashamed" (Dinerstein 1999, 240). Most often, exaggerated pride is followed by ridicule, which is why the cool person reduces pride to nothingness. The other extreme, being ashamed or embarrassed, leads to similarly dramatic results, and the cool person empties himself of shame, too.

Trying to play one's roles "excellently" can easily become pretentious. "Doing nothing" is thus the only option, as the example of dandyism demonstrates better than anything else. Given the absurd character of so many of Brummell's actions, he was constantly running the risk of looking ridiculous. However, according to Barbey, "Brummell was never ridiculous" ("le ridicule ne l'atteignait jamais," 1897, 76; 1879, 51). The reason is that one can only be ridiculous when doing *something*. And one can only be ridiculous when one is—at least to some extent—sincere about what one is doing. Avoiding sincerity (which is so closely linked to pride) prevents embarrassment and ridicule. Too much sincerity leads to kitsch, which is why the dandy attempts to simply *be*, through play, without committing himself to a purpose. The aforementioned example of Molière's Alceste demonstrates best that too much sincerity becomes ridiculous. Baudelaire even noted the "difficult art [of] being sincere without being absurd" (1986a, 9). The best alternative is genuine pretending, which means not to *do* (with a purpose) but to *play* without engagement. It means to play seriously without taking one's own person seriously.

The topic of coolness can also be linked to the previously mentioned theme of the "game in which the winner loses," which Sartre sees as the existential model of dandyism. In this game, the player has been disowned of the victory beforehand because it has been decided that he loses when he wins and that he wins when he loses. He is thus forced to stay cool no matter what happens. Such a game prevents both pride and embarrassment, and the winner cannot be proud because, in the end, he lost. Nor can he be embarrassed. This strange game bears a profound link with dandyism. It can even be seen as symbolizing Brummell's own life, which Marie-Christine Natta has summarized as "the story of seduction and failure." It is this double aspect of Brummell's life, and not the straightforward success story of a careerist, that attracted Barbey and many others (Natta 1989, 26–27). Were the dandy's life mere success, it would be kitsch. At the same time, Brummell's life story is not one of dramatic ups and downs, which would be kitsch, too. The aesthetics of cool advocates a dedramatized quality. Sartre's peculiar game shows that winning is cool but that being ready to do anything to win is not. Of course, the eternal loser is no cool person, either, but the cool player is rather the one who is indifferent to winning or losing. For Mocchia, "A lost battle is always more chic than a crushing victory." Mocchia even speaks of the "elegance of the vanquished" (2019, 63).

Nothing is less chic than fighting for an ideal, and the dandy gambles merely in order to beat boredom. Losing and still keeping a straight face is one of the coolest behaviors one can imagine, which is why the young English aristocracy had been explicitly taught such behavior at Eton: the pupils "never breathe a word about their loss. It was in order to be Man, in order to be a person of endurance that they risked hereditary acres so desperately," writes T. H. White (1950, 68). The purpose of playing is playing and not winning, and playing only in order to win is uncool.

In a Kantian "aesthetic" sense, the game should have no exterior purpose because if it does, there is the danger that the players will become proud or conceited. But then again, being proud or conceited is not an ethical default. Being ridiculous is not unethical either, it is simply uncool. The game in which the loser wins is thus a game in which no player is striving to be excellent, which is precisely why it is a cool game. The "loser wins" game prevents players from becoming extreme, fanatic, or kitsch, though at the same time, it remains a "real" game. The "loser wins" game has nothing to do with the philanthropist charity game in which the winner gives his gain to the loser, either. This is rather the game that Oscar Wilde criticized. In a society permeated by ethics and "philanthropist busybodies," the loser is to be rewarded, too. The loser is permitted to win because we are supposed to have "sympathy with failures," and "prizes should always be given on moral grounds to those who come in last in the race" (Wilde 1919, 179). Both Zhuangzi and Wilde are against all competitiveness, and this is perfectly well expressed in Sartre's "the loser wins" game. Wilde writes in his Zhuangzi review: "It is the race that he objects to; and as for active sympathy, which has become the profession of so many worthy people in our own day, he thinks that trying to make others good is as silly an occupation as 'beating a drum in a forest in order to find a fugitive'" (1919, 179). In the "the loser wins" game, no ranking is possible. The competitiveness of those who distribute names and titles is deconstructed through the absurdity that this game establishes. As mentioned, Daoism also holds the conviction that one should not be "all-too Daoist," which suggests, according to Moeller and D'Ambrosio, "paradoxical models of skillfulness through disowning skills" (2018, 162). The people who are playing the "loser wins" game are playing like idiots, and this is precisely what makes them cool. The conclusion is that both moralists (who are always trying to win their cases) and totally immoral people (who are equally always trying to win) are uncool.

Cool behavior and cool aesthetics do not look for perfection but accept the mismatch between form (or what Daoists would call the "name") and content. To be cool means that my subjective feeling is not required to match my outward expression. Any *total* overlap of form and content leads to kitsch. The kitsch man is not the Daoist Perfect Man but rather the All-Too-Perfect Man. Kitsch is an "all-too perfect" art that spells out everything (good, bad, beautiful, ugly) too clearly.

"Flow" and "Pure Experience"

Many scholars[3] have seen similarities between the *Zhuangzi*'s idea of flow and the famous concept of flow developed by the psychologist Mihaly Csíkszentmihályi. Csíkszentmihályi describes how during an "optimal experience" of flow, people feel "strong, alert, in effortless control, unselfconscious, and at the peak of their abilities" (1990, 1). Csíkszentmihályi himself analyzes in his book *Flow: The Psychology of Optimal Experience* (1990) the story of the butcher Ding by concentrating on the notion of *you*, which he calls a "total autotelic experience" (150–51, 269). *Telos* means goal, and autotelic means "goal in itself." The autotelic experience is thus "an end in itself. Even if initially undertaken for other reasons, the activity that consumes us becomes intrinsically rewarding" (67). Flow is an optimally focused mental state leading to productivity and creativity. There are certainly some resemblances between flow and *you* though in the end, both might not entirely overlap. The problem is, as Csíkszentmihályi points out himself, that the Daoist condition of "forgetfulness" is not contained in his concept of flow, which is still "the result of a conscious attempt to master challenges, [whereas] *you* occurs when the individual gives up conscious mastery" (150). Zhuangzi's flow accentuates forgetfulness of both the self and the goal; but then again, Csíkszentmihályi relativizes this difference because, in his interpretation of the *Zhuangzi*, for butcher Ding, "after all the obvious levels of skill and craft (*chi*) have been mastered, the *you* still depends on the discovery of new challenges (. . .), and on the development of new skills." For this psychologist, skill is not entirely unconscious but emerges from a "gradual focusing of attention on the opportunities for action in one's environment" (151).[4]

Given that so many specialists of Eastern thought have been interested in Csíkszentmihályi's psychologically established concept of flow, it is surprising that another author went comparatively unnoticed: there is some resemblance between *you* and William James's concept of "pure experience." James's "pure experience" has already been absorbed into Eastern philosophy because it strongly influenced the Japanese philosopher Nishida Kitaro in his early years and initiated his unique philosophy of *basho*, which is a "place" determined by nothingness. These thoughts laid the foundation of the famous Kyoto School. Csíkszentmihályi, in his main work on flow, mentions James only once and then only very briefly when talking about the limits of consciousness.[5] Nishida reformulated James's "pure experience" in the context of Zen Buddhism and, along the way, reconceptualized some traditional Japanese ideas by using a Western framework, an approach that would become the trademark of his philosophical style.

In Zen Buddhism, no-mind corresponds to a musician's absorption into music. No-mind is forgetful about the act of playing but, at the same time, it is pure awareness. As has been explained in chapter 3, "The person of no-mind sees the objects of the world as neither real nor unreal, as neither independent substances nor dreams or illusions" (Kasulis 1985, 44). No-mind (*wuxin* 無心) is also important in Daoism as it leads to fluid behavior that does not need to constantly think about correct rules. Nishida thus establishes a connection between no-mind and pure experience.

James developed the idea of pure experience in his *Essays in Radical Empiricism* (1912), which Nishida read immediately after its publication (see Botz-Bornstein 2004, 11–15). For James, empiricism is the antithesis of rationalism, an idea that would become the point of departure of Nishida's analyses of "self-consciousness" in Buddhism and "self-awakening." In pure experience, the ego disappears, action becomes effortless, and a feeling of fullness emerges. Any clinging to the ego would prevent this emergence. Nishida is particularly interested in the fact that James's pure experience is an immediate experience in the sense of a prereflexive experience. It is an experience made in the moment when subject and object are not yet separated, that is, in the moment when the individual's intellect is not yet present to recognize the subject in the form of a subject experiencing an object.

Since it is an experience in which the "I" forgets itself, it must be different from Csíkszentmihályi's flow. From the point of view of pure experience, subjectivity and objectivity are intellectual abstractions, and the division of experience into "consciousness" and "content" is only undertaken by human reason *after the experience* (see James 1912, 9). In the moment they are experienced, these pure experiences are without subjectivity; and only because there is no subjectivity can the perceptions and actions of pure experience become fluid. James's model very much overlaps with the Zen Buddhist and Daoist position described in chapter 3. Zen experience is a state of mind "in which there is no 'I' and no 'self' but only an 'it' which plays" (Toshimitsu 1973, 53).

In Daoism, there is also the idea of a pure presence that ignores the future "in the sense of worries about future stages of existence—such as death, which will only irritate and eventually spoil the enjoyment of pure presence." This pattern emerges from Guo Xiang's commentary on the butterfly dream allegory (see Moeller 2004, 97), which permits us to say that pure experience would take place within this pure presence in which intellect has not yet established different levels of time: "Unlike Western conceptions of eternity, which tend to devalue all that is merely temporal, the Daoist concept of timelessness affirms the realm of temporality and of passing time" (100).

Pure experience is also like the act of miming described in chapter 6 because, strictly speaking, there is no experience of "something" whereas ordinary experience, or what is also called "perceptual experience," always represents an experience *of something*. From the Zen Buddhist point of view, this "something" produces the *illusion* of logic and coherence, but this coherence should not be confused with the coherence of the flow, which is not the flow of something perceived by an ego. In ordinary experience, coherence is established and perceived from a fixed and subjective point of view. In pure experience, coherence depends neither on the experience of a concrete "I" nor of a concrete "what," but it is coherent in and of itself. It therefore comes close to cool actions and to rambling (*you*). There is a nonknowledge of the "what" that is experienced. In Zen *no kenkyu*, Nishida refers to James's statement that newborn babies or humans in a semicoma from drugs, etc., might have "pure experiences" (1912, 93). The reference to the child is telling since in Daoism, too, the child player is seen to be free of all conscious faculties. Even the Daoist ruler is "an infant that does not yet smile" (Moeller 2006, 67). Pure experience in Nishida's understanding is a subject-less state of "spiritual naiveté" that can lead to artistic creativity. Artistic experiences are often "pre-conceptual" in the sense that they are not mastered by a conceptualizing intellect. One can also say that this experience is "cool" because it takes place not only before reasoning but also before feeling. It gives the impression of unfolding itself "all alone," that is, of taking place without any conscious effort, from the part of a subject, to establish a logic or a coherence. Therefore, Ellen Zhang's suggestion to divide "flow" or "you" into preexperiential and postexperiential units is not pertinent. Zhang writes: "How can one give an account of a flow experiences and make an evaluative judgment when he/she is in a state of 'forgetfulness'? It is quite obvious that these experiences are only apprehended after the fact, when one is no longer in flow. My suggestion to solve this dilemma is to make a distinction between [flow] experience itself and the post-experiential account, interpretation and evaluation of that experience" (2019, 81). In Zen Buddhism and Nishida's philosophy, the experiences are precisely not supposed to be apprehended after the fact, which is what gives it the status of coolness.

Coolness against the Ethics of Warmth

Instead of remaining the floating joke that it was initially meant to be, PC became a serious ideology. It was no longer determined by the "cool" irony that it had stood for at its beginnings. It was no longer used for cool play, but its main purpose had become to push society from a cool aesthetic that still knew and recognized play and seduction, to a "warmer" ethics where everything needed be spelled out in terms of rules. I insist on the cool/warm dichotomy because it illustrates something that might not be clear at first sight. PC is not "cool"; on the contrary, it is connected to the "warm" politics of empathy and feeling that had become dominant on the left in the 1970s. PC is the latest development of the "authenticity movement" that has been described in chapter 4. The purpose of the cultural revolutions of the 1960s was to finish with the "cold" conformist postwar society that was still so strongly determined by sincerity. Conservative Western societies had crushed not only the authentic individual but also all possible authentic relationships between individuals. To become expressively authentic and to interact with individuals in equally authentic ways was seen as the "warm" option that would have to be enforced within modern societies that were perceived as cold and heartless. Authenticity was warm whereas the inauthentic self was "cold." The inauthentic person was criticized as distanced, formal, *entfremdet*, and sexually inhibited, whereas the authentic self was venerated as being liberated from all social conditionings and able to go straight toward others to spontaneously embrace them. Fast forward fifty years and we see that the name of the Mediterranean refugee rescue ship *Open Arms* is not random but still firmly inscribed in this culture.

The age of authenticity is the age of warmness, and coolness is seen as the repression of warm feelings. The authentic person also assumes the fullness of their sensuality and sentimental expressions. In the anticool age of warm sentiment, men begin to cry, which is considered the peak of authenticity. One cannot imagine a crying dandy. The dandy, already suspect since the 1970s because of his urban, antinature posture, definitively becomes a negative figure. In a recent master's thesis on dandyism one can find, in the first pages the following: "There are men today whose idiosyncrasies strike us as dandyish: their unrestrained narcissism, their fastidiousness about clothes and personal hygiene, their inclination to alcohol and drug abuse, their eating disorders, their fear and depression problems, their megalomaniac and self-destructive schemes, their sense of failure and a grating void inside, their poor self-image, their incapacity of steady relationships, their subsequent loneliness, their fits of uncontrollable emotions, their manipulative philandering, and their unquenchable thirst for success" (Van Dooren 2006, 2). The original and much more complex concept of coolness that has been presented in the preceding sections is entirely neglected. Dandyism is misrepresented, too, as it is mistakenly linked to the Romantic era when the "fashionable were obliged to present themselves, at first sight, as ill and unhappy; [when] they had to possess something negligent about the person, long nails, a partial beard, not shaved, but allowed to grow a little, neglectfully, during their preoccupation with despair; [when they had] locks of straggling hair; a profound gaze, sublime, errant and fatal." This is how Chateaubriand describes the situation *before* dandyism (1848, 43), whereas Brummell's starched neckcloth and his reassertion of male self-control in the realm of fashion symbolized the reaction *against* melancholic decadence and carelessness of the Romantic Boehme as well as against the overdressed state of Prince George. Melancholy and self-destruction are rather the ways of the fake dandy or the *gagà* (see Mocchia di Coggiola 2016, 6).

Of course, the new "culture of warmth" is not actually new. Already Oscar Wilde sensed the rise of warmth in his Victorian England where people suffered, according to him, from the sordid necessity of living for others. In his "The Soul of Man under Socialism" (1891) Wilde ironically suggests that socialism should relieve us from that obligation. This means that what he resents is not so much the puritanical coldness for which the Victorian age is famous but, as he makes clear in his review of the *Zhuangzi*, the Victorian ethics of (hypocritical) altruism. In ancient China there were "no Humanitarian Societies, no dull lectures about one's duty to one's neighbor" and "there was no chattering about clever men, and no laudation of good men" (Wilde 1919: 180).

Victorian society already presented those features that Christopher Lasch would describe, in the 1970s, as the "victim ethics" of late capitalist societies. In Lasch's time, the term "political correctness" was not yet in use, but his criticism goes in the same direction: "Having overthrown feudalism and slavery and then outgrown its own personal and familial form, capitalism has evolved a new political ideology, welfare liberalism, which absolves individuals of moral responsibility and treats them as victims of social circumstance. It has evolved new modes of social control, which deal with the deviant as a patient and substitute medical rehabilitation for punishment" (Lasch 1979, 218). Wilde's hypocritically altruistic Victorian society has very much evolved into a society of victims and benefactors. Wilde saw Zhuangzi as an alternative, as he found similarities between the morally hyperactive busybodies of his time and the do-gooders described in the Zhuangzi. And he would have criticized the culture of warmth of the 1960s in the same terms. Longxi Zhang links the *Zhuangzi* story of Hundun (Chaos)[6] and his "philanthropist" fellow kings directly to Wilde. Hundun used to invite the kings Shu and Hu from the neighboring empires to his house. One day, Shu and Hu wanted to repay Hundun for his kindness and said, "'Men all have seven orifices for the purpose of seeing, hearing, eating, and breathing, while this (poor) Ruler alone has not one. Let us try and make them for him.' Accordingly they dug one orifice in him every day; and at the end of seven days Chaos (Hundun) died" (*The Normal Course for Rulers and Kings*, chap. 7). Zhang concludes that "for Zhuangzi, as Wilde rightly argued, it is best to leave others alone in their original, natural condition" (L. Zhang 2016, 32). Hu and Shu were showing Hundun a lot of warmth, which was finally destructive.

Initially, one could have thought that the revolutionaries of the 1960s and Wilde would be on the same side of the protest culture spectrum. Both were against an overly sincere morality of the cold bourgeoisie. However, the opposite is the case. Wilde is on the side of coolness, whereas the revolts are on the side of warmness, which is also why Slingerland finds that "Zhuangzi would have made fun of the 1960s hippies *as well as* their parents" (2014, 142; my italics). Oscar Wilde was against the cold puritan Victorian morals, which, paradoxically, preached ethical warmth by systematically intertwining coldness with the busybody warmth of enforced ethical goodness. However, Wilde did not break out in a rhapsody of warmth when encountering Victorian coldness but developed a peculiar kind of coolness. The Victorian world is thus not so different from our present neoliberal world where rigid economic coldness is combined with PC warmth.

The cultural cool-warm dichotomy becomes very flagrant in Western societies from the 1960s onward. In the 1969 film *Easy Rider*, Peter Fonda and Dennis Hopper might look "cool" with their bikes and sunglasses, but the appearance is deceptive. Underneath the cool surface of tough men lurks the relentless protest against a cold capitalist society (see Geiger 2015). Even the coolest-looking people search for warm and authentic sentiments. The hippie movement created rural enclaves of bohemian alternative life, and the choice of nonurban locations was consistent with the prevalent ethics of warmness since the coldest of all places is the city. Being most radically opposed to nature, the city houses all cold phenomena from industrial *Entfremdung* to overly sincere bourgeois morality. The city is a grim reality and lacks soul. As a result, the dandy, this urban creature who seems to enjoy that kind of environment, becomes the enemy of the bohemian. Schiffer is thus right when conceptualizing the hippie as an "anti-dandy" (2010, 62). Very early Georg Simmel had warned in his "Big Cities and Spiritual Life" (1903) of the flâneur, whom he called blasé. As mentioned, the flâneur is necessarily blasé because the overstimulation of the senses that is so current in modern cities requires the blasé as a defense (Simmel1995, 121). Of course, according to Simmel, becoming blasé in modern life is only the destiny of intelligent people. Stupid people are simply dull and do not even perceive these stimuli. Being blasé is very rational, which makes it cold in return: it is a form of cold rationality (117). Against this, natural life enables a spontaneity that has been lost in the city.

When stiff sofas were replaced with soft Indian cushions, this was not merely an aesthetic choice but also a political statement and therefore a matter of ethics. The politically conservative bourgeoisie was cold, and both coldness and warmth would quickly become ethicized and politicized. Other expressions of this new sensibility were nature protection and emotionally guided sympathies toward minorities. The "other" needed to be not only warmly embraced but also protected. "Warm" was authentic, and "cool" became inauthentic and hypocritical in a moral sense. This is intriguing to say the least, since there is substantial literature that defines coolness precisely as an expression of authenticity. As I mentioned previously, such estimations of "cool as authenticity" are basically wrong, but it is interesting to note how the value of cool could morph into its opposite over time. For many, cool was initially supposed to give a solid chunk of authenticity to the image of the Black man for whom "being cool" was often "the only source of pride, dignity, and worth" (Majors and Billson 1992, 30). I mentioned Norman Mailer, but there are many more examples. Being cool was being "true to oneself" in the sense of keeping one's dignity. Strangely, and in contradiction with everything that has been said in this book about coolness, it was also often seen as sincere, which further illustrates the strong link between sincerity and authenticity. The authenticity paradigm, when linked to black culture, could even be spelled out in terms of race, which would then, once again, be evaluated in terms of warmth. Lisa Nakamura finds that in *The Matrix*, the Wachowski brothers' insistence on Black style is more than a visual fad and "that blackness is represented as the source of human agency in this techno-future" (2005, 132). The Black race adopts the quality of being warm (interestingly it also adopts the quality of being real). Claudia Springer finds this problematic and detects a "racist paradigm [in the idea of] associating black people with authenticity and life and white people with artifice and death" (2005, 92, 94). In *The Matrix*, ethnic people represent human warmth, whereas the robots are white. "Warm," "authentic," and "real" are here interlinked concepts.

The racist reproach is sketchy; but historically speaking, the linking of these concepts is not surprising. Were Enlightenment concepts such as freedom and equality not predestined to culminate one day in an ideal of warmth?[7] In an ideal and enlightened society, equal members embrace each other warmly, and the members of this society's minorities are warmly embraced, too. The latter would not happen during the Enlightenment, but later, in the twentieth century, it would become an ethical requirement for many. Eventually, the ethicization and politization of warmth led to PC, as warmth needed to be formalized in terms of norms and rules. The aim of PC is to make societies warmer, and it does so, among other things, by designing a vocabulary of authenticity.

The ethical approach toward human warmth necessarily develops social epistemologies of relativity. The other can only be fully embraced if we establish, in parallel, that s/he is never entirely wrong. Therefore, PC creates rules to guarantee every individual's right to "being right." Alan Bloom, a fierce critic of PC *avant l'heure*, has shown how a sort of PC thinking emerges from "postmodern" relativism. For PC everybody is right (except those who are against PC): "The relativity of truth is not a theoretical insight but a moral postulate, the condition of a free society" (2008, 25). Indeed, relativity is not only the postulate of a *free* society but also of a *warm* society.

Richard Rorty's writings on ethics fully support the necessity of such a warm embrace of the other. In *Truth and Progress* (1998), Rorty explains that moral progress is possible only if we increase "our ability to see more and more differences among people as morally irrelevant—to see the differences between people's religions, genders, races, economic status, and so on as irrelevant to the possibility of cooperating with them for mutual benefit" (1998, 11). Though Rorty speaks—misleadingly, I would say—of moral irrelevance, this approach should not be confused with a Daoist equalization of essences. It is not an equalization taking a purely amoral perspective by seeing differences of race, gender, etc., as *inessential*. For Rorty such essences do exist, but it is our moral duty to see them as *irrelevant*. This remains an ethical approach fed by the ethics of warmth; it is not fed by *wuxin* (no-mind) or by amoral coolness. In an essay on "Human Rights," Rorty advocates the progress of sentiment, which "consists in an increasing ability to see the similarities between ourselves and people very unlike us as outweighing the differences" (1998, 181). To recognize what is "human" in human rights we need empathy. Rorty's approach is not based on a free roaming amoral attitude and the refusal to make any ethical statements. It is rather based on an ethics of relativization that he defends just like one can defend any ethical argument. His relativism does not lead to the amoral detachment recommended by Daoism. His relativism does not follow a nonethics of forgetting in which the protagonist slips into a fluid self, always lingering between this and that and not knowing if they are awake or dreaming. Rorty's relativism is not the Zhuangzist or dandyist equalization of differences. Instead, it simply declares differences to be irrelevant on ethical grounds; differences are not inessential on nonethical grounds.

The Cold War justified the need of warmth more than ever before. The Russian enemy, cold as they—almost literally—were, had to be embraced if the arms race was ever going to stop. The peace movements of the 1980s sincerely believed that warmth was the equivalent of peace. Post–Cold War politics of warmth is no less impressive. Activities like lifestyle coaching, meditation, and wellness Buddhism emerged from the same "warmth requirements" that the cultural left has cultivated since the 1970s. A part of this alternative has been commercialized Daoism. Cool is seen as cold and therefore as negative. The cool person has a lack of sentiment toward others and is egocentric like Bret Easton Ellis's protagonist in *American Psycho* (1991) or like the protagonists in Michel Houellebecq's novels. Barack Obama might have been perceived as a "cool" president, but what made him most popular was that he could replace white coldness with Black humanity. He was cool the way Peter Fonda and Dennis Hopper were in *Easy Rider*: cool but with an "authentic" warm kernel underneath the surface. Obama spread his warmth in the midst of cold terrorism and the cold financial crisis of 2008. Cold stands here for decadence and inner emptiness, and coolness is attached to this negative term. The sophistication that clung to coolness since its inception in an African American context is here entirely lost. In a culture where the cold and the warm are judged ethically, coolness can survive, at best, as a commercial gadget. "This is cool" still remains the "most widely diffused slang term for approval among American high-school and college students" (Liu 2004, 78), which means that cool has mainly become "cool buying power." This is absurd since the original meaning of being "hip" (to which cool is linked) has been "not to be duped by the world around one when faced with an assault of one's being" (Monson 1995, 399).

In chapter 4, I described how the first "Dionysian phase" of a progressive "ideology of warmth" became formalized in the 1990s, and how it eventually turned into PC. The desired "warm approach" toward the other was recast as the "politically correct approach." The warmth requirements remained as strong as they were in the 1960s. From today's perspective, PC might look cold and formal to its opponents, but it does symbolize the last stage of a chain of attempts desperately trying to obtain some human warmth in a world of coldness.

As a result, cool becomes negative, as was shown by quoting from the above master thesis. German anthropologist Annette Geiger demonstrates that by 2010, cool was definitely "out," and as an explicit example of what the new culture of warmth vehemently rejects, Geiger names the decline of the dandy. In magazines from 2010 onward, handsome men are not cool dandies but radiate a "bittersweet hint of melancholy—passive, narcissistic and gloomy" (Geiger 2015, 90). The reason is that society no longer desires the cool man but rather the authentic man: "Genuine charm and charisma must be authentic, warm-hearted and rich in sentiment, whereas coolness is fabricated, artificial, and constructed" (90). Again, warm is authentic; cool is fake.

Geiger is aware that such thoughts misconstrue the initial idea of coolness and dandyism. The misconstrual is partly due to the reduction of cool to the consumption of certain fashion products, that is, to a commercialized form of cool. However, this might actually be the *result* of warmness culture (which misrepresents cool), rather than the *cause*. Regardless, cool was ultimately objectified because only as an objectified item is it allowed to function in capitalist structures. A further reason for the misconstrual of cool is that in this culture, the "human" has been ethicized, which permitted the insertion of the idea of the "human" into an ethics and ideology of warmth. All this propelled the decline of coolness. Commercialized cool is also a populist cool because it delivers prefabricated clichés of cool behavior to the masses. Again, this contradicts the original idea of coolness, which becomes most obvious when we look back at dandyism and Daoism. Both have the reputation of being elitist (be it only because of their strange rationalism) and are thus opposed to populism. We perceive a big change when we consider that in the African American context, cool has been a survival technique, or that even Stoicism recommended *apatheia* as a serious ascetic philosophy. Daoism also has the characteristics of such a survival technique, as it represents a way of life, not only a religion or philosophy.

The rebellious component of coolness is lost, too. If we think of the dandy's eternal state of being *revolté*, which pushed him to take existential risks when provoking his aristocratic environment, we see how much cool has degenerated into a gadget; and this entire transformation happened under the influence of the ideology of warmness. Within the ethicizing context of the "culture of warmth," coolness *could* only be misconstrued. PC, which is the formalized version of the "culture of warmth," makes real cool behavior impossible because cool becomes incorrect as it is opposed to warmth. Beyond that, it has been shown above that cool is incorrect by definition. Dandyism and Daoism are splendid illustrations of the fact that cool is *always* incorrect.

In warm societies, cool is considered fake, but this does not mean that the "real" cool had ever been authentic. As this book has made clear, cool is *always* pure play and cannot be authentic, which is just another reason why the culture of warmth had to reject it. Cool has qualities that *can* only be genuinely pretended. As a matter of fact, few people are able to accept risks, be independent, or have self-control without the slightest trace of what Sartre called *angoisse*. This means that all those who master these activities are not *authentically* cool but simply play; and this is the only way coolness can *emerge*. It cannot be created or implanted as a ready-made essence. The dandy masters these capacities very well: he is not cool because he is authentic, nor is he cool because he is more ethical. More ethical would mean being less formal, less *entfremdet*, less sexually inhibited, and "warmer." The dandy is none of these but simply plays a role that becomes his genuine role while he is playing. He has nothing to gain from playing this role, neither materially nor ethically. Again, this does not mean that he is more ethical: he is not less greedy, less arrogant, or less blasé than the high-class people he caricatures. He is simply cooler than them because he is only playing them.

Andy Warhol

The dandy is anti-PC, but his stance differs very much from what emerges today in anti-PC right-wing politics. To let this book end on a more forward-looking and constructive note, I suggest that dandyism's and Daoist incorrectness comes close to Pop Art. Carter Radcliff found that "the Baudelairean dandy is a recent ancestor of the avant-gardist" (2001, 102), and Tristan Tzara said that Zhuangzi was "just as dada as we are" (Lee 2004, 126), which establishes a link between dandyism/Daoism and modern art. Some have noted strong correlations between Andy Warhol and dandyism because Warhol's critique of elite culture, formulated while he himself was a member of the most snobbish elite, follows the principles of dandyism. Deeper parallels can be traced between Warhol and the "Daoist" approach. In his art, Warhol deals with images in a "Daoist" way by emptying them of signification. Many of Warhol's works are the result of a disinvestment or disownment. The print images of Marilyn Monroe, for example, are infinitely repeated until there remains neither authentic image nor real person. There is nothing that could be commented upon in terms of ethics either. Like dandyism and Daoism, Pop Art refuses to be sincere. Marc Le Bot identifies Warhol with a dandy and describes the emptying of reality that Warhol undertakes in a way reminiscent of a Daoist principle: "The dandy is elsewhere, which fascinates us. He is not in oppositions of wealth and poverty, good taste and bad taste, utility value and exchange value, useful and useless expenditure, reality and simulations. (. . .) He is on the side of death and of all dichotomies because he transcends them" (1990, 6).

For Susan Sontag, this aesthetics would be the aesthetics of camp because camp "makes no distinction between the unique object and the mass-produced object" but "transcends the nausea of the replica" (1982, 289). Oscar Wilde formulated precisely this sensibility when declaring that a doorknob could be as admirable as a painting, thus announcing "the equivalence of all objects" (Sontag 1982, 289). Again, this sounds very much like a Daoist equivalization of things: Wilde's statement should not be understood as (populist) relativism because he does not hold that *all* doorknobs and paintings are admirable. His intention is rather to widen aesthetic criteria without attempting to leave the conventional realm of elitism.

The seriality of Warhol's work presents a stereotype. However, the word "stereotype" should not be understood negatively. By producing stereotypes, Warhol overcomes dichotomies and practices the equalization of fake and authentic. A work of art represents a totality that can be neither critiqued nor defended. Standards like good art or bad art can only be established by basing our judgment on external criteria, but Pop Art cannot be judged in this fashion. Many of the criteria that we use in art are external criteria, and authenticity and sincerity are among the most prominent ones. However, authenticity and sincerity are ethical criteria and have no place in aesthetics. Warhol wrenches art from all moral essences, and he does so more radically than most artists before him. The result is a kind of dandyist-Daoist absurdity.

Warhol obtains an absolute freedom that can only be gained once the world is emptied of all ethical meaning. Warhol's approach leads not to relativism but to indifference in the Daoist or Zen Buddhist sense. It is the indifference of nonknowledge that is also proper to the dandy, who calls it *ennui*, *dédain*, or phlegm. Someone once asked Brummell which lake he liked the most in the Lake District, at which point he turned to his valet and asked: "Robinson, which lake do I admire?" His indifference toward names and titles is motivated by the same nonknowledge. "Johnson and Thompson—and Thompson and Johnson, are really so much the same kind of thing.'" He does not care because he has reached the "equalization of things." Things work similarly for Warhol. He paints a can of soup though he could have painted anything else. Which one does he prefer? He does not care.

Conclusion

We are living in a world in which the authenticity politics of "being yourself" or "Just do it" is advertised as cool. On the one hand, this is understandable because in a world full of copies, to attain the status of authenticity can easily appear as the best way to live a meaningful life. On the other hand, and paradoxically, this mechanism submits everybody to the dictatorship of authenticity. Even worse, it is often not clear at all what "authenticity" is supposed to mean. Despite calls for authenticity and spontaneity such as "Just do it" or "Obey your thirst" (Sprite), it is rarely explained what it really means to live an authentic life. Dandyism and the *Zhuangzi* free us from the imperative of authenticity and suggest a philosophy of coolness in the sense of "emptiness" that grants independence beyond all ethical imperatives, even those of authenticity and sincerity. "Being yourself" is the last thing a Daoist or a dandy would advocate. Be it simply because they have no selves.

Would the eighteenth- and nineteenth-century dandy, if he lived today, have to repeat the same feats as he did 150 years ago? The main problem he would face is that he would have to juggle between left- and right-wing politics, which, I am afraid, would exhaust him. Dandyism cannot be used for politics. Nor is dandyism a self-help philosophy. Contrary to many of today's "warm" pop philosophies, dandyism gives no instructions for reaching happiness. It simply shows a way to survive in a world dominated by both formal coldness and busybody warmness. In this world it has become increasingly difficult to be "cool." Just like Daoism, dandyism is a survival technique for people in difficult situations. It shows how a person coming from a lower social class can participate in the game of high society without being totally hypocritical and without having to abandon his critical distance. Survival is not guaranteed through revolution or by following a better ethics. One must simply learn certain social techniques, master ceremonies, and engage in some theatrical play. The first African American masters of Black coolness would have given the same advice. That said, by doing all this, the dandy and the Daoist also fulfill a political task in an indirect fashion. They "unsettle permanently all the configurations of power [and] prevent them—right or left" (Hall 1994, 182). This is how Stuart Hall defines the task of politics in a postindustrial society.

This book has advocated overcoming the concepts of sincerity and authenticity currently saturating our cultures through the concept of genuine pretending. Genuine pretending circumvents both fanaticism and relativism, two terms that are closely linked to sincerity and authenticity. Genuine pretending has a predominantly aesthetic orientation and does not attempt to produce a counterethics of any sort. Instead, it deconstructs ethics through aesthetics. One of the principal results is politeness because politeness is an aesthetic gesture based on nonknowledge. Polite incorrectness emphasizes style, smoothness, contemplation, and fluidity; and as an ethico-aesthetic standard, it can put forward trust, compassion, empathy, wit, and irony. Politeness is not hypocritical, but it is never authentic either. Nor is it ever perfect. It is "useless" in the sense of apolitical, which is why it is never intrusive. Politeness does not try to impose upon or target selected groups but rather passes over many ethical and political issues. Despite this "smoothness," in this book, politeness could be formulated as necessarily anarchic as it disparages any idea of correctness.

In this book's narrative, kitsch became a keyword encompassing the productions of both fanaticism and relativism in all walks of life. Kitsch is an existential pattern that dandyism and Daoism combated by using coolness, irony, and distanciation. It is for this reason that the dandy and the Daoist could appear as the opponents of PC. The ideas of dandies and Daoists can thus be used to undermine the religion, ethics, and the aesthetics of kitsch that have become increasingly pervasive in the twenty-first century. Daoism and dandyism, when fighting Confucianism and snobbism respectively, have demonstrated how important it is to depoliticize and to deethicize human behavior. Above that, they have also shown that the fight against snobbish PC should not be led along ethicizing and politicizing lines: this would contradict its own principles. Ethics is most efficiently combated with aesthetics.

This book also suggested amoral coolness and Daoist "doing nothing." The purpose is certainly not to embrace commercial cool or to end up with drug abuse, depression, or eating disorders. "Of petty uselessness great usefulness is achieved," says the *Zhuangzi*, but what is this great usefulness? I presented Warhol as an example to show that this kind of coolness is meant to be creative and productive. Daoism invested much time into bodily cultivation and aesthetic appreciation; Brummell invested in clothes, but theoretically *anything* can be done in a Daoist-dandyist fashion. It is important to remain spontaneous and natural and to avoid politicization, to be productive without becoming a busybody, and to be creative without searching for novelties. Avoid careerism, mysticism, as well as revolutionary activities. Engage in absurdities but never look ridiculous. Never see life as a drama. Most importantly, do not care about what it means to be cool.

Notes

Notes to the Introduction

1. Zhuangzi is a historical figure who lived in the fourth century BC in China whereas the *Zhuangzi* is a compilation of his and others' writings to which I will refer most of the time. "Zhuangzi" refers thus to the author whereas "the *Zhuangzi*" refers to the Daoist anthology.

2. *Analects* (*Lunyu* 論語) *Book XIII*, chapter 3, verses 4–7, 263–64.

3. "犬可以為羊." Legge translates: "A dog might have been (called) a sheep." In Miscellaneous Chapters 天下—Tian Xia. I am using many different translations of the *Zhuangzi* and indicate the choice by mentioning the name of the translator in brackets. When no name is used, the translation comes from James Legge, that is, from the online *Chinese Text Project* (see Zhuangzi in bibliography).

4. Giles's translation is problematic, but it has become popular and was also read by Wilde, which is why I include it here. I will discuss Giles's translation in chapter 3 and compare it with Hans-Georg Moeller's translation.

5. McCormack's two pieces "From Chinese Wisdom to Irish Wit: Zhuangzi and Oscar Wilde" (2007a) and "Oscar Wilde: As Daoist Sage" (2017) are certainly the most important sources. Isobel Murray has done pioneering work in her article "Oscar Wilde's Absorption of 'Influences': The Case History of Chuang Tzu" (1971). Further sources are Günther Debon's, *Oscar Wilde und der Taoismus* (1986), a master's thesis by Ding Xiaoyu entitled *Oscar Wilde and China in Late Nineteenth Century Britain: Aestheticism, Orientalism, and the Making of Modernism* (University of Hong Kong 2012), as well as a text by brother John Albert on Zhuangzi and Wilde published by the Thomas Merton Center.

6. Seventy-six years separate the birthdates of Brummell and Wilde, and when Wilde was born, Brummell had already been dead for fourteen years. The linking element between both is represented by Charles Baudelaire who is thirty-three years older than Wilde and forty-three years younger than Brummell.

Baudelaire was nineteen when Brummell died, and Wilde was thirteen when Baudelaire died. Baudelaire can be called the "middle generation" of dandyism. Brummell: 1778–1840; Baudelaire: 1821–1867; Wilde: 1854–1900.

7. Similar points can be made about other "politically incorrect" movements such as the ancient Greek Cynics and the Eastern Fools for Christ movements. During the fourth and third centuries BC, Greek civilization underwent key periods of social transformation, and the Cynics responded to these social changes denying the legitimacy of the existing political systems and denouncing the upper rulers (see Yang 2007). Catherine Kolomeytseva draws a link between dandyism and the Eastern Fools for Christ movements, which occurred in the Russian orthodox tradition though they also existed in Byzantium. Dandyism and Eastern Fools for Christ are, for her, "two sides of the same coin: social crises, a need for change in morality" (Kolomeytseva).

8. This is also the headnote to chapter 4 in Giles's translation. In this book, translations from the *Zhuangzi* usually come from Legge's version on the *Chinese Text Project*, unless otherwise indicated.

9. Yangzi or Yang Zhu (楊朱), 440–360 BC. The Yangist school was prevalent at the time of Mencius. Yangzi's ideas appear primarily in the Huainanzi, Lüshi Chunqiu, Mengzi, and possibly the Liezi and Zhuangzi. The Liezi contains a chapter about Yang Zhu but could be a later forgery.

10. Of course, such overpoliticization is not the sole domain of leftism. These topics become politicized through right-wing discourse, too.

Notes to Chapter 1

1. *Analects*, Book XIII, chap. 3, verses 4–7, 263–64.

2. Chinese writers in the classical period speak of words only as *ming* (names) (see Hansen 2000, 49).

3. *Ming shi* occurs in the *Zhuangzi* in *The Normal Course for Rulers and Kings* (應帝王) [5], where Hu-zi meets a wizard who is confused by Hu-zi's constantly changing identity. It also appears in the Geng-sang Chu (庚桑楚) [14] in the miscellaneous chapters where those who "multiply their approvals and disapprovals, determining what is merely nominal and what is real" are criticized. "They go on to conclude that to themselves must the appeal be made in everything, and to try to make others adopt them (. . .). In this way they consider being employed in office as a mark of wisdom, and not being so employed as a mark of stupidity, success as entitling to fame, and the want of it as disgraceful." They have unreflectively internalized a "differentiating method." In *Ze-yang* (則陽) [11], Da-gong Diao explains: "The Yin and Yang reflected light on each other, covered each other, and regulated each the other. (. . .). Likings and dislikings,

the avoidings of this and movements towards that, then arose (in the things thus produced), in their definite distinctness; (. . .) Words can describe them and knowledge can reach to them; but with this ends all that can be said of things. Men who study the Dao do not follow on when these operations end, nor try to search out how they began: with this all discussion of them stops."

4. The disagreement about the status of philosophical language, that is, how language is supposed to describe reality, is responsible (among other things) for the divide between analytic and continental philosophy. In the 1930s, during the "debate" between Heidegger and Carnap, this gap appeared for the first time. Carnap held that most of what philosophers have written is semantically empty, and he called such discourse "pseudostatements." The most typical of such "pseudostatements" was Heidegger's "The Nothing itself nothings" from *Being and Time* (see Carnap 1932). For Carnap, words needed to correspond to actually existing things.

5. *Wang* (忘) can concern the forgetting of time, as in the *Qiwulun* (chap. 12): "Let us forget the lapse of time; let us forget the conflict of opinions. Let us make our appeal to the Infinite, and take up our position there." Important is also the forgetting of the body, as says *The Seal of Virtue Complete* (德充符) (chap. 1): "So it is that when one's virtue is extraordinary (any deficiency in) his bodily form may be forgotten. When men do not forget what is (easily) forgotten, and forget what is not (easily) forgotten, we have a case of real oblivion." Or in *The Great and Most Honoured Master* (大宗師) (chap. 6) it is said: "Fishes forget one another in the rivers and lakes; men forget one another in the arts of the Dao." *Sang* (喪) can concern the losing of consciousness as described at the beginning of the *Qiwulun* (chap. 1): "Nan-Guo Zi-Qi was seated, leaning forward on his stool. He was looking up to heaven and breathed gently, seeming to be in a trance, and to have lost all consciousness of any companion." And loss can be overcome. About the wise man without feet in *The Seal of Virtue Complete* (chap. 1), it is said: "Though heaven and earth were to be overturned and fall, they would occasion him no loss. His judgment is fixed regarding that in which there is no element of falsehood; and, while other things change, he changes not." But it is not appropriate to get lost in vulgar things, as stated in *Correcting the Nature* (繕性) (chap. 3): "They who lose themselves in their pursuit of things, and lose their nature in their study of what is vulgar, must be pronounced people who turn things upside down." More on "forgetting" will follow in chapter 7.

6. *Mencius*, Book 3, Part B.

7. The School of Names is one of six recognized main philosophical movements, and it normally comprises seven scholars: Deng Xi, Yin Wen, Hui Shi, Gongsun Long, Cheng-gong Sheng, Huang Gong, and Mao Gong. The leaders were Hui Shih and Gongsun Long. It was no real school or movement,

but the label was coined much later, in the second-century BC. Sometimes the members of the School of Names are also called dialecticians, and Western scholars can refer to them as "Sophists." Since almost all writings of the school were lost, there is almost no firsthand knowledge about their philosophies, with the exception of a few brief texts attributed to Gongsun Long. Everything we know about them comes from other texts, especially the *Zhuangzi and Xunzi*. The School of Names did not discover any new laws, nor did they develop syllogistic reasoning; but they affected all the other schools that were active during the fourth century (see Mair 1994, xxiv).

8. The "logic chopping" aspect has become famous through Gongsung Long's "White Horse Discourse" (*Baimalun*) where he treats the color of a white horse as a thing separable from the horse's shape and concludes: "The white is not the horse. A white horse is a horse together with white" (see Graham 1978, 173). The idea is to treat the name "white horse" (*baima* 白马) as a single name.

9. Zhuang Zhou, Gongsun Long, and Hui Shi spent time together at the Jixia Academy.

10. Such logical theories are not necessarily self-sufficiently logical but can be traced to age-old sociological patterns requiring that "every social role should be designated by only one title, corresponding to a fixed set of duties or expectations" (Eno 2016). About the alignment of names and actualities Gongsun Long wrote that "to fulfill the position of one's position is 'correct.' To take what has been corrected to correct what has not been corrected is to introduce doubt about what has been corrected. What is corrected is the character [of a position] as actuality. To correct its character as actuality is to correct its name" (Eno 2016). We must identify each person's unique role through the name and make the function match the name. It emerges from a further reading of Gongsun Long that he found language actually too arbitrary and that nothing can be proved through language. According to Eno, this would make Gongsun Long a "Confucian champion, defending against the challenges of Mohist rationalism, challenges that Mohist logicians were attempting to strengthen" (Eno 2016).

11. Also called *Tao Te Ching* or *Laozi* (*Lao-tzu*).

12. The debate took place between Jordan Peterson, Stephen Fry, Michelle Goldberg, and Eric Dyson.

13. One could say that Daoism creates what Mircea Eliade calls a symbolic religious language. I am not saying that Daoism is a symbolism, but I mean that from a Daoist point of view, the language we use is never literal. Daoist language is not a symbolic language but a symbolic *religious* language in Eliade's understanding. In various works (1959, 1991) Eliade explains that human beings use religious language in a symbolic, nonliteral way. Human beings are essentially symbolic beings (*homo symbolicus*), and a religious statement is never about facts in the world. Therefore, it cannot be refuted by citing facts. Rather,

it is via symbolic religious language that human beings are able to express their experiences with reference to coherent structural worlds of meaning. PC takes language literally and thinks that its words relate directly to facts. It is not a *religious* symbolic language but believes that a certain pronoun can directly represent a certain part of gender reality, or, as we have seen above, of genetic reality. From Eliade's point of view, this approach comes close to superstition.

14. Confucianism has been associated with sexist practices such as foot binding, child-brides, and female infanticide. Lise Li-Hsiang asks: "How does one identify the 'sexist' components of Confucianism as a whole? (. . .) Is there an inevitable causal link between 'Confucianism and 'sexism'? In short, is 'Confucianism' sexist through and through?" (Li-Hsiang 2006, 15).

15. In the *Zhuangzi*, the Perfect Unity is "no action" that is, "a constant manifestation of spontaneity" (*Correcting the Nature*, 繕性 2). In *The Seal of Virtue Complete* (德充符) (chap. 6) Zhuangzi explains to Huizi that the Perfect Man "always pursues his course without effort (自然) and does not (try to) increase his (store of) life." In *The Normal Course for Rulers and Kings* (應帝王) (chap. 3) a nameless man gives Tian Gen the advice: "Allow all things to take their natural course; and admit no personal or selfish consideration—do this and the world will be governed." *Ziran* is important in music. In *The Revolution of Heaven* (天運) (chap.3), the musician Di explains that his performance "corresponded to the spontaneity (apparent in nature). "In the last part (of the performance), I employed notes which did not have that wearying effect. I blended them together as at the command of spontaneity." The most famous application of *ziran* is the case of Lao Dan who replies to Confucius in *Tian Zi-fang* 田子方 [4] that water "does nothing, but it naturally acts so (無為而才自然矣)." *Ziran* is also important in the Dao De Jing where it is declared that "the law of the Dao is its being what it is (道法自然)."

16. Ames derives this conclusion from the *Lao Tzu*, chapters 17, 3, and 57. *Tu hua* is also "individualization," a term that Guo Xiang, who is credited with the first revision of the *Zhuangzi*, developed.

17. "A seal always precedes the impression, but a hub always coexists with the spokes" (Moeller 2018, 147).

18. For example: "Although it be so, there is affirmed now life and now death; now death and now life; now the admissibility of a thing and now its inadmissibility; now its inadmissibility and now its admissibility. (The disputants) now affirm and now deny; now deny and now affirm. Therefore the sagely man does not pursue this method, but views things in the light of (his) Heaven (-ly nature), and hence forms his judgment of what is right" (5).

19. I am not suggesting that Peterson's few repetitive sentences on Daoism in his *Twelve Rules of Life: An Antidote to Chaos* reflect anything relevant for Daoism.

20. The Dhammapada is a collection of the sayings of Buddha.

Notes to Chapter 2

1. See especially Tominaga (1983), Wienpahl (1958), and Gudmunsen (1977). Tominaga's refers to "the inexpressible resort to silence," that is, the fact that "Lao Tzu and Chuang Tzu are in agreement with the early Wittgenstein that there are realities that cannot be expressed or described in terms of written or spoken words" (Tominaga 137). Tominaga likens Ch'an Buddhism's *wu* (enlightenment experience) to Wittgenstein's "the mystical" as mentioned in the *Tractatus*. See also Botz-Bornstein (2004), Goodman (1976), Hudson (1973), Rieman (1977), Kalupahana (1977), Waldo (1978), and Thurman (1980), and Anderson (1985). Publications on Wittgenstein and Eastern thought appear between 1973 and 1985 and do then, curiously, cease.

2. Dandyism has been compared with ancient Greek philosophical tradition like the Cynics, too (see Kolomeytseva).

3. In *Enjoyment in Untroubled Ease* (逍遙遊) [3], Jian Wu gives an account of a "Spirit-like man (. . .) who drove along the flying dragons, rambling and enjoying himself beyond the four seas." In the *Qiwulun* [11], the Perfect Man is described as one who "mounts on the clouds of the air, rides on the sun and moon, and rambles at ease beyond the four seas (而遊乎四海之外). Neither death nor life makes any change in him, and how much less should the considerations of advantage and injury do so!" In *Qiwulun* [12], a Master is described as "finding his enjoyment outside the dust and dirt (of the world) (而遊乎塵垢之外)."

4. D'Ambrosio points out that Confucius himself is recorded to have detested the drawing of lines as imaginary restrictions as well: "In the Analects Confucius expresses concern for students who map out what they can and cannot do before getting started. But Confucius criticizes his students for yang-based reasons: he is worried that people do not work hard enough, and that they draw lines that limit their own effort" (D'Ambrosio 2017: 34).

5. Originally, *wuwei* emerged from Confucianism, but it can also be found in the *Zhuangzi*, where it is used for fundamental statements such as: "This is the Dao; there is in It emotion and sincerity, but It does nothing and has no bodily form (無為無形)." *The Great and Most Honored Master* (chap. 3). *The Normal Course for Rulers and Kings* (chap. 6) says: "Non-action (makes its exemplifier) the lord of all fame; non-action (serves him as) the treasury of all plans; non-action (fits him for) the burden of all offices; non-action (makes him) the lord of all wisdom." In *Tien Xia* (chap. 5) it is said about the ancient Daoist that "He does nothing, and laughs at the clever and ingenious (無為也而笑巧). And in *Cutting open Satchels* (胠篋) (chap. 3) one complains: "The plain and honest-minded people are neglected, and the plausible representations of restless spirits received with pleasure; the quiet and unexciting method of non-action is put away, and pleasure taken in ideas garrulously expressed."

6. One must consider that the Laozi were part of a more ancient society, where "everything was relatively tranquil, secure, unhurried, and balanced" (Li

2019, 89). The *Laozi*'s "non-striving" conveys this kind of social ideal. In *wuwei* everything is "natural" or "spontaneous," to the point that Li Zehou likens it to "an animal-esque existence, ignorant and without knowledge or desire, and without any particular direction" (89).

7. The etymological origin of the word "dandy" remains unclear. The word appears in 1780 in a Scottish border ballad though in a context unrelated to later meanings. See "Dandy" in Oxford English Dictionary.

8. The Victorian era reaches from 1837 to 1901. Wilde lived from 1854 to 1900.

9. More precisely, the period before the reign of Prince Regent George, that is, the latter part of George II's reign, as well as the period of the reign of George IV's brother William IV, can be included in the Regency period, too.

10. These philosophical schools also disappeared, of course, because in a unified empire, many posts for political advisers of Feudal Lords had become redundant.

11. The Confucian term *junzi* (君子), literally a person of high stature is often translated as "gentleman" or "superior person."

12. The *Liezi* (列子) is a Daoist text attributed to Lie Yukou (fifth or fourth century BC).

13. The *Zhuangzi* begins with a transformation: "In the Northern Ocean there is a fish, the name of which is Kun—I do not know how many li in size. It changes [化] into a bird with the name of Peng" (*Enjoyment in Untroubled Ease* [chap. 1]). Heaven and earth are "transforming powers" and *hua* can be seen in connection with *wuwei*: "The ancients "did nothing and all things were transformed (無為而萬物化)" (*Heaven and Earth* [chap. 1]).

14. "L'idée de Dieu nous laisse froids; la nature nous laisse froids; nous n'avons que l'esprit du monde qui n'a pas d'intérêt vrai à nous offrir, et à qui nous n'avons rien à préférer" (Barbey 1926–27, 151).

15. Arnold concedes that "Hellenism may thus actually serve to further the designs of Hebraism" because it introduces "life and movement into that side of us with which alone Hebraism concerns itself, and awakens a healthier and less mechanical activity there" (117).

16. Parallels between Wittgenstein and Daoism or Zen Buddhism have been noted by several authors (see note 1 of this chapter).

17. Marie-Christine Natta (2001) and Joël Fusco (2013) mention this phrase. It has been used in various places, but I could not trace its origin.

Notes to Chapter 3

1. *Qi* is a sort of nondoing that can be similar to fasting, as is shown in *The Full Understanding of Life* (達生) (11). The worker Qing makes a bell stand that impresses the marquis of Lu, and when asked how he proceeded to achieve

this feat, he explains: "I did not venture to waste any of my power, and felt it necessary to fast in order to compose my mind [必齊以靜心]. After fasting for three days [齊三日], I did not presume to think of any congratulation, reward, rank, or emolument (which I might obtain by the execution of my task); after fasting five days [齊五日], I did not presume to think of the condemnation or commendation (which it would produce), or of the skill or want of skill (which it might display). At the end of the seven days [齊七日], I had forgotten all about myself." The character is similar to 齋 (zai), which means fasting, and is used in xinzhai, 心齋 (fasting of the heart).

2. I call him/her "he" to avoid confusion in this paragraph.

3. Xu is linked to xinzhai (心, see above note 1). In Man in the World, Associated with other Men (人間世) [2] it is said that "Where the (proper) course is, there is freedom from all pre-occupation [虛者]; such freedom is the fasting of the mind [心齋也]."

4. Japanese mushin. 心 (xin) means most generally "heart" but also mind or intelligence.

5. Paradoxically, Mengsun approaches reality, which is again linked to the dream theme: "He was more awake than others were (孟孫氏特覺). (. . .) And we all have our individuality which makes us what we are as compared together; but how do we know that we determine in any case correctly that individuality? Moreover you dream that you are a bird, and seem to be soaring to the sky; or that you are a fish, and seem to be diving in the deep. But you do not know whether we that are now speaking are awake or in a dream."

6. The authors refer to the fourth chapter "Man in the World, Associated with other Men," where these terms can be found from 4.1 to 4.3, for example in chap. 3, "He who is in the position of a minister or of a son has indeed to do what he cannot but do. Occupied with the details of the business (in hand), and forgetful of his own person (忘其身), what leisure has he to think of his pleasure in living or his dislike of death?"

7. The character 同 commonly means "same" or "like." Stevenson explains that it also signifies "objects under the same cover" or objects with the "same background," which refers to the above "background noise." He refers to Harbaugh's *Chinese Characters* (Stevenson 2006, 326n27).

8. On Levet's definition of neo-feminism see Botz-Bornstein 2020.

9. On the process of the large-scale deculturization of modern life see Botz-Bornstein 2019.

10. "Le Je qui figure aux rêves est un élément du système de l'instant. Il n'est pas quelqu'un qui se retrouve finalement dans telles caractéristiques. Mais le quelqu'un, au contraire, qui se fait autre, qui dépend du reste actuel" (Valéry 1974, 173; from *Cahiers* XIX, 86). For more on the ego-less dream see Botz-Bornstein 2007.

11. "Où l'échange entre choses et images est encore tâtonnement, indétermination *réelle*, primitive (. . .) plus vraie en un sens que la solution de la veille unique" (Levaillant 1979, 17).

12. "Le rêve veut être précis. Il ne veut pas être précisé. Ce qui ne peut être précisé et périrait de l'être" (1979, 95; from Cahier V, 1914).

13. "Tout ce qui ferait l'importance de cette recherche est TUE par le langage" (173).

14. In the language of early Chinese philosophy *shi-fei* 是非 would mean "is-is not," "right-wrong," "ought-ought not." *Qiwulun* (chap. 7) says that in ancient times "Some held that at first there was not anything. (. . .) A second class held that there was something, but without any responsive recognition of it (on the part of men). A third class held that there was such recognition, but there had not begun to be any expression of different opinions about it (而未始有是非也). It was through the definite expression of different opinions about it that injury ensued to (the doctrine of) the Dao. Therefore, as is said (chap. 6), the sagely man brings together a dispute in its affirmations and denials (是非) and rests in the equal fashioning of Heaven.

15. See Mocchia di Coggiola about ancestors of the *gagà* (see chap. 7) or those imitative dandies who emerged in 1840 (2016, 52).

16. It must be noted that there is no personalized and gendered possessive pronoun in Chinese. "Its" is identical to "his" or "her."

17. Butler uses the pronouns "they/their."

18. This was the incident that ultimately led Wilde to jail, as he attempted to sue the Marquess for libel (Marjoribanks 1932, 213).

19. "Cette correction, que l'artiste opère par son langage et par une redistribution d'éléments puisés dans le réel, s'appelle le style et donne à l'univers recréé son unité et ses limites, à donner sa loi au monde" (Camus 1965, 672).

20. "Tonescale" in Zora Neale Hurston's "Glossary of Harlem Slang" (contained in the short story *Spunk* from 1925).

21. It was published again in a 2011 congressional document titled: "The Constitutional Commission on Justice and Citizenship." A list of all 136 was published in *USA Today*: https://www.usatoday.com/story/sports/soccer/2014/07/08/136-variations-of-brazilian-skin-colors/12373343/.

Notes to Chapter 4

1. See Yaning An's article on *cheng* where An lists different translations. Legge first rendered *cheng* as "sincerity" (Legge 1893), which was generally accepted. Later, scholars introduced various other translations, such as "perfection" (Wieger 1917), "truth" (Bruce 1923; Enkar 1927) "realness" (Hughes 1942), and

"integrity" (Graham 1958). "Scholars sticking to 'sincerity' added further explanations and described 'cheng' as 'both an ethical and an ontological category'" (Schwartz 1985, 405). Joseph Needham (1956, 468) suggested, that "the word [cheng] is so untranslatable and at the same time so important that it probably ought to be retained in mere transliteration, like *dao* and *li*" (An, 157–58).

2. D'Ambrosio (2015) provides a good summary of those writings that identify Daoism with the search for authenticity: Coyle 1998, Carr and Ivanoe 2010, and Michael 2015. Daniel Coyle writes: "Thus *zhen*, as implemented in the Zhuangzi, denotes 'authenticity' within a transforming world, genuineness in the Nietzschean sense of being true to oneself" (1998, 199). The latter contrasts the constructed self (*wo* 我) with the authentic self (*wu* 吾).

3. In *Xu Wu-gui* (徐無鬼) [10], the Great Man is characterized as one who has accomplition but "does not seek for it," and *cheng* has described it as "the perfect sincerity of the Great Man (大人之誠). In *Perfect Enjoyment* (至樂) (chap. 1), the *cheng* of "meritorious officers" is questioned. They are regarded by the world as good but "I do not know whether the goodness (誠) ascribed to them be really good or really not good. If indeed it be considered good, it is not sufficient to preserve their persons alive."

4. It is rather Confucius who aims with his idea of sincerity at real and authentic feeling when saying: "As for mourning, real grief is to be preferred over formalities" (*Analects* 3.4). Inner feeling of mourning is more important than mere ritual.

5. More specifically, Heidegger wants to "de-structure" the understanding of being as it has existed since antiquity as well as in Descartes's *cogito*. The latter perceives being from the point of view of a subject ("I," reason, spirit, or person) and never questions being in terms of temporality, that is, in terms of what transcends the static point of view of the "I." Heidegger also shows that Kant uncritically adopted these Cartesian positions and never undertook an analysis of subjectivity in terms of time.

6. *Qiwulun* (chap. 12) says: 忘年忘義. Literally meaning, "Forget time, forget *yi* (Legge translates it as "Let us forget the lapse of time; let us forget the conflict of opinions").

7. Buddhism developed a rich discourse on the problem of identity. The Buddhist position rejects the notion of a continuous self or a personal identity as Buddhist thinkers were forced to reconcile the doctrine of the "no-self" (Sanskrit *anātman*) with the human experience of selfhood and continuity.

8. The term "sprezzatura," often mentioned together with dandyism, predates dandyism and has been important in Italy since the Renaissance. It was elucidated for the first time in 1524 by Baldassare Castiglione in his *The Book of the Courtier* (*Il Libro del Cortegiano*). Castiglione did not invent the term but invested it with a plurality of new signifiers. *Sprezzatura* (literally "contempt") is an "artful dishevelment" that is never excessive and can become a habitus. Central are the elements of dissimulation and grace, the latter of which is

"fleeting and quasi unattainable": "Without the existence of grace, we can understand neither affection, to which [sprezzatura] is opposed, nor sprezzatura itself, which is (. . .) the fortunate result of a successful public performance" (Paulicelli, 101; my trans.).

9. "Avec quel dédain de grand air, par exemple, il [le dandy] sut accepter le grade d'officier dans un des premiers régiments de l'armée, grade que tout autre fat de sa naissance et de son âge aurait considéré comme un rêve" (Boulenger 1907, 7).

10. Berlin, 139. Since Berlin relies so much on German Romanticism, it is interesting to note that in German, the word "sincere" does not really exist, except if one accepts the very technical term "integer." Berlin uses "integrity" in the above passage. The Latin word "sincere" moved into English and Romance languages but not into German. In German, "aufrichtig" would come closest to it, but it should be translated as "upright." Like "sincerity," "integrity" is a word of Latin origin, and *integer* means "whole." The sincere person's will forms a whole and is not split into two parts: into egoistic desire on the one hand and intellectually assumed moral obligations on the other. Sincerity settles somewhere between honesty and seriousness and can be characterized as a sort of moral seriousness.

11. See Fuhrer 2004, especially his chapter 3, "The Rediscovery of Georg Simmel's Work on Culture."

12. Marx formulated the *Entfremdungstheorie* (theory of alienation) in the *Economic and Philosophic Manuscripts* (1844).

13. To be fair, one needs to say that these thinkers refrained from framing the authentic in Romantic terms as an essential self that can be thought independently of the world. Heidegger's self is determined by Being-in-the-World, and Sartre's idea of true freedom is not otherworldly but engaged. Any belief in a ready-made "true self" is false or "bad faith," too. Therefore, in some way, this "existentialist" cultivation of authenticity can be related to Daoism. See David Cooper's criticism of Moeller and D'Ambrosio in Cooper et al. 2019. For D'Ambrosio, any Daoist "authenticity" has little in common with existentialist authenticity and "key aspects such as uniqueness, authorship and ownership are completely lacking in the Zhuangzi." The *zhen* person "does not stand out or apart from others but becomes so completely in line with the situation that it is deemed identical" (2015, 374).

14. According to Trilling, this connection happened through the sublime, which is related—though in a complex fashion—to the authentic (95). Both the authentic and the sublime are aesthetic ideals that differ from the ideal of beauty.

Notes to Chapter 5

1. I use Victor Mair's translation (1994, 324). I also provide the translation of Höchsmann and Yang, which brings out certain components of the passage

more clearly: "I was frightened." "What frightened you?" "I went into ten soup shops on the way and in five of them I was served soup free of charge." "But why did that frighten you?" Liezi replied, "Even when the inward true nature is not clearly manifested, the body betrays it, giving an outward shine. This outward shine overwhelms men's minds, making them, on slim evidence, treat you as noble or venerable. From this, afflictions will arise" (Höchsmann and Yang 2006, 301).

2. See in *Enjoyment in Untroubled Ease*: "The Perfect man has no (thought of) self (至人無己)."

3. See *The Seal of Virtue Complete* [6] "The Dao gives him his personal appearance (and powers); Heaven gives him his bodily form; and he does not by his likings and dislikings do any internal harm to his body (身)."

4. *Tian Xia* chap. 5, trans. Legge. I also provide Victor Mair's translation:

> "To one who does not dwell in himself,
> The forms of things will manifest themselves.
> His movement is like water,
> His stillness is like a mirror.
> His response is like an echo,
> Indistinct as though it were absent,
> Quiet as though it were pure.
> In sameness there is harmony,
> In getting there is loss." (1994, 341)

5. "Just Do It" is a trademark of the shoe company Nike and was coined in 1988. It was meant to be both "universal and intensely personal" (von Borries 2018, 37).

6. An *arhat* is one who has gained insight into the true nature of existence and has achieved *nirvana*.

7. Hans-Georg Gadamer highlights, in a discussion of aesthetic perception, the necessity of a "space for play": "Every work of art leaves the person who responds too it a certain leeway, a *Spielraum* to be filled in by himself" (1993, 117).

8. A famous passage in *The Seal of Virtue Complete* (chap. 6) reads: "Huizi said to Zhuangzi, 'Can a man indeed be without desires and passions [*wuqing*]?' The reply was, 'He can.' 'But on what grounds do you call him a man, who is thus without passions and desires?' Zhuangzi said, 'The Dao gives him his personal appearance (and powers); Heaven gives him his bodily form; how should we not call him a man?' Huizi rejoined, 'Since you call him a man, how can he be without passions and desires?' An explanation follows at the end of the paragraph: "You deal with your spirit as if it were something external to you, and subject your vital powers to toil. You sing (your ditties), leaning against

a tree; you go to sleep, grasping the stump of a rotten dryandra tree. Heaven selected for you the bodily form (of a man), and you babble about what is strong and what is white."

9. One can suggest that today, the anonymity of the internet serves as such a mask.

10. See Botz-Bornstein 2011, 94–95 and 127–28 for a more extended discussion of Sontag's thoughts on camp.

11. XXIV. L'homme de goût doit toujours savoir réduire le besoin au simple. XXVI. La prodigalité des ornements nuit à l'effet. XXVIII. En toute chose, la multiplicité des couleurs sera de mauvais goût (Balzac 1854, 67).

12. See Stevenson 2006, 304. Stevenson analyzes Serres's elaboration of chaos theory in physics (nonlinear dynamics) as described in *Genesis* (1995) and *The Parasite* (1982).

Notes to Chapter 6

1. It is the headnote to chapter 4 in Giles's translation, which influenced Oscar Wilde in the choice of the subtitle to *The Critic as Artist* (see chapter 3).

2. Same headnote to chapter 4 in Giles's translation.

3. Moeller explains the particularity of those myths: "The God of the Bible (. . .) created the world, but *tian* [heaven] in classical Chinese *is* the world. (. . .) *Tian* is *natura naturans*: "nature naturing." The "ten thousand processes and events (*wan wu*)," an expression for "all things that are happening," are not the creatures of a *tian* that stands independent of what is ordered; rather, they are constitutive of it. On this basis, *tian* can be described as the emergent orders negotiated out of the dispositions of the many particulars that are constitutive of it, human beings being no exception" (Moeller 2006, 44).

4. "Le Mime n'imite rien. Et d'abord il n'imite pas. Il n'y a rien avant l'écriture de ses gestes. Rien ne lui est présent. (. . .) la mime ne suit aucun livret préétabli" (*La Dissémination*, 221).

5. "Les rêves sont vérité mais exprimée comme exprime la pantomime" (from *Cahier* XV [1931]).

6. *The Great Most Honored Master* (chap. 6).

Notes to Chapter 7

1. I follow Clement Greenberg's classic paradigm. He famously suggests that avant-garde is the opposite of kitsch (Greenberg 1961 [1939]).

2. "En se faisant dandy, un homme devient un meuble de boudoir, un mannequin extrêmement ingénieux, qui peut se poser sur un cheval ou sur

un canapé, qui mord ou tette habituellement le bout d'une canne, mais un être pensant . . . jamais ! L'homme qui ne voit que la mode dans la mode est un sot. La vie élégante n'exclut ni la pensée ni la science : elle les consacre" (Balzac 1854, 68).

3. "Tout en se flattant d'être snob,—et parce qu'il s'en flatte—cesse de l'être" (Boulenger 1907, 29).

4. Through contacts with high-profile politicians who stayed in his house, Brummell's grandfather could assure his son William a position at the Treasury (see Kelly 2006, 1). William, George's father, became secretary to Prime Minister Lord North and accumulated a considerable fortune, part of which he very wisely invested in the colonies.

5. The Prince of Wales was also called "the most overdressed man in Europe" (Kelly 2006, 40).

6. 1837 is the year of Victoria's accession to the throne, although the beginning of the Victorian Era may even be rounded off to 1830. Many scholars mark the beginning from the passage of the first Reform Bill in 1832.

7. "Qu'est-ce donc que cette passion qui, devenue doctrine, a fait des adeptes dominateurs, cette institution non écrite qui a formé une caste si hautaine? C'est avant tout le besoin ardent de se faire une originalité, contenue dans les limites extérieures des convenances" (Baudelaire 1885, 93).

8. "L'eau en liberté m'est insupportable; je la veux prisonnière, au carcan, dans les murs géométriques d'un quai." The statement is reported by the painter Schanne (1887, 231–32).

9. Li refers to the famous phrase of Xunzi in the "Li lun" 禮論 of "mastering destiny and making use of it" (19.95.1).

10. "Je voulus faire comme lui, être plus que belle, c'est-à-dire coquette, coquette pour lui, comme il l'était pour le monde" (Baudelaire 2002, 16).

11. "Ils ne pouvaient, dandies forcenés, se définir que par rapport à ces ennemis, prendre forme que dans le combat acharné" (Camus 1965, 224).

12. ". . . ne peut ni ne veut vivre l'être ou l'existence jusqu'au bout" (Baudelaire, p. 90). His existence is "retenue, fugace, toute semblable à une odeur" (204). Baudelaire "n'est jamais tout à fait là, ni tout à fait visible, il reste en suspens entre le néant et l'être" (200).

13. Lady Hester Stanhope was a British socialite and is famous for her archaeological expedition to Syria in 1815 where she tried to find a treasure following a map printed in a medieval Italian manuscript. Such textual uses for archeological purposes were new at the time. See Silberman 1984.

14. "A ce jeu de 'perd qui gagne' c'est le vainqueur qui, en tant que vaincu remporte la victoire" (113–14).

15. According to Jean d'Ormesson, the dandy therefore emerges as the first "philosopher (. . . .) "who strives to remain continuously detached from both snobbism and anti-snobbism" (d'Ormesson 1963, 453).

16. "Un dandy peut mettre s'il veut dix heures à sa toilette, mais une fois faite, il l'oublie" (Barbey 1895, 311n22).

17. It has been referred to in note 1 of chapter 1 of this book.

Notes to Chapter 8

1. "Un dandy peut être un homme blasé, peut être un homme souffrant; mais, dans ce dernier cas, il sourira comme le Lacédémonien sous la morsure du renard" (1885, 93; trans. modified).

2. See chapter 5 note 8 of this book.

3. See Moeller 2011, 25; Slingerland 2014, n42; Christopher Kirby 2017; Fraser 2014, Nathaniel Barrett 2011; Chris Jochim 1998; P. J. Ivanhoe 1993.

4. *Wuwei* as an action that is as effortless as an inaction, does also capture Csíkszentmihályi's idea of flow. Csíkszentmihályi does not mention it, but Slingerland points to the parallel.

5. He refers to James's early *Principles of Psychology* (1880).

6. Hundun (混沌) is a legendary faceless being in Chinese mythology and also the primordial chaos in Chinese cosmogony.

7. The link between freedom-equality and warmth might look counterintuitive, but one must consider that Enlightenment *philosophes* also suggested a more obvious warmth component in the form of "fraternity," which does not push the individual towards the universal through the use of reason but suggests the "warmer" communitarianism as a supplementary option (see Conty 2017).

Bibliography

Albert, John. 1987. "Two Studies in Chuang Tzu: Thomas Merton and Oscar Wilde." In *The Merton Seasonal* 12, no. 1: 5–14. Available on A//merton.org/ITMS/Seasonal/12/12-1Albert.pdf.
Amann, Elisabeth. 2015. *Dandyism in the Age of Revolution: The Art of the Cut.* Chicago: University of Chicago Press.
Ames, Roger T. 1981. "Taoism and the Androgynous Ideal." *Historical Reflections / Réflexions Historiques* 8, no. 3: 21–45.
Ames, Roger T. 2016. Introduction to *Wandering at Ease in the Zhuangzi*, edited by Roger Ames, 1–14. New York: State University of New York Press.
An, Yanming. 2004. "Western 'Sincerity' and Confucian 'Cheng.'" *Asian Philosophy* 14, no. 2: 155–69.
Anderson, Tyson 1985. "Wittgenstein and Nâgârjuna's Paradox." *Philosophy East and West* 35, no. 2: 157–69.
Anonymous. 1844. "Beau Brummell." *Blackwood's Edinburgh Magazine* 8, 769–84. https://www.gutenberg.org/files/23529/23529-h/23529-h.htm.
Antliff, Mark. 1998. "Cubism, Futurism, Anarchism: The 'Aestheticism' of the 'Action d'art' Group, 1906–1920." *Oxford Art Journal* 21, no. 2: 101–120.
Arnold, Matthew. 1869. *Culture and Anarchy: An Essay in Political and Social Criticism.* London: Smith, Elder & Co.
Ashelford, Jane. 1996. *The Art of Dress: Clothes and Society 1500–1914.* London: National Trust.
Baecque, Antoine de. 1997. *The Body Politic: Corporeal Metaphor in Revolutionary France, 1770–1800.* Stanford: Stanford University Press.
Balzac, Honoré de. 1854 [1830]. *Traité de la vie élégante.* Paris: Librairie Nouvelle.
Barbey d'Aurevilly, Jules. 1897. *Of Dandyism and of George Brummell.* London: Dent. French translation: *Du Dandysme et de George Brummell.* Paris: Alphonse Lemerre, 1879 [1845].
Barbey d'Aurevilly, Jules. 1926–27. *L'Amour impossible* in *Œuvres complètes* Vol. 9. Paris: Bernouard.

Bashford, Bruce. 2017. "'Even Things That Are True Can Be Proved': Oscar Wilde on Argument." In *Philosophy and Oscar Wilde*, edited by M. Bennett, 53–71. New York: Palgrave.

Baudelaire, Charles. 1986a [1863]. *The Painter of Modern Life and other Essays*. Translated by J. Mayne. New York: Da Capo. French translation: *Le Peintre de la vie moderne* (Œuvres complètes III). Paris: Calmann Lévy, 1885.

Baudelaire, Charles. 1986b. *Fusées; Mon Cœur mis a nu; La Belgique deshabillée; Amoenitates Belgicae*. Paris: Gallimard.

Baudelaire, Charles. 2002 [1847]. *La Fanfarlo*. Paris: Éditions du Boucher.

Baudrillard, Jean. 1990 [1970]. *Seduction*. Montreal: New World Perspectives.

Benemann, William E. 2006. *Male-Male Intimacy in Early America: Beyond Romantic Friendships*. New York: Harrington Park.

Benjamin, Walter. 1972. *Passagenwerk* in *Gesammelte Werke* V, ed. R. Tiedemann and H. Schweppenhäuser. Frankfurt: Suhrkamp.

Bennett, Michael Y., ed. 2017. *Philosophy and Oscar Wilde*. New York: Palgrave.

Berkson, Mark A. 2005. "Conceptions of Self/No-Self and Modes of Connection: Comparative Soteriological Structures in Classical Chinese Thought." *Journal of Religious Ethics* 33, no. 2: 293–331.

Berlin, Isaiah. 2013 [1965]: *The Roots of Romanticism*. Princeton, NJ: Princeton University Press.

Berman, Paul. 1992. "Introduction: The Debate and its Origins." In *Debating P.C.: The Controversy over Political Correctness on College Campuses*, edited by P. Berman., 1–25. New York: Dell.

Billeter, Jean François. 2013. *Notes sur Tchouang-tseu et la philosophie*. Paris: Allia.

Bloom, Allan. 2008 [1987]. *The Closing of the American Mind*. New York: Simon and Schuster.

Botz-Bornstein, Thorsten. 1995. "Rulefollowing in Dandyism: Style as an Overcoming of Rule and Structure." *Modern Language Review* 90: 285–95.

Botz-Bornstein, Thorsten. 2004. *Place and Dream: Japan and the Virtual*. Amsterdam: Rodopi.

Botz-Bornstein, Thorsten. 2007. "Dreams in Buddhism and Western Aesthetics: Some Thoughts on Play, Style, and Space." *Asian Philosophy* 17, no. 1: 65–81.

Botz-Bornstein, Thorsten. 2011. *The Cool-Kawaii: Afro-Japanese Aesthetics and New World Modernity*. Lanham: Lexington-Rowman & Littlefield.

Botz-Bornstein, Thorsten. 2019. *The New Aesthetics of Deculturation: Neoliberalism, Fundamentalism and Kitsch*. London: Bloomsbury.

Botz-Bornstein, Thorsten. 2020. "Review of Bérénice Levet, *Libérons-nous du féminisme*." In *Gender, Place and Culture* 27, no. 8 (2020): 1219–1222.

Boulenger, Jacques. 1907. *Les Dandies*. Paris: Ollendorf.

Brown, Joanna. 2006. "Nothing but a Name Mysteriously Sparkling." *Jane Austen Magazine*, February 9. https://www.janeausten.co.uk/beau-brummell-nothing-but-a-name-mysteriously-sparkling/.

Bulwer-Lytton, Edward. 1840. *Pelham or Adventures of a Gentleman*. London: Chapman and Hall.
Butler, Judith. 1990. "Performative Acts and Gender Constitution: An Essay in Phenomenology and Feminist Theory." In *Performing Feminisms: Feminist Critical Theory and Theatre*, edited by Sue-Ellen Case, 519–31. Baltimore: Johns Hopkins University Press.
Butler, Judith. 1993. *Bodies that Matter: On the Discursive Limits of 'Sex.'* New York: Routledge.
Campbell, John. 1851. *Negromania*. Philadelphia: Campbell & Power.
Camus, Albert. 1965. *L'Homme revolté* in *Essais* ed. by R. Quilliot and L. Faucon. Paris: Gallimard.
Carassus, Emilien, 1971. *Le Mythe du dandy*. Paris: Colin.
Carnap, Rudolf, 1932, "The Elimination of Metaphysics Through Logical Analysis of Language." In *Logical Positivism*, edited by A. J. Ayer, 60–81. New York: Free Press.
Carr, Karen, and Philip Ivanhoe. 2010. *The Sense of Antirationalism: The Religious Thought of Zhuangzi and Kierkegaard*. Seattle: CreateSpace.
Chan, Sin Yee. 2003. "The Confucian Conception of Gender in the Twenty-First Century." In *Confucianism for the Modern World*, edited by D. Bell and H. Chaibong, 312–33. Cambridge: Cambridge University Press.
Chateaubriand, François-René de. 1836. *Essais sur la littérature anglaise* tome II. Paris: Gosselin et Furne.
Chateaubriand, François-René de. 1848 [2005]. *Memoirs from Beyond the Grave (Mémoires d'Outre-Tombe) Book XXVII*. Translated by A. S. Kline. London: The London Embassy. https://www.poetryintranslation.com/PITBR/Chateaubriand/ChateaubriandMemoirsBookXXVII.php.
Clary, Sasha. 2018. "Society Has an Unhealthy Obsession with Genitals and Body Parts." *Healthline.com*, May 11. https://www.healthline.com/health/womens-health/having-a-vagina-trans-woman#2.
Confucius. 1971. *Confucian Analects: The Great Learning, and The Doctrine of the Mean*. Translated by James Legge). New York: Dover.
Confucius. 2003. *Analects: With Selections from Traditional Commentaries*. Trans. and commentaries by Edward Slingerland. New York: Hackett.
Confucius. 2006–2019. *Analects*. Chinese Text Project. https://ctext.org/analects.
Conty, Arianne. 2017. "Liberty, Equality, and/or Fraternity: The Aporia of Democracy in Immanuel. Kant and John Rawls." *Dialegesthai*, June 27, 2017. https://mondodomani.org/dialegesthai/acon01.htm. Last accessed on 2.14.2021.
Conze, Edward. 1959. *Buddhism: Its Essence and Development*. New York: Harper & Brothers.
Cooper, David E., Paul D'Ambrosio, and Hans-Georg Moeller. 2019. "Decoding the 'Zhuangzi': A Debate on Hans-Georg Moeller and Paul J. D'Ambrosio's 'Genuine Pretending.'" *Los Angeles Review of Books*, September 15.

Coyle, Daniel. 2016. "On the *Zhenren*." In *Wandering at Ease in the Zhuangzi*, edited by R. Ames, 197–210. Albany: State University of New York Press.
Crandell, Michael Mark. 1983. "On Walking without Touching the Ground" *Experimental Essays on Chuang-tzu*, edited by V. Mair, 125–39. Honolulu: University of Hawai'i Press.
Csíkszentmihályi, Mihaly. 1990. *Flow: The Psychology of Optimal Experience*. New York: Harper and Row.
D'Ambrosio, Paul. 2015. "Authenticity in the Zhuangzi? Contemporary Misreadings of *Zhen* 真 and an Alternative to Existentialism." *Frontiers of Philosophy in China* 10, no. 3: 353–79.
D'Ambrosio, Paul J. 2017. "Imagination in the Zhuangzi: The Madman of Chu's Alternative to Confucian Cultivation." *Asian Philosophy* 27, no. 1: 30–42.
D'Ormesson, Jean. 1963. "Arrivisme, snobisme, dandysme." *Revue de métaphysique et de morale* 68: 443–59.
De Botton, Alain. 2008. "Political Correctness vs. Politeness." In *The Book of Life: An Emotional Education*. Harmondsworth: Penguin. https://www.theschooloflife.com/thebookoflife/political-correctness-vs-politeness/.
Debon, Günther. 1986. *Oscar Wilde und der Taoismus*. Bern: Peter Lang.
Derrida, Jacques. 1972. *La Dissémination*. Paris: Seuil.
Derrida, Jacques. 1987. *Psyché: Inventions de l'autre I*. Paris: Gallilée.
Dinerstein, Joel. 1999. "Lester Young and the Birth of Cool" in *Signifyin(g), Sanctifyin(g), & Slam Dunking: A Reader in African American Expressive Culture*, edited by G. Caponi, 239–78. Boston: University of Massachusetts Press.
Ding, Xiaoyu. 2012. *Oscar Wilde and China in Late Nineteenth Century Britain: Aestheticism, Orientalism, and the Making of Modernism*. Hong Kong: University of Hong Kong Press.
Dorfles, Gillo. 1968. *Kitsch: The World of Bad Taste*. New York: Bell.
Eliade, Mircea. 1959. *The Sacred and the Profane: The Nature of Religion*. Translated by Willard Trask. Boston: Houghton Mifflin Harcourt.
Eliade, Mircea. 1991. *Images and Symbols: Studies in Religious Symbolism*. Translated by Philip Mairet. Princeton, NJ: Princeton University Press.
Ellmann, Richard. 1988. *Oscar Wilde*. New York: Alfred Knopf.
Eno, Robert. 2016: "Logicians and Philosophers of Language: Hui Shi, the Later Mohists, and Gongsun Long." https://chinatxt.sitehost.iu.edu/Thought/Logic_and_Language.pdf.
Feldman, Jessica. 1993. *Gender on the Divide: The Dandy in Modernist Literature*. Ithaca, NY: Cornell University Press.
Fox, Sharon Louise. 2016. *Dandy as Disease: Gender Hygiene and British Nineteenth-Century Literature*. Thesis 1471. http://scholarworks.uark.
Fraser, Chris. 2011. "Emotion and Agency in Zhuangzi." *Asian Philosophy* 21, no. 1: 97–121.

Fraser, Chris. 2012. "Landscape, Travel, and a Daoist View of the 'Cosmic Question.'" http: //cjfraser.net/images/2012/12/Fraser-LandscapeDaoist_7Dec2012.pdf.
Fraser, Chris. 2017. "School of Names." In *The Stanford Encyclopedia of Philosophy*, edited by Edward N. Zalta. https://plato.stanford.edu/archives/spr2017/entries/school-names.
Fuhrer, Urs. 2004. *Cultivating Minds: Identity as Meaning-Making Practice*. London: Psychology Press.
Funayama, Toru. 2019. "Translation, Transcription, and What Else? Some Basic Characteristics of Chinese Buddhist Translations as a Cultural Contact between India and China." In *Buddhism and the Dynamics of Transculturality*, 85–100. Berlin: de Gruyter.
Gadamer, Hans-Georg. 1993. "Die Aktualität des Schönen: Kunst als Spiel, Symbol und Fest." In *Gesammelte Werke Band 8: Ästhetik und Poetik I: Kunst als Aussage*. Tübingen: Mohr-Siebeck.
Geiger, Annette. 2015. "Cool ist out: Warum James Bond heute weinen muss und die Avantgarde immer weniger Gefühle zeigt." In *Coolness: Zur Ästhetik einer kulturellen Strategie und Attitüde*, edited by A. Geiger, G. Schröder, and Ä. Söll, 85–104. Berlin: Transcript Verlag.
Giles, Herbert, trans. 2019 [1889]. *Chuang Tzu: Mystic, Moralist, and Social Reformer* [trans. of the Zhuangzi]. Glasgow: Good Press.
Goodman, Russell. 1976. "Style, Dialectic, and the Aim of Philosophy in Wittgenstein and the Taoists." *Chinese Journal of Philosophy* 3, no. 2: 145–57.
Graham, A. C., trans. 2001. *Chuang-Tzu: The Inner Chapters*. Indianapolis and Cambridge: Hackett.
Graham, A. C. 1978. *Later Mohist Logic, Ethics and Science*. Hong Kong: Chinese University Press.
Greenberg, Clement. 1961. "Avantgarde and Kitsch." In Greenberg's *Art and Culture: Critical Essays*. Boston: Beacon.
Gudmunsen, Chris. 1977. *Wittgenstein and Buddhism*. London: Macmillan.
Hall, Stuart. 1994. "Some 'Politically Incorrect' Pathways through PC." In *The War of Words: The Political Correctness Debate*, edited by S. Dunant, 164–83. London: Virago.
Hansen, Chad. 1983. "A Tao of Tao in Chuang-Tzu." In *Experimental Essays on Chuang-tzu*, edited by V. Mair, 24–55. Honolulu: University of Hawai'i Press.
Hansen, Chad. 2000. *A Daoist Theory of Chinese Thought: A Philosophical Interpretation*. Oxford: Oxford University Press.
Harden, Nathan. 2012. *Sex and God at Yale: Porn, Political Correctness, and a Good Education Gone Bad*. New York: Thomas Dunne Books-St. Martin's Press.
Heidegger, Martin. 1980. *Being and Time*, Translated by J. Macquarrie and E. Robinson. Oxford: Blackwell.

Heidegger, Martin. 1986 [1927]. *Sein und Zeit*. Tübingen: Niemeyer.
Heidegger, Martin. 1996. *Being and Time*. Translated by Joan Stambaugh. New York: State University of New York Press.
Hess, Amanda. 2019. "How 'Political Correctness' Went from Punch Line to Panic." In *Political Correctness: Too Far or Not Far Enough?*, edited by Alex Ward, 93–97. New York: Rosen.
Höchsmann, Hyun, and Yang Guorong, trans. 2006. *Zhuangzi* (Longman Library of Primary Sources in Philosophy). New York: Pearson Longman.
Huang, Yong. 2010. "The Ethics of Difference in the Zhuangzi." *Journal of the American Academy of Religion* 78: 1, 65–99.
Hudson, H. 1973. "Wittgenstein and Zen Buddhism." *Philosophy East and West* 23, no. 4: 471–81.
Huizinga, Johan. 1970. *Homo Ludens*. London: Temple Smith.
Hurston, Zora Neale. 1997 [1925]. *Spunk: A Collection of Short Stories*. Boston: DaCapo.
Izutsu, Toshihiko. 1982. *Towards a Philosophy of Zen Buddhism*. Boulder: Pranja.
Izutsu, Toshihiko. 1983. *Sufism and Daoism: A Comparative Study of Key Philosophical Concepts*. Berkeley: University of California Press.
Izutsu, Toyo and Toshiko Izutsu. 1981. *The Theory of Beauty in the Classical Aesthetics of Japan*. The Hague: Nijhoff.
Jackson, Russell. 1997. "The Importance of Being Earnest" in *The Cambridge Companion to Oscar Wilde*, edited by P. Raby, 161–78. London: Cambridge University Press.
Jahanbegloo, Ramin. 2011. *Conversations with Isaiah Berlin*. London: Halban.
James, William. 1912. *Essays in Radical Empiricism*. New York and Boston: Longmans & Green.
Jesse, William. 1844. *The Life of George Brummell*. 2 vols. London: Saunders and Otley.
Jochim, Chris. 2016. "Just Say No to 'No Self' in *Zhuangzi*" in *Wandering at Ease in the Zhuangzi*, edited by R. Ames, 35–74. Albany: State University of New York Press.
Kalupahana, David J. 1977. "The Notion of Suffering in Early Buddhism Compared with Some Reflections of Early Wittgenstein." *Philosophy East and West* 27, no. 4: 423–31.
Kant, Immanuel. 1908 [1790]. *Kritik der Urteilskraft*, in *Kants gesammelte Schriften* XV. Edited by Königl. Preussischen Akademie der Wissenschaften. Berlin: Reimer.
Kant, Immanuel. 1911 [1781]. *Kritik der reinen Vernunft* (Kants Werke IV). Berlin: Reimer. English translation: *Critique of Pure Reason*. New York: Dover 1900.
Kasulis, Thomas. 1985. *Zen Action Zen Person*. Honolulu: University of Hawai'i Press.
Kelly, Ian. 2006. *Beau Brummel: The Ultimate Man of Style*. New York: Free Press.

Kjellberg, Paul. 1994. "Skepticism, Truth, and the Good Life: A Comparison of Zhuangzi and Sextus Empiricus." *Philosophy East and West* **44**, no. 1: 111–133.
Knox, Melissa. "Homo Ludens: Oscar Wilde's Philosophy." In *Philosophy and Oscar Wilde*, edited by M. Bennett, *107–32*. New York: Palgrave.
Kohn, Livia, ed. 2015b. *New Visions of the Zhuangzi*. St. Petersburg: Three Pines Press.
Kohn, Livia. 2015. "Forget or Not Forget? The Neurophysiology of *Zuowang*." In *New Visions of the Zhuangzi*, edited by Livia Kohn, 161–179. St. Petersburg: Three Pines Press.
Kolomeytseva, Catherine B. 2020. "Dandyism and the Holy Fool Phenomenon as Two Extreme Aspects of Spiritual Quest." *Global Journal of Human Social Science* (St. Petersburg), 20, no. 8.
Kors, Alan Charles, and Harvey Silverglate. 1999. *The Shadow University: The Betrayal of Liberty on America's Campuses*. New York: Simon and Schuster.
Lasch, Christopher. 1979. *The Culture of Narcissism: American Life in an Age of Diminishing Expectations*. New York: Norton.
Le Bot, Marc. 1990. "Andy Warhol: Le Dandysme d'aujourd'hui" in *Esprit* 165: 10, 5–9.
Lea, John. 2008. *Political Correctness and Higher Education: British and American Perspectives*. New York: Routledge.
Lee, Tosi. 2004. "Fire Down Below and Watering, That's Life: A Buddhist Reader's Response to Marcel Duchamp" in *Buddha Mind in Contemporary Art*, edited by Jacquelyn Bass and Mary Jane Jacob. Berkeley: University of California Press.
Legge, James, trans. 1891. *The Zhuangzi* available on *The Chinese Text Project* on https://ctext.org/zhuangzi.
Legge, James, trans. 1891b. *Dao De Jing* available on *The Chinese Text Project* on https://ctext.org/dao-de-jing.
Legutko, Ryszard. 2016. *The Demon in Democracy: Totalitarian Temptations in Free Societies*. New York: Encounter Books.
Lessing, Doris. 1992. "Political Correctness." *New York Times*, June 22.
Lethen, Helmut. 1994. *Verhaltenslehren der Kälte: Lebensversuche zwischen den Kriegen*. Frankfurt: Suhrkamp.
Levaillant, Jean. 1979. "Avant Rêve" in Paul Valéry, *Questions du rêve (Cahiers Paul Valéry III)*. Paris: Gallimard, 13–19.
Levet, Bérénice. 2018. *Libérons-nous du féminisme*. Paris: Editions de l'observatoire.
Levinovitz, Alain. 2012. "The Zhuangzi and You 遊: Defining an Ideal Without Contradiction" in *Dao: A Journal of Comparative Philosophy* 11, 479–96.
Li, Xiaofan Amy. 2018. "Playful You in the *Zhuangzi* and Six Dynasties Literati Writing." *Journal of the British Association for Chinese Studies* 8, no. 2: 1–28.

Li, Zehou. 2009. *The Chinese Aesthetic Tradition*. Honolulu: University of Hawai'i Press.
Li, Zehou. 2019. *A History of Classical Chinese Thought*. New York: Routledge.
Li-Hsiang, Lisa Rosenlee. 2006. *Confucianism and Women: A Philosophical Interpretation*. Albany: State University of New York Press.
Liu, Alan. 2004. *The Laws of Cool: Knowledge Work and the Culture of Information*. Chicago: University of Chicago Press.
Loos, Adolf. 1962 [1898]. "Die Herrenmode." In *Ins Leere gesprochen*, 19–25. Munich: Herold.
Lundberg, Brian. 2016. "A Meditation on Friendship." In *Wandering at Ease in the Zhuangzi*, edited by R. Ames, 211–18. Albany: State University of New York Press.
Mailer, Norman. 1970 [1957]. *The White Negro: Superficial Reflections on the Hipster*. San Francisco: City Lights.
Mair, Victor, ed. 1983b. *Experimental Essays on Chuang-Tzu*. Honolulu: University of Hawai'i Press
Mair, Victor H., trans. 1994. *Wandering on the Way: Early Taoist Tales and Parables of Chuang Tzu* [translation of the *Zhuangzi* with Introduction]. London: Bantam.
Mair, Victor. 1983a. "Chuang-Tzu and Erasmus: Kindred Wits" in *Experimental Essays on Chuang-Tzu*, edited by V. Mair, 85–100. Honolulu: University of Hawai'i Press.
Majors, Richard, and Janet Mancini Billson. 1992. *Cool Pose: The Dilemma of Black Manhood*. New York: Lexington.
Makeham, John. 2016. "Between *Chen* and *Cai*: Zhuangzi and the Analects." In *Wandering at Ease in the Zhuangzi*, edited by R. Ames, 75–100. Albany: State University of New York Press.
Marjoribanks, Edward. 1932. *Carson the Advocate*. London: Macmillan.
Marsden, Pat. 2016. "William Brummell (1777–1853). Who Owned the Wivenhoe House Estate from 1811–1853." In *Wivenhoe's History*. https://www.wivenhoehistory.org.uk/content/topics/people-2/william-brummell-1777-1853.
Mattice, Sarah. 2017. "Daoist Aesthetics of the Everyday and the Fantastical." In *Artistic Visions and the Promise of Beauty: Cross-Cultural Perspectives*, edited by K. Higgins, S. Maira, and S. Sikka, 251–65. New York: Springer.
McCormack, Jerusha. 2007. "From Chinese Wisdom to Irish Wit: Zhuangzi and Oscar Wilde." *Irish University Review* 37, no. 2: 302–21.
McCormack, Jerusha. 2017. "Oscar Wilde: As Daoist Sage." In *Philosophy and Oscar Wilde*, edited by M. Bennett, 73–103. New York: Palgrave.
Mencius (Ke Meng). 2003. *Mencius*. Translated by D. C. Lau. Hong Kong: Chinese University Press.
Michael, Thomas. 2015. "Hermits, Mountains, and Yangsheng in Early Daoism." In *New Visions of the Zhuangzi*, edited by Livia Kohn, 149–64. St. Petersburg: Three Pines Press.

Michéa, Jean-Claude. 2008. "Michéa avec MAUSS." *Revue du MAUSS permanent*. http://archive.wikiwix.com/cache/?url=http%3A%2F%2Fwww.journaldumauss.net%2Fspip.php%3Farticle308.

Mocchia di Coggiola, Massimiliano. 2016. *Il Gagà*. Cesena: Giubilei Regnani.

Mocchia di Coggiola, Massimiliano. 2019. *Il Dandy*. Milan: Alcatraz.

Moeller, Hans-Georg, trans. 2013. *Daodejing*. Chicago: Open Court.

Moeller, Hans-Georg, and Andrew K. Whitehead. 2020. *Critique, Subversion, and Chinese Philosophy: Socio-Political, Conceptual, and Methodological Challenges*. London: Bloomsbury.

Moeller, Hans-Georg, and Paul D'Ambrosio. 2018. "Authority without Authenticity: The *Zhuangzi*'s Genuine Pretending as Socio-Political Strategy." *Religions* 9, no. 398: 1–11.

Moeller, Hans-Georg, and Paul J. D'Ambrosio. 2017. *Genuine Pretending: On the Philosophy of the Zhuangzi*. New York: Columbia University Press.

Moeller, Hans-Georg. 1999. "Zhuangzi's 'Dream of the Butterfly': A Daoist Interpretation." *Philosophy East and West* 49, no. 4: 439–50.

Moeller, Hans-Georg. 2004. *Daoism Explained: From the Dream of the Butterfly to the Fishnet Allegory*. Chicago: Open Court.

Moeller, Hans-Georg. 2006. *The Philosophy of the Daodejing*. New York: Columbia University Press.

Moeller, Hans-Georg. 2008. "Idiotic Irony in the *Zhuangzi*." In *Chinese Literature: Essays, Articles, Reviews (CLEAR)* 30: 117–23.

Moeller, Hans-Georg. 2009. *The Moral Fool: A Case for Amorality*. New York: Columbia University Press.

Moeller, Hans-Georg. 2015. "Paradoxes of Health and Power in the Zhuangzi." In *New Visions of the Zhuangzi*, edited by L. Kohn, 70–81. St Peterburg, FL: Three Pines Press.

Moeller, Hans-Georg. 2020. "Genuine Pretending." In *ODIP: Online Dictionary of Intercultural Philosophy*, edited by T. Botz-Bornstein. https://www.Odiphilosophy.com/genuine-pretending.

Moeller, Hans-Georg. 2020b. "The King's Slaughterer—or, the Royal Way of Nourishing Life." *Philosophy East & West* 70, no. 1: 1–19.

Moers, Ellen. 1960. *The Dandy: Brummell to Beerbohm*. New York: Viking.

Monson, Ingrid. 1995. "The Problem with White Hipness: Race, Gender, and Cultural Conceptions in Jazz Historical Discourse." *Journal of the American Musicological Society* 18, no. 3: 396–422.

Mou, Bo. 2020. "Wuwei." In *ODIP: The Online Dictionary of Intercultural Philosophy*, edited by T. Botz-Bornstein. https://www.odiphilosophy.com/wuwei2.

Müller, Max. 1880. *Dhammapada* Vol. 1. Edited by F. Max Müller. Oxford: Clarendon Press.

Murray, Isobel. 1971. "Oscar Wilde's Absorption of 'Influences': The Case History of Chuang Tzu." *Durham University Journal* 64, no. 1:1–13.

Nakamura, Lisa. 2005. "The Multiplication of Difference in Post-Millenial Cyberpunk Film: The Visual Culture of Race in the Matrix Trilogy." In *The Matrix Trilogy: Cyberpunk Reloaded*, edited by Stacey Gillis, 126–37. London: Wallflower.

Natta, Christine. 1989. Introduction to Barbey d'Aurevilly, *Du dandysme de Georges Brummell de J. Barbey d'Aurevilly*, 1–28. Paris: Plein Chant.

Natta, Marie-Christine. 2011. *Grandeur sans convictions: Essai sur le dandysme*. Paris: Editions du Felin.

Nishida, Kitarô. 1990. *Inquiry into the Good*. Translated by Masao Abe and Charles Ives. New Haven, CT: Yale University Press.

Oxford English Dictionary. 1989. "Dandy." Oxford: Oxford University Press.

Özbey, Sonya. 2018. "Undermining the Person, Undermining the Establishment in the Zhuangzi." In *Comparative and Continental Philosophy* 10, no. 2: 123–39.

Patterson, Orlando. 1972. "Toward a Future that Has no Past: Reflections on the Fate of Blacks in the Americas." In *The Public Interest* 27, 25–67.

Paulicelli, Eugenia. 2019. *Moda e letteratura nell'Italia della prima modernità. Dalla sprezzatura alla satira*. Milan: Meltemi.

Perry, Ruth. 1992. "Historically Correct." In *The Women's Review of Books* 9, no. 5: 14–15.

Peterson, Jordan, Stephen Fry, Eric Dyson, and Michelle Goldberg. 2018. *Political Correctness Gone Mad?* London: One World.

Peterson, Jordan. 2016. "The Right to Be Politically Incorrect: Why I Refuse to Use Genderless Pronouns." *National Post*, November 8. https://nationalpost.com/opinion/jordan-peterson-the-right-to-be-politically-incorrect.

Pichois, Claude, and Jean-Paul Avice. 2002. *Dictionnaire Baudelaire*. Tusson: Du Lerot.

Pountain, Dick, and David Robins. 2000. *Cool Rules: Anatomy of an Attitude*. London: Reaktion.

Radcliff, Carter. 2001. "Dandyism and Abstraction in a Universe Defined by Newton." In *Dandies: Fashion and Finesse in Art and Culture*, edited by S. Fillin-Yeh, 101–26. New York: New York University Press.

Raphals, Lisa. 1994. "Skeptical Strategies in the 'Zhuangzi' and 'Theaetetus,'" *Philosophy East and West* 44, no. 3: 501–26.

Reader, Simon. 2017. "Wilde at Oxford: A Truce with Facts." In *Philosophy and Oscar Wilde*, ed. M. Bennett, 9–27. New York: Palgrave.

Ribeiro, Aileen. 2002. "On Englishness in Dress." In *The Englishness of English Dress*, edited by Christopher Breward, Becky Conekin, and Caroline Cox, 15–28. Oxford: Berg.

Rieman, Fred. 1977. "On Linguistic Skepticism in Wittgenstein and Kung-sun Lung." *Philosophy East and West* 27, no. 2: 183–93.

Rorty, Richard. 1998. *Truth and Progress: Philosophical Papers*. Cambridge: Cambridge University Press.

Rosemont, Henry Jr. 1997. "Confucian and Feminist Perspectives on the Self." In *Culture and Self*, edited by D. Allen, 63–82. Boulder, CO: Westview.
Roslak, Robyn S. 1991. "The Politics of Aesthetic Harmony: Neo-Impressionism, Science, and Anarchism." *Art Bulletin* 73, no. 3: 381–90.
Rouart, Jullien. 1979. "La Tentation du rêve chez Paul Valéry." *Questions du rêve (Cahiers Paul Valéry III)*, 1–35. Paris: Gallimard.
Sainte-Beuve, Charles Augustin. 1866. "Flâneur and flânerie." In *Grand dictionnaire universel du XIXe siècle*. 1–35. Vol. 8. Paris: Larousse.
Sartre, Jean-Paul. 1947. *Baudelaire*. Paris: Gallimard.
Sartre, Jean-Paul. 1967. *Baudelaire: A Critical Study*. New York: New Directions
Sax, Leonard. 2002. "How Common is Intersex? A Response to Anne Fausto-Sterling." *Journal of Sex Research* 39, no. 3: 174–178.
Scaraffia, Giuseppe. 1981. *Dizionario del dandy*. Roma-Bari: Laterza.
Schanne, Alexandre Louis. 1887. *Souvenirs de Schaunard: Édition ornée de deux portraits: Schaunard à vingt ans et Schaunard aujourd'hui*. Paris: Charpentier.
Schiffer, Daniel Salvatore. 2010. *Le Dandysme, dernier éclat d'héroïsme*. Paris: PUF.
Sellman, James. 2016. "Transformational Humor in the Zhuangzi." In *Wandering at Ease in the Zhuangzi*, edited by R. Ames, 163–74. Albany: State University of New York Press.
Shusterman, Richard. 2003. "Rap as Art and Philosophy." In *A Companion to African American Philosophy*, edited by Tommy Lott and John P. Pittman, 419–28. Oxford: Blackwell.
Sigurðsson, Geir. 2020. "Pedagogical Self-Subversion and Critical Becoming in Early Confucian Philosophy." In *Critique, Subversion, and Chinese Philosophy: Socio-Political, Conceptual, and Methodological Challenges*, edited by H.-G. Moeller and A. Whitehead, 9–20. London: Bloomsbury.
Silberman, Neil Asher. 1984. "Restoring the Reputation of Lady Hester Lucy Stanhope." *Biblical Archaeology Review* 10: 68–75. https://www.baslibrary.org/biblical-archaeology-review/10/4/5.
Simmel, Georg. 1995 [1903]. "Die Grosstädte und das Geistesleben." In *Aufsätze und Abhandlungen*, 116–31. Frankfurt: Suhrkamp.
Skaja, Henry G. 2016. "How to Interpret Chapter 16 of the Zhuangzi: 'Repairers of Nature.'" In *Wandering at Ease in the Zhuangzi*, edited by R. Ames, 101–24. Albany: State University of New York Press.
Slingerland, Edward. 2004. "Conceptions of Self in the Zhuangzi: Conceptual Metaphor Analysis and Comparative Thought." *Philosophy East and West* 54, no. 3: 322–42.
Slingerland, Edward. 2007. *Effortless Action: Wu-wei as Conceptual Metaphor and Spiritual Ideal in Early China*. Oxford: Oxford University Press.
Slingerland, Edward. 2014. *Trying Not to Try: The Art and Science of Spontaneity*. New York: Crown.

Sontag, Susan. 1982. "Notes on Camp." In *Against Interpretation and Other Essays*, 275–92. New York: Octagon.
Springer, Claudia. 2005. "Playing it Cool in the Matrix." In *The Matrix Trilogy: Cyberpunk Reloaded*, ed. S. Gillis, 89–100. London: Wallflower.
Stanhope, Lady Hester. 1845. *Memoirs of the Lady Hester Stanhope* Vol. 1. London: Colburn.
Stearns, Peter N. 1994. *American Cool: Constructing a Twentieth Century Emotional Style*. Albany: State University of New York Press.
Sternberg, Jacques. 1972. *Kitsch*. London and New York: Academy Editions/St. Martin's Press.
Stevenson, Frank W. 2006. "Zhuangzi's 'Dao as Background Noise." *Philosophy East and West* 56, no. 2: 20, 301–31.
Suhr, Stephanie, and Sally Johnson. 2003. "Re-visiting 'PC': Introduction to Special Issue on 'Political Correctness.'" *Discourse & Society* 14, no. 1: 5–16.
Szilágyi, Anna. 2017. "A Linguist Explains How the Far-Right Hijacked Political Correctness." *Quartz*, January 18. https://qz.com/886552/a-linguist-explains-how-the-far-right-hijacked-political-correctness.
Tacium, David. 1998. "Le Dandysme et la crise de l'identité masculine à la fin du XIXe siècle: Huysmans, Pater, Dossi." PhD diss., Université de Montréal.
Takaki, Ronald. 1979. *Iron Cages: Race and Culture in 19th-Century America*. Oxford: Oxford University Press.
Taylor, Charles. 2007. *A Secular Age*. Cambridge, MA: Harvard University Press.
Theodor, Ithamar, and Zhihua Yao. 2013. *Brahman and Dao: Comparative Studies of Indian and Chinese Philosophy and Religion*. Lanham, MD: Lexington.
Thomas, Clarence. 2007. "The Justice Nobody Knows" CBS. September 27. https://www.cbsnews.com/news/clarence-thomas-the-justice-nobody-knows/.
Thurman, R. A. F. 1980. "Philosophical Nonegocentrism in Wittgenstein and Candeakîrti in their Treatment of the Private Language Problem." *Philosophy East and West* 30, no. 3: 321–37.
Todorov, Tzvetan. 1973. *The Fantastic: A Structural Approach to a Literary Genre*. Cleveland: Case Western Reserve University Press.
Tominaga, Thomas. 1983. "Ch'an, Taoism, and Wittgenstein." *Chinese Journal of Philosophy* 10: 127–45.
Toshimitsu, Hasumi. 1973. *Elaboration philosophique de la pensée du zen*. Paris: La pensée universelle.
Trésor de la langue française. "Dandy." https://www.le-tresor-de-la-langue.fr/definition/dandy. Accessed March 10, 2020.
Trilling, Lionel. 1972, *Sincerity and Authenticity*. Cambridge, MA: Harvard University Press.
Ueda, Shizuteru. 1984. *Die zen buddistische Erfahrung des Wahr-Schönen*. Frankfurt: Insel.

Valéry, Paul. 1973. *Cahiers I* (Pléiade). Paris: Gallimard.
Valéry, Paul. 1974. *Cahiers II* (Pléiade). Paris: Gallimard.
Valéry, Paul. 1977. *Mes Théâtres (Cahiers Paul Valéry II)*. Paris: Gallimard.
Valéry, Paul. 1979. *Questions du rêve (Cahiers Paul Valéry III)*. Paris: Gallimard.
Valéry, Paul. 1986. *Cartesius redivivus (Cahiers Paul Valéry IV)*. Paris: Gallimard.
van Dooren, Tanja. 2006. *From Brummell to Byron: The Story of Early Nineteenth-Century British Dandyism*. Master's thesis, LUCA School of Arts Brussels.
Van Norden, Bryan W. 1996. "Competing Interpretations of the Inner Chapters of the 'Zhuangzi.'" *Philosophy East and West* 46, no. 2: 247–68.
Van Norden, Bryan W. 2016. "Zhuangzi's Ironic Detachment and Political Commitment." *Dao: A Journal of Comparative Philosophy* 15:1–17.
von Borries, Friedrich. 2018. *Who's Afraid of Niketown? Nike Urbanism, Branding and the City of Tomorrow*. Rotterdam: Episode.
Voskuil, Lynn. 2004. *Acting Naturally: Victorian Theatricality and Authenticity*. Charlottesville: University of Virginia Press.
Waldo, Ives. 1978. "Nāgārjuna and Analytic Philosophy." *Philosophy East and West* 28, no. 3: 287–98.
Ward, Robert Plumer. 1825. *Tremaine, or the Man of Refinement*. London: Henry Colburn.
Waterton, Matthew. 2016. "Kendall Jenner 'Appropriating' Ballerina Culture Shows How Ridiculous the Cultural Appropriation Debate has Become." *The Independent*, September 26. https://www.independent.co.uk/voices/kendall-jenner-cultural-appropriation-political-correctness-notting-hill-carnival-a7331111.html.
Watson, Burton, trans. 2013 [1968]. *The Complete Works of Zhuangzi*. New York: Columbia University Press.
White, T. H. 1950. *The Age of Scandal*. London: Jonathan Cape.
Wienpahl, Paul. 1958. "Zen and the Work of Wittgenstein." *Chicago Review* 12, no. 2: 67–72.
Wilde, Oscar. 1899 [1895]. *Importance of Being Earnest*. London: Smithers and Co.
Wilde, Oscar. 1919 [1890]. "A Chinese Sage." In *A Critic in Pall Mall: Being Extracts from Reviews and Miscellanies*, 177–87. London: Methuen.
Wilde, Oscar. 1962. *The Letters of Oscar Wilde*. Edited by Rupert Hart-Davis. London: Rupert Hart-Davis Limited.
Wilde, Oscar. 1992 [1890]. *The Picture of Dorian Gray*. Ware, UK: Wordsworth Editions.
Wilde, Oscar. 2000 [1905]. *De Profundis* in *The Complete Works of Oscar Wilde: De Profundis, "Epistola: in Carcere et Vinculis."* Edited by R. Jackson, I. Small, and J. Bristow. Oxford: Oxford University Press.
Wilde, Oscar. 2003 [1895]. "An Ideal Husband." In *Complete Works of Oscar Wilde*, edited by M. Holland, 515–82. London; HarperCollins.

Wilde, Oscar. 2005. *The Prose of Oscar Wilde*. New York: Cosimo.
Wilde, Oscar. 2007a [1891]. *The Critic as an Artist* in *The Complete Works of Oscar Wilde: Vol. IV*, edited by J. Guy, 140–200. Oxford: Oxford University Press.
Wilde, Oscar. 2007b [1891]. *The Decay of Lying* in *The Complete Works of Oscar Wilde Vol. IV*, edited by J. Guy, 73–107. Oxford: Oxford University Press.
Wilde, Oscar. 2007c [1891]. *Soul of Man under Socialism* in *The Complete Works of Oscar Wilde: Vol. IV*, edited by J. Guy, 231–68. Oxford: Oxford University Press.
Wilson, Elisabeth. 1995. "The Invisible Flâneur." In *Postmodern Cities and Spaces*, edited by S. Watson and K. Gibson, 59–79. Oxford: Blackwell.
Wilson, John K. 1995. *The Myth of Political Correctness: The Conservative Attack on Higher Education*. Durham, NC: Duke University Press.
Wittgenstein, Ludwig. 1980. *Vermischte Bemerkungen = Culture and Value* (bilingual). Chicago: University of Chicago Press.
Wittgenstein, Ludwig. 2012 [1921]. *Tractatus Logico-Philosophicus*. Chelmsford, MA: Courier Corporation.
Woodcock, George. 2004 [1962]. *Anarchism: A History of Libertarian Ideas and Movements*. Peterborough, ON: Broadview.
Woolf, Virginia. 1935. "Beau Brummell." In *Common Reader Second Series*, 85–89. New York: Harcourt.
Yang, Juping. 2007. "Behavior and Attitude towards the World: A Comparative Analysis between the Cynics and the School of Zhuangzi." *Frontiers of History in China* 2, no. 1: 60–73.
Young, George Malcolm. 1936. *Victorian England: Portrait of an Age*. Oxford: Oxford University Press.
Zhang, Ellen Y. 2019. "Forgetfulness and Flow: 'Happiness' in Zhuangzi's Daoism." *Science, Religion and Culture* 6, no. 1: 77–84.
Zhang, Longxi. 2016. "Elective Affinities? Two Moments of Encounter with Oscar Wilde's Writings." In *Writing China: Essays on the Amherst Embassy (1816) and Sino-British Cultural Relations*. Cambridge: D. J. Brewer.
Ziporyn, Brook, trans. 2009b. *Zhuangzi. The Essential Writings With Selections from Traditional Commentaries*. Indianapolis: Hackett.
Ziporyn, Brook. 2009. "Zhuangzi as Philosopher" https://www.hackettpublishing.com/zhuangziphil.
Ziporyn, Brook. 2012. *Ironies of Oneness and Difference: Coherence in Early Chinese Thought; Prolegomena to the Study of Li*. Albany: State University of New York Press.

Index

absurdity, 13, 46–47, 56, 66, 142, 153, 172, 184
Advaita Vedanta, 34
Aestheticism (British), 50–52, 114
aesthetization, 48–49
amorality, 66–67, 139, 15, 169, 1801
Analects, 15–16, 141–42, 196n4
anarchy, 51–57, 65, 188
Ancien Régime, 89
androgynous, 29–30, 113
angoisse, 183
arhat, 108, 202n6
aristocracy, 4, 44, 125, 132–35, 132, 155, 182
Aristotle, 148, 154, 162
Arnold, Matthew, 51, 53–54, 197n15
art, 111–12; (Chinese), 46–47, 148
artificial, 77, 108, 124, 146–50, 182
atheism, 168
authenticity, 18, 23, 73, 80, 85–115, 121–23, 125–28, 132, 143–44, 163–69, 176–84, 187–88, 200n2, 200n4, 201n13, 201n14. See also *zhen* 真
avant-garde, 53, 114, 131, 183, 203n1

Balzac, Honoré de, 132, 136, 164; *The Treatise of Elegant Living*, 115

Barbey d'Aurevilly, Jules, 39, 49, 144–45, 153, 155–56, 160, 170, 197n14
Baudelaire, Charles, 4, 42, 44, 45, 55, 98, 114–15, 120–22, 133, 144, 146, 149–50, 154, 160–62, 170, 191n6
Baudrillard, 77, 124
beauty, 39, 53, 68, 71–72, 120–21, 146, 150, 161, 169, 202n14
Benjamin, Walter, 40, 49, 74, 119
Berlin, Isiah, 90, 201n10
blasé, 132–33, 161, 178–79
Bloom, Alan, 10, 31, 180
Body. See *shen*
bohemians, 92, 136–37
bourgeois, 6, 9, 11, 44, 88, 91–92, 115, 139, 155, 160, 178–79
Brummell, George, 4–5, 6, 11–13, 38–39, 41–42, 44, 46, 56, 78, 115, 121–22, 125, 129, 135–35, 145–46, 152–53, 155, 160, 170, 185, 191n6
Buddhism, 33–35, 173, 181, 200n7
Butler, Judith, 79–80, 123
Butterfly parable, 2, 72–73, 76–77, 87, 123
Byron, George Gordon, 133, 137

camp, 113–14, 167–68, 203n10

Camus, Albert, 56, 81, 152, 155
careerist, 4, 134–35, 140, 144
Carnap, Rudolf, 16, 193n4
catharsis, 148
chaos, 7, 20–21, 26–27, 30–31, 51, 69, 76–77, 108, 167, 177–78
cheng 诚 (sincerity), 62, 84–85, 101, 199–200n1
china (porcelain), 50
Confucianism, 1–3, 15–16, 18, 20, 23, 29–30, 38, 46–47, 59–62, 65, 87–88, 101, 103, 106–108, 140–43, 149, 151, 154, 195n14, 196n4, 200n4
contingency, 54, 82, 105, 108, 110, 127–28, 162
coolness, 135, 138, 159–68, 175–83, 187, 188, 189
correcting names. *See* rectification of names
cosmos, 48, 64, 75, 162
Count d'Orsay, 115, 156
creation myths, 122
Critic as Artist, The (Wilde), 39, 50, 65, 111–13, 129, 148, 203n1
Cromwell, Oliver, 44
Csíkszentmihályi, Mihaly, 172–75, 205n4
Cubism, 53
culture, 21–26
Cynicism, 37, 160, 196n2

dandy (etymology), 197n7
Daodejing, 20, 21, 39, 67, 70, 162
Daoism (history), 45
de 德 (virtuosity), 84, 120, 120, 159, 161
Debord, Guy, 50
deconstruction, 65, 86, 86, 172, 188
dédain, 65–66, 89, 136, 185, 201n9
Delacroix, Eugene, 137

Derrida, Jacques, 86, 123, 127
Descartes, René, 90, 200n5
dialecticians, 75–76, 194n7
différance, 79
dignity, 90, 166, 179
Ding (butcher), 48, 145, 172–73
Diogenes of Sinope, 12
Dionysian, 95–97, 136
Dōgen, 73
Dorfles, Gillo, 114
d'Ormesson, Jean, 136, 204n15
dream, 41, 73–75, 77–78, 123, 127

Easy Rider, 178
ecology, 146
ego, 72–74, 121
Eliade, Mircea, 77, 194–95n13
emergence, 122, 126
emptiness, 34, 55, 85, 110, 153, 181, 187. *See also sunyata*
Enlightenment, 23, 87, 89–93, 96, 98, 103, 179, 180, 205n7
ennui, 89, 133, 120, 136, 153, 185
Entfremdung (alienation), 94, 176, 178, 183, 201n12
Epicureanism, 160
equalization, 11, 27, 31, 61–64, 72, 167, 180–81, 184–85. *See also qi* (齊)
essentialism, 7, 27–28, 30–35, 60–64, 72, 75, 102, 110
ethics, 66–70, 78, 138–39, 160, 167, 169
excellence, 119–20, 145, 154–56, 167, 169, 170
existence, 21, 26, 33, 60, 63, 68, 75, 77, 156, 162, 168, 202n6

fantastic, 47–48
feminism, 27, 30, 62–63, 71, 76–77, 80
flâner, 5, 37–41, 74, 87, 120–22

flâneur, 5, 38–41, 45, 49, 50, 74, 114–15, 120, 133, 137–38, 149, 155, 178
flow, 40–41, 61, 68, 130, 137, 146, 157, 164–65, 172–75, 205n4
fops, 45
forgetting. See *wang*
Fry, Stephen, 54, 96
Futurism, 53

Gadamer, Hans-Georg, 126, 202n7
gagà, 137–38
gambling, 160, 171
game. See play
Gaudiya Vaisnava, 158
gender, 5, 17, 20–27, 31, 68–69, 78, 106; gender and sex, 24–25
gender bending, 80
gender blindness, 81–82
gender fluid, 1, 17, 59–60, 64, 106
gender gifted, 1, 17, 59
gender theory, 25, 79
genuine, 12, 30, 56, 85, 98, 107–14, 125–26
genuine pretending, 70, 77, 91, 108–12, 124–25, 127, 152, 156–57, 163–65, 188
George (Prince of Wales), 6, 42, 44–45, 70, 115, 138, 177, 197n9
Gongsun Long, 19, 193–94n7
grace, 54, 56, 57, 138, 142, 153, 200n8, 201n8
Gray, Dorian, 12, 89, 150
Greenberg, Clement, 203n1
Guo Xiang, 73, 174, 195n16

Hall, Stuart, 9, 16, 22, 97
heart-mind (*xin* 心), 101, 102, 198n4
Hegel, Georg Wilhelm Friedrich, 49
Heidegger, Martin, 16, 19, 86, 94, 193n4, 200n5, 201n13
hermeneutics, 19

Hinduism, 158
Homo Ludens, 156–58
homosexuality, 80–81, 113
hua 化 (transformation), 2, 47, 48, 77; self-transformation (*tu hua* 獨化), 30, 48, 195n16, 167; transformation of things (*wu hua* 物化), 128, 197n13
Huizi, 4, 18–19, 144, 195n15, 202n8
Huizinga, Johan, 156–58
humor, 11, 46, 48, 76, 109, 145
Hundred Schools of Thought (*zhuzi baijia*), 18 45
Hundun, 177–78, 205n6
Hurston, Zora Neale, 199n20
Huysmans, Karl Joris, 114–14, 150

identity, 2, 9, 21–23, 27, 59, 77, 86–88, 90, 92, 102, 108–109, 124, 154, 163, 165; gender identity, 28, 32, 63, 68–69, 79; identity appropriation, 99, 143; identity in Buddhism, 200n7; identity politics, 10, 18, 121, 168, 200n7
idiotic, 126, 62, 163–64
inclusive language, 1, 8
incroyables, 39
individualism, 9, 91, 95–96, 154
intersex, 62
irony, 8, 76, 110, 163, 165–66

James, William, 173–75
jazz, 159–60
Jesse, William, 133
jeunes gens, 39
ji 己. See self
Joyce, James, 37

Kabuki, 124
Kant, Immanuel, 116–17, 147
Kierkegaard, Søren, 87

kitsch, 68, 110–17, 131–32, 163–64, 167, 169–70, 172, 188
Kropotkin, Peter, 52–53
Kyoto School, 173

language, 1–2, 7–8, 15–24, 40–41, 47, 52, 54, 59–61, 74, 79, 96, 105, 114, 116, 193n4; language in Buddhism, 33–35
language correction. *See* rectification of names
Laozi (Lao-tzu), 29, 62, 78, 143, 194n11, 196–97n6
Lasch, Christopher, 177
leftism, 9–10, 60–61, 96–97
li 理, 34, 108, 194n13, 200n1
liberalism, 9, 177
Liezi (Lie Yukou), 46, 101–102, 192n9, 197n12, 200n1
Lions (cultural movement), 78, 137–38
Locke, John, 90

macaronis, 45, 81
MacDonald, George, 51
Mahayana, 34
Mailer, Norman, 168
Mallarmé, 123, 127
Mao, 8
mask, 65, 111–12, 144, 203n9
Matrix, The, 179
melancholy, 177, 182
Mencius, 15, 18, 28, 62, 140, 143, 192n9
#metoo, 62
miming, 123, 127
ming shi 名實 (correspondence of names), 15, 18, 192n3
Mohists, 6, 15, 19, 142, 144, 194n10
Molière, 112, 134
muscadins, 39

Musset Alfred de, 137

Nagarjuna, 34
nature, 146–49; acting naturally, 148–49
Needham, Joseph, 200n1
negativity, 151–52
Neo-Confucianism, 28
Neo-Impressionism, 53
newspeak, 24, 60
Nietzsche, Friedrich, 54, 94, 200n2
nihilism, 124, 136
nirvana, 202n6
Nishida, Kitaro, 173–75
nominalism, 16–20, 22; in Buddhism, 33–34
no-mind. See *wuxin* 無心
non-action, 196n5
nonbinary, 17, 25, 64
Nothingness, 34, 78, 85, 153, 173. See also *wu*
Nyaya and Vaisesika schools, 34

Obama, Barack, 181
Orwell, George, 24

Parker, Charlie 159
passivism, 81
Pelham, 56–57, 65, 154
Perfect Man, 22, 25, 119, 165, 172, 195n15, 196n3, 202n2
Peterson, Jordan, 10, 21, 32, 54, 67, 195n19
philanthropy, 5, 43, 48, 57, 65, 168, 171, 177
philosophes, 205n7
phlegm, 11, 39–40, 53, 54, 56, 64–67, 89, 161, 163, 185
Plato, 116–17
play, 6, 61, 64, 77, 80–81, 89, 105–106, 109, 127, 146, 148, 150, 156–58, 161, 167, 171, 176

Poe, Edgar Allan, 114, 120–21, 145
polite incorrectness, 166, 188
politeness, 7, 55–56, 67, 69, 166, 188
political correctness (PC), 1–2, 6–11, 16–17, 22–27, 31–32, 54–60, 88, 97, 105, 115–16, 129, 175–78, 180
Pop Art, 183–84
poseur, 107, 143–44
pride, 42, 112, 121, 126, 131, 134, 145–46, 169–70
pronouns, 1, 5, 16–17, 21–22, 25–35, 41, 53–61, 63, 64, 68–75, 81, 87, 90, 96, 97, 98, 105, 107–10, 113, 117, 195, 199n16
pure experience (James), 173–75
puritanism, 3, 5, 44–45, 53–54, 92, 97, 139, 152, 177–78

qi 齊 (equal), 63
Qin Dynasty, 45
Qiwulun, 59, 156, 196n3, 193n5, 199n14
queer theory, 80–81

Rabelais, François, 37
racism, 179–80
Reagan, Roland, 9, 91
rectifcation of names (zheng ming 正名), 15, 18, 43; rectification of language, 17, 57, 88, 109
Regency Period, 4, 44, 197n9
relativism, 26, 31–32, 84–85, 167, 180–81
Restauration (English), 44
Restoration (French), 38
Revolution (French), 90
revolution, 13, 154–56, 166
right-wing (American), 97–98
Robber Zhi, 7, 169
roleplay, 99, 111, 128, 154
Romanticism, 137, 177

Rorty, Richard, 180–81
Rousseau, Jean-Jacques, 87
Ruskin, John, 51

Sainte-Beuve, Charles, 39
sang 喪 (losing), 18
Sartre, Jean-Paul, 83, 86, 145, 152, 153, 170–71, 201n13
School of Names, 4, 18, 193–94
scientism, 43
seduction, 76–78, 161, 176
self, 84–88, 128; ji 己, 102–105
self-awakening, 173–74
selfie, 94
self-transformation (tu hua 獨化). See hua
Serres, Michel, 30, 116
Seurat, George, 53
sexism, 195
shen 身 (body), 102, 202n3
shi-fei 是非 (right-wrong), 199n14
Signac, Paul, 53
Simmel, Georg, 93, 132–33, 178–79, 201n11
sincerity, 84–85, 89–90, 201n10. See also cheng
skepticism, 17, 26, 40, 54, 68, 74, 80, 125, 128, 154, 163
slavery, 159, 165–66
snob, 4, 131–36, 139–43, 154–55
socialism, 52, 72, 117
Sontag, Susan, 113–14, 167–68, 184
Sophists, 194
spleen, 133
spontaneity (zìrán 自然), 5, 16, 30, 40, 51, 53–54, 95, 104, 120, 122, 132–33, 143–45, 179, 187, 189, 195n15, 197n6
sprezzatura, 89, 137, 200–201n8
Stoicism, 152, 160, 182

sublimation, 13, 6, 90, 98
sublime, 147, 176, 201n14
sunyata, 34
sunyavada, 34
svabhava, 33
symbols, 30–31, 34, 69, 74, 77, 79, 194–95n13

Taylor, Charles, 91–95, 115, 128
Thatcher, Margaret, 9, 91
tian, 203n3
Todorov, Tzvetan, 47
tolerance, 6, 64
transculture, 105
transformation. See *hua*
transgender, 5, 17, 25, 32
transgression, 11, 56, 161, 166
transsexualism, 62
Tremaine, 131, 156
Trilling, Lionel, 89–91, 134, 147–48

Upanishadic philosophy, 34
uselessness, 4–7, 39, 42, 45–46, 81, 121, 142, 188–89

Valéry, Paul, 73–74, 123–24, 198n10
Victorian Age, 3, 45, 90–91, 138; Victorian ethics, 53–54, 177, 197n8
virtue, 39, 48, 62, 89–90, 97, 101, 106, 119, 143, 169, 143, 168–69, 193n5 101, 168
virtuosity, 120, 160–62. See also *de* 德

wang 忘 (forgetting), 18, 63, 70, 156–57, 193n5
Warhol, Andy, 183–85
Warring States, 18, 45

Weimar Republic, 92
Wilde, Oscar, 2–6, 42–43, 46–51, 52–53, 65, 67–68, 125, 147, 162, 171, 177–78, 184
Wittgenstein, Ludwig, 37, 52, 64, 196n1, 197n16
wu 無 (negating), 18, 34, 55, 200n3
wuqing 無情 (nonfeeling), 111, 162, 202n8
wuwei 無為, 39, 52, 55, 61–62, 135, 140–42, 144, 146, 149, 159, 196n5, 197n13, 205n4
wuxin 無心 (no-mind), 11, 54, 64, 73, 103, 173, 180, 198n4

xiaoyaoyou 逍遙游 (carefree wandering), 5
xin. See heart-mind
xinzhai 心齋 (fasting of the heart), 70, 198n1 and n3
Xunzi, 15, 28, 140, 194, 204n9
Yan Hui, 20, 65, 166

yi 義 (role), 86, 70, 200n6
yin-yang, 28, 30
you (遊), 5, 31, 37–40, 55, 64, 104, 119–22, 157, 165, 172–75, 198n5
Young, Lester, 170

Zen Buddhism, 33–35, 46, 65–66, 70, 88, 108, 151, 172–75, 196n1
zhen 真 (authenticity), 65, 85, 108, 200n2, 201n13
zheng ming 正名. See rectification of names
zhenren 真人 (true person), 65, 108
Zhu Xi, 28
zìrán 自然. See spontaneity
zuowang, 64, 121

www.ingramcontent.com/pod-product-compliance
Lightning Source LLC
Chambersburg PA
CBHW020652230426
43665CB00008B/402